Domains and Types in

Relational Theory and SQL

Shedding Some Light on

a Widely Misunderstood Concept

C. J. Date

Published by:

115 Linda Vista, Sedona, AZ 86336 USA
https://www.TechnicsPub.com

Cover design by Lorena Molinari

First Printing 2024

Printed in the United States of America.

ISBN, print ed.   9781634625449
ISBN, Kindle ed.   9781634625524
ISBN, PDF ed.   9781634625531

domain *n.* area, authority, bailiwick, business, concern, demesne, department, discipline, dominion, empire, estate, field, jurisdiction, kingdom, lands, orbit, pidgin, policies, power, province, realm, region, scope, speciality, sphere, sway, territory.
—Chambers 20th Century Thesaurus
(Chambers, 1980)

type *n.* a class of expressions, or of the entities they represent, that can all enter into the same syntactic relations.
—E. J. Borowski and J. M. Borwein:
Collins Dictionary of Mathematics, 2nd ed.
(Collins, 2002)

A major purpose of type systems is to avoid embarrassing questions about representations, and to forbid situations in which these questions might come up.
—Luca Cardelli and Peter Wegner:
"On Understanding Types, Data Abstraction, and Polymorphism"
ACM Computing Surveys 17, No. 4 (December 1985)

May this be a light to you in dark places, when all other lights go out.
—J. R. R. Tolkien (but very slightly reworded here):
The Fellowship of the Ring (1954)

To the memories garnered from my years in the great State of California, with thanks and much appreciation

About the Author

C. J. Date is an independent author, lecturer, researcher, and consultant, specializing in relational database technology. He is best known for his book *An Introduction to Database Systems*, 8th ed. (Addison-Wesley, 2004), which has sold around a million copies at the time of writing and is used by several hundred colleges and universities worldwide. He is also the author of numerous other books on database management and related matters, including most recently:

- From Morgan Kaufmann: *Time and Relational Theory: Temporal Databases in the Relational Model and SQL* (with Hugh Darwen and Nikos A. Lorentzos, 2014)

- From O'Reilly: *View Updating and Relational Theory: Solving the View Update Problem* (2013); *SQL and Relational Theory: How to Write Accurate SQL Code*, 3rd ed. (2015); *The **New** Relational Database Dictionary* (2016); *Type Inheritance and Relational Theory: Subtypes, Supertypes, and Substitutability* (2016)

- From Apress: *Database Design and Relational Theory: Normal Forms and All That Jazz*, 2nd ed. (2019)

- From Technics: *Logic and Relational Theory: Thoughts and Essays on Database Matters* (2020); *Fifty Years of Relational, and Other Database Writings: More Thoughts and Essays on Database Matters* (2020); *Stating the Obvious, and Other Database Writings: Still More Thoughts and Essays on Database Matters* (2020); *E. F. Codd and Relational Theory, Revised Edition: A Detailed Review and Analysis of Codd's Major Database Writings* (2021); *Database Dreaming: Relational Writings Revised and Revived* (two volumes, 2022); *On Cantor and the Transfinite* (2023); *Keys, Foreign Keys, and Relational Theory* (2023); *The Relational Model for Database Management Version 2 – A Critical Analysis* (2024); *Database Technology: Nulls Considered Harmful* (2024)

Mr Date was inducted into the Computing Industry Hall of Fame in 2004. He enjoys a reputation that is second to none for his ability to explain complex technical subjects in a clear and understandable fashion.

C o n t e n t s

Preface

This tale grew in the telling. Very little of it is really new, but recent events have made me realize, rather forcefully, that it needed telling again. What happened was this: A certain well known consultant—I'm not going to name him here—asked me if I'd be prepared to review the draft of a book he was writing on database design, and I said I would be. Now, most of what he had to say in that draft was solid and useful (based as it was on considerable practical experience), and I concurred with almost all of it—but there was one point he and I simply couldn't manage to agree on, despite repeated attempts on both our parts to understand where the other was coming from, as they say. To be specific, he insisted on treating domains and types as if there were a logical difference between them, and I don't believe there is.

Well, let me interrupt myself right there. Actually, in SQL, there *is* a difference between domains and types—but that's because what SQL calls "domains" have almost nothing to do with domains in their original relational sense. In fact, when it was first defined, SQL had nothing to say about domains, as such, at all. Subsequently, however, a construct by that name was added to the language—that happened with the 1992 version of the SQL standard, known officially as SQL:1992—but, to repeat, that new construct was and is quite different from the relational concept of the same name. Nor is that construct supported by many of the mainstream SQL products; and even if it were I wouldn't use it, regarding it as I do as, to put it politely, not very useful.

Unfortunately the picture is muddied still further by the fact that Codd himself—inventor of the relational model, and hence the person responsible for introducing the term into the database arena—never made it 100% clear what he thought a domain was, either. Now, I'll have quite a lot more to say regarding domains as Codd saw them in the body of this book; however, the significant point for present purposes is simply that, like my consultant friend, Codd too claimed there was a logical difference between domains and types. In my opinion, though, his arguments in that connection never stood up to careful analysis. In fact, he and I had numerous debates on the topic all through the late 1980s and on into 1990s (it was one of the biggest points of contention between us). The substance of those debates—the arguments pro and con—can be found if you're interested in Chapter 11 ("A Type Is a Type Is a Type") of my book *Database Dreaming Volume I* (Technics, 2022).

Just as an aside, I note that actually I did manage, eventually, to get Codd to agree that domains and types were the same thing after all. That happened on June 30th, 1994. (A red letter day!—I noted it in my diary at the time.) Unfortunately, however, he never went so far as to admit as much in writing. So far as I know, at any rate.

In fairness, let me add that it took me quite a while to understand the point myself: the point, that is, domains and types were indeed one and the same thing. The first of my writings to acknowledge the fact—the first to conclude that there weren't two concepts here but only one—was probably the fourth edition of my book *An Introduction to Database Systems* (published by Addison-Wesley in the mid 1980s, though of course written a year or two earlier). Earlier editions never drew that same conclusion: at least, not explicitly. So the widespread lack of proper appreciation of this matter, in the industry at large, might be partly my fault! If so, then I apologize, profusely.[1]

Anyway, the point of the present book is to explain as carefully as I can just what domains, also known as types, are really all about. As I've said, little of it is really new—almost everything I have to say in what follows I've already said elsewhere in some book or other publication[2]—but I've never gathered all of the material into one place like this before. I'm also not aware of any other book that's devoted to the topic, nor one that covers quite the same territory; thus, I do believe, or hope, that this book can serve a useful purpose, even though as I say the content is mostly not new.

Structure of the Book

The book consists of five long chapters and two appendixes:

- Chapter 1 ("Preliminaries") lays some groundwork; in particular, it goes into the basics of the issue of domains vs. types in some detail. It also introduces the running example; explains what *The Third Manifesto* is all about; and provides some crucial and fundamental definitions. Subsequent chapters all build on this material.

---

[1] On the other hand, let me point out for what it's worth that the fourth edition of my *Introduction* book did at least predate the first version of the SQL standard. Thus, the committee members responsible for the standard at that time could have set the matter straight, if they'd wanted to.

[2] But the material in question is so widely scattered, over so many different books and other publications, that it would be much too complicated (not to say tedious) to give a detailed publishing history here, and I'm not even going to try.

■ There are three quotes, or maxims, that I try to follow as guidelines in my technical writing in general:

1. In teaching at an elementary level, one must tell the truth, nothing but the truth, but not the *whole* truth (W. A. Hurwitz).

2. It is downright sinful to teach the abstract before the concrete (Z. A. Melzak).

3. Writing can be either readable or precise, but not at the same time (Bertrand Russell).

With these precepts in mind, I've divided the core material of this book, on type theory as such, into two separate chapters. Chapter 2 ("Types and Domains: The Basics") covers the fundamentals in a tutorial, "once over lightly" manner. Chapter 4 ("Types: A Closer Look") then covers some of the same territory, but it does so rather more carefully, and (more important, perhaps) it also introduces much new material.

■ Chapters 3 ("Types and Domains in SQL: The Basics" and 5 ("Types in SQL: A Closer Look") treat the corresponding SQL material in similar fashion. That is, Chapter 3 consists of a tutorial treatment of the fundamentals, while Chapter 5 goes into a lot more detail.
Note: I should explain that what I mean by SQL throughout this book is the standard version of that language, not some commercial dialect or other implemented version. What's more, I follow the standard in assuming the pronunciation "ess cue ell" (not "sequel"), therefore saying things like "an SQL statement," not "a SQL statement."

As for the appendixes, both are included primarily for reference. Appendix A contains the text of *The Third Manifesto*, in full. Appendix B provides formal definitions for many of the terms and concepts introduced in the body of the book.
A couple of further remarks on the book's structure:

■ As you can see from the foregoing overview, the theoretical material and the SQL material are interleaved. My rationale for presenting it in such a fashion was this: Rightly or wrongly, I felt it would be unnecessarily confusing to treat type theory as such in its entirety, in depth and in full detail, and then to drop back down to a more elementary level again in order to explain the basics of SQL's support. I hope you agree. I also felt it would be not only confusing but actively misleading to cover the SQL material before the theoretical material. Again, I hope you agree.

- Every chapter includes a set of exercises, and I recommend strongly that you not skip them. In most cases answers are provided too, and those answers often go into rather more detail than the material in the chapter as such does.

Finally, note that the book contains almost nothing on the subject of type inheritance. Now, you might think that rather an odd omission for a book that's supposed to be all about types. But the fact is, type inheritance is a huge subject in itself! I've already written a whole book about it—viz., *Type Inheritance and Relational Theory* (O'Reilly, 2016)—and that book is almost 600 pages long. It's also a somewhat separate, or separable, subject; and what I wanted to do with the present book was cover the basic ideas of type theory as such, together with SQL's support for those ideas, without getting sidetracked or distracted by the (huge!) additional complexities of type inheritance.

That's the end of the preamble; now on to the book proper. I hope you enjoy it, and I hope too that you learn something from it.

C. J. Date
Morristown, Vermont
2024

Chapter 1

Preliminaries

The relational model is the foundation of all modern general purpose database systems. It was first described by its inventor, E. F. ("Ted") Codd, in a landmark paper in 1969:

■ "Derivability, Redundancy, and Consistency of Relations Stored in Large Data Banks," IBM Research Report RJ599 (August 19th, 1969)

Codd then went on to revise this paper slightly and publish it again, under a different title, in the journal *Communications of the ACM* (*CACM*):

■ "A Relational Model of Data for Large Shared Data Banks," *CACM 13*, No. 6)June 1970)

And it's this revised paper that's generally credited with being the seminal paper in the field—certainly it's much more widely read, and referenced, than its 1969 predecessor—though such treatment is a little unfair in a way to the original 1969 version.

Anyway, regardless of which of the foregoing papers is cited as the origin, there can be no question that it was Codd's invention, the relational model, that first put the field of database management on a sound theoretical footing. Everybody in the field knows that. But what isn't quite so generally known, perhaps, is that the relational model requires a further theoretical footing of its own: namely, a supporting theory of *data types* (types for short, or *domains* as Codd called them in those early papers). The requirement for such a theory arises most obviously, albeit not exclusively, from the fact that the relational model requires every attribute of every relation to be of some type.

The foregoing state of affairs provides a large part of the motivation for the work my colleague Hugh Darwen and I have been involved in ever since the early 1990s. The work in question goes by the generic name of *The Third Manifesto*, or just the *Manifesto* for short (I'll explain that name later in this chapter). The primary objectives of the *Manifesto* are, and always were, twofold:

1. To provide a careful description of the relational model as such (and thereby to provide a kind of abstract blueprint for the design of a database language)

2. To provide an appropriate theory of types to support the relational model

To elaborate briefly:

■   Regarding the first objective, it's true that we dotted a few *i*'s and crossed a few *t*'s that Codd left undotted or uncrossed in his own writings; in other words, we performed a few minor tidying activities here and there. However, the model as we describe it in our *Manifesto* doesn't depart in any essential respect from the original vision as documented by Codd in his early papers.

■   Regarding the second objective, the relational model certainly does assume that types exist, as I've said; however, nowhere does it spell out just what those types must be or what properties those types must have. Nor should it! The fact is, the relational model and the supporting type theory are to a considerable degree independent of one another (they're *orthogonal*, to use the jargon). Thus, something else we tried to do in our *Manifesto* was define a theory of types that seemed to us to be "in the spirit of" the relational model (inasmuch as such a claim makes any sense); more specifically, we tried to define a theory of types that seemed to us to work well with that model.

One last introductory point: Of course, this book is intended for database professionals, and so I assume you're familiar with such terms as *database management system* (DBMS); *database administrator* (DBA); *relation*; *attribute*; *tuple* (rhymes with "couple," and short for *n*-tuple); *key*; *foreign key*; *base relation*; *view*; *projection*; *join*; *SQL*; and so on. However, let me say a few words regarding the terms *relation*, *attribute*, and *tuple* in particular. Those terms are, of course, the relational analogs of the SQL terms *table*, *column*, and *row*, respectively—but as I hope you know, there are some significant logical differences in each case. I'm not going to explain or discuss those differences just yet (I'll give precise definitions later in the chapter); here let me just note that throughout this book I'll use the formal relational terms when I'm describing relational matters, but SQL terms when I'm talking about SQL.

> *Aside:* The foregoing paragraph makes reference to the concept of *logical difference*, a concept that derives from a dictum of Wittgenstein's:
>
> > **All logical differences are big differences**.
>
> This notion is an extraordinarily useful one; as a "mind tool," it's a great aid to clear and precise thinking, and it can be very helpful in pinpointing and analyzing some of the confusions that are, unfortunately, all too common in the computing world. I'll be appealing to it many times in the pages ahead. *End of aside.*

THE SUPPLIERS AND PARTS DATABASE

If you've read other books of mine, you'll know that I almost always use the same basic example to illustrate the various points I need to make: namely, the familiar—not to say hackneyed—suppliers and parts database. What's more, I generally go on to say this (quoting now from my book *SQL and Relational Theory*, 3rd ed., O'Reilly, 2015):

> I apologize for dragging out this old warhorse yet one more time, but I believe that using the same example in a variety of books and other publications can help, not hinder, learning.

So here we go again ... First of all, the database contains three relvars, called S (suppliers), P (parts), and SP (shipments of parts by suppliers), respectively. (*Note:* If the term *relvar* is unfamiliar to you, I'll be explaining it in a few moments.) The picture overleaf shows a set of sample values for these relvars; examples later in the book will assume these actual values, where it makes any difference. The intended interpretation is as follows:

- *Suppliers:* Relvar S represents *suppliers under contract*. Each supplier has one supplier number (SNO), unique to that supplier; one name (SNAME), not necessarily unique (though the SNAME values in the picture do happen to be unique); one status value (STATUS), representing some kind of ranking or preference level among available suppliers; and one location (CITY).

- *Parts*: Relvar P denotes *parts* (more accurately, *kinds* of parts) *used in the enterprise.* Each kind of part has one part number (PNO), which is unique; one name (PNAME), not necessarily unique; one color (COLOR); one weight (WEIGHT), in pounds avoirdupois; and one location where parts of that kind are stored (CITY).

- *Shipments*: Relvar SP represents *shipments* (it shows which parts are shipped, or supplied, by which suppliers). Each shipment has one supplier number (SNO), one part number (PNO), and one quantity (QTY). There's at most one shipment at any given time for a given supplier and given part, and the combination of supplier number and part number is thus unique to the shipment in question. Note that the sample values include one supplier, supplier S5, with no shipments at all.

S

SNO	SNAME	STATUS	CITY
S1	Smith	20	London
S2	Jones	10	Paris
S3	Blake	30	Paris
S4	Clark	20	London
S5	Adams	30	Athens

P

PNO	PNAME	COLOR	WEIGHT	CITY
P1	Nut	Red	12.0	London
P2	Bolt	Green	17.0	Paris
P3	Screw	Blue	17.0	Oslo
P4	Screw	Red	14.0	London
P5	Cam	Blue	12.0	Paris
P6	Cog	Red	19.0	London

SP

SNO	PNO	QTY
S1	P1	300
S1	P2	200
S1	P3	400
S1	P4	200
S1	P5	100
S1	P6	100
S2	P1	300
S2	P2	400
S3	P2	200
S4	P2	200
S4	P4	300
S4	P5	400

Now, what the foregoing figure actually depicts is three *relations*, or more precisely three relation *values*: namely, the relation values that happen to exist in the database at some particular time. But if we were to look at the database at some different time, we would probably see three different values appearing in their place. Thus, S, P, and SP in that database are really *variables* (relation variables, to be precise, or *relvars* for short). For example, suppose S currently has the value—the relation value, that is—shown in the figure, and suppose we delete the set of tuples (actually there's only one) for suppliers in Athens:

```
DELETE S WHERE CITY = 'Athens' ;
```

After this DELETE, S looks like this:

SNO	SNAME	STATUS	CITY
S1	Smith	20	London
S2	Jones	10	Paris
S3	Blake	30	Paris
S4	Clark	20	London

Conceptually, what's happened here is that the old value of S has been replaced in its entirety by a new value. Of course, the old value (with five tuples) and the new one (with four) are very similar, in a sense, but they certainly are different values. In fact, the DELETE just shown is logically equivalent to, and indeed shorthand for, the following *relational assignment:*

```
S := S MINUS ( S WHERE CITY = 'Athens' ) ;
```

As with all assignments, the sequence of events here is that (a) the *source expression* on the right side of the assignment symbol (":=") is evaluated and then (b) the value resulting from that evaluation (a relation value in the case at hand, since the expression in question is a relational expression) is then assigned to the *target variable* on the left side (a relation variable, in the case at hand), with the overall effect already explained.

Aside: The foregoing DELETE statement and the relational assignment it's equivalent to are both formulated in a language called **Tutorial D** (note the boldface)—see the section *"The Third Manifesto,"* later in this chapter, for further explanation—and I'll be using that language as a basis for coding examples throughout the relational portions of this book. Now, **Tutorial D** is intended as far as possible to be pretty much self-explanatory; however, I'll explain specific features of that language as and when we encounter them, if further explanation seems to be needed at the time. *End of aside.*

So DELETE is shorthand for a certain relational assignment. And, of course, an analogous remark applies to INSERT and UPDATE also—they too are basically just shorthand for certain relational assignments. In fact, relational assignment is the only update operator that's included in the relational model as such, because of course it's the only update operator we need, logically speaking. *Note:* I follow the usual convention throughout this book in using the generic term *update* to refer to the INSERT, DELETE, and UPDATE (and assignment) operators considered collectively. When I want to refer to the UPDATE operator specifically, I'll set it in all caps as just shown.

So there's a logical difference between relation values and relation variables.[1] The trouble is, the database literature has historically used the same term, *relation*, for both concepts, and that practice has certainly led to confusion (confusion, I might add, that persists in some circles to this very day). Throughout this book, therefore, I'll distinguish very carefully between the two from this point forward: I'll talk in terms of relation values when I mean relation values, and relation variables when I mean relation variables. However, I'll also abbreviate *relation value*, most of the time, to just *relation* (exactly as we abbreviate *integer value* most of the time to just *integer*). And I'll abbreviate *relation variable* most of the time to **relvar**; for example, I'll say the suppliers and parts database contains three *relvars* (three base relvars, to be precise, where a base relvar is a relvar that—unlike a view, for instance—isn't defined in terms of other relvars).

Here then are **Tutorial D** definitions for relvars S, P, and SP:

```
VAR S BASE RELATION
    { SNO     SNO ,
      SNAME   NAME ,
      STATUS  INTEGER ,
      CITY    CHAR }
    KEY { SNO } ;

VAR P BASE RELATION
    { PNO     PNO ,
      PNAME   NAME ,
      COLOR   COLOR ,
      WEIGHT  WEIGHT ,
      CITY    CHAR }
    KEY { PNO } ;
```

---

[1] I'll have a lot more to say about the logical difference between values and variables in general in Chapter 4.

```
VAR SP BASE RELATION
    { SNO    SNO ,
      PNO    PNO ,
      QTY    QTY }
    KEY { SNO , PNO }
    FOREIGN KEY { SNO } REFERENCES S
    FOREIGN KEY { PNO } REFERENCES P ;
```

What's more, I'll take the foregoing definitions (like the language **Tutorial D** itself, in fact) to be more or less self-explanatory; in particular, I'll assume you're familiar with the relational key and foreign key concepts, as I've said. However, please note the following:

■ The keyword BASE indicates that the relvar being defined is a base relvar specifically and not some other kind, such as a view. (As a matter of fact, the relvars mentioned in this book will always be base relvars specifically, barring explicit statements to the contrary.)

■ Purely for definiteness, I assume that types INTEGER and CHAR are system defined and types SNO, PNO, NAME, COLOR, WEIGHT, and QTY are user defined. See Chapters 2 and 4 for further explanation.

■ Relvars S, P, and SP have keys {SNO}, {PNO}, and {SNO,PNO}, respectively.
    Note: In the figure, I've marked the attributes participating in those keys with double underlining. Such double underlining is usually taken to mean the keys in question are, specifically, the *primary* keys for the pertinent relvars. However, **Tutorial D** deliberately provides no way of—in particular, no explicit syntax for—distinguishing between primary and other keys, referring to them all as just keys, unqualified.

THE THIRD MANIFESTO

The first version of *The Third Manifesto* as such was published in March 1995,[2] though Darwen and I had been thinking about the idea of producing such a document for several years prior to that time. It—that first version, I mean—was

---

[2] Specifically, in *ACM SIGMOD Record 24*, No. 1 (March 1995). However, we also published an informal description of what it contained ("Introducing ... *The Third Manifesto*") earlier that same year, in *Database Programming & Design 8*, No. 1 (January 1995).

quite short, occupying as it did a total of just eleven pages (and several of those contained only acknowledgments, references, and other boilerplate matter), and it consisted in essence of a series of prescriptions, proscriptions, and what we called "very strong suggestions." The general idea was that, in order to be "*Manifesto* compliant," as it were, a system would certainly have to abide by all of the prescriptions and proscriptions, but it might choose to ignore some of the suggestions.

Being so short, the *Manifesto* was of course very terse—so terse, in fact, that we wrote an entire book of nearly 500 pages to explain it:

■ C. J. Date and Hugh Darwen: *Foundation for Object / Relational Databases: The Third Manifesto* (Addison-Wesley, 1998)

The title of this book requires some explanation. Note first that, technically speaking, "*The Third Manifesto*" is only the subtitle; the main title, which is to say the title as such, is *Foundation for Object / Relational Databases*. Of course, we would have liked it to be the other way around—as far as we were concerned, the *Manifesto* as such was what the book was all about—but it was explained to us, in words of one syllable, that bookstores shelve their wares by title, not subtitle, and so our title simply had to contain the crucial word *database* somewhere. That's why "*The Third Manifesto*" was only the subtitle: essentially just for marketing reasons.[3]

Second, why did we say, or suggest, in our chosen title that the *Manifesto* was a foundation for "object / relational" databases specifically? Well, I'll answer this question, in part, by quoting from the book itself:

> *The Third Manifesto* is a detailed proposal for the future direction of data and database management systems (DBMSs).[4] Like Codd's original papers on the relational model, it can be seen as an abstract blueprint for the design of a DBMS and the language interface to such a DBMS. In particular, it lays the foundation for what we believe is the logically correct approach to integrating relational and object technologies—a topic of considerable interest at the present time, given

---

[3] Actually the book had what might be called a "subsubtitle" too: viz., *a detailed study of the impact of objects and type theory on the relational model of data, including a comprehensive proposal for type inheritance.* What's more, that "subsubtitle" itself went through a couple of interesting changes in later editions. To be specific, first, the reference to objects was dropped; second, *comprehensive **proposal for** type inheritance* became *comprehensive **model of** type inheritance* (boldface added for emphasis).

[4] Please note the logical difference between a DBMS and a database! Unfortunately, the industry very commonly uses the term *database* when what it means is either some DBMS product, such as Oracle, or the particular copy of such a product that happens to be installed on a particular computer. I do *not* follow this usage in this book. The problem is, if you call the DBMS a database, what do you call the database?

the recent appearance in the marketplace of several "object / relational" DBMS products (sometimes called *universal servers*). Perhaps we should add immediately that we do not regard the idea of integrating relational and object technologies as just another fad, soon to be replaced by some other briefly fashionable idea. On the contrary, we think that object / relational systems are in everyone's future—a fact that makes it even more important to get the logical foundation right, of course, while we still have time to do so.

As this extract says, there was indeed a lot of interest at the time in integrating object and relational technologies. First of all, the early 1990s had seen numerous proposals for DBMSs based not on the relational model but rather on some kind of object model. Well, we can now see, with hindsight, that those proposals were never going to go very far; but that fact wasn't so clear at the time, and there were even those who were claiming that "the object model," whatever that might be, would eventually—possibly even quite soon—replace the relational model. As a consequence, the possibility of a system that got the best of both worlds, as it were, did seem an attractive one. The trouble was, it seemed to us that the database community in general was going after this objective in a fatally flawed way. To be specific, people were designing systems on the basis of an incorrect assumption: namely, the assumption that the relational concept that most closely resembled the object *class* concept was the concept of a relation as such—or a *relvar*, really, but this latter term wasn't in wide use at the time.[5] We characterized this mistake at the time, rather rudely, as **The First Great Blunder**.[6] To us, by contrast, it seemed clear that the true relational analog of an object class was neither a relation nor a relvar, but rather a *type* (a domain, if you prefer) Thus, part of our goal in writing our book was simply to promulgate what we regarded as the right way to go about building object / relational systems, and in particular to help the community avoid that "great blunder," if we could.

All of that being said, I'm sorry to have to say too that our chosen title was partly a matter of marketing once again. The term *object / relational* sounds rather quaint now, but the fact is that object / relational databases were a pretty hot topic at the time (all of the mainstream DBMS vendors were describing their products as object / relational, at least to some degree). This

---

[5] Not that it is now, either. But it should be.

[6] There was a second "great blunder" also: viz., allowing relations in the database to contain pointers. Both "blunders" are examined in depth in my book *An Introduction to Database Systems*, 8th ed. (Addison-Wesley, 2004) and elsewhere. Moreover, I'll be examining the second in particular in Chapters 3 and 5 of the present book as well,.

state of affairs notwithstanding, it was our opinion at the time (and still is) that a true "object / relational" system would be nothing more nor less than a true relational system[7]—which is to say, it would be a system that supports the relational model, with all that such support entails—and true relational systems were (and still are) what the *Manifesto* was supposed to be a foundation for. So we went along with the idea of using the term *object / relational* in our title, even though it was essentially just a marketing term, dreamt up by the "relational" DBMS vendors at the time to disguise the fact that their original "relational" products weren't really very relational at all.[8]

Be all that as it may, it was that 1998 book that contained, among much else, the first published description of the **Tutorial D** language. To elaborate briefly: The main purpose of that book was, of course, to describe and explain *The Third Manifesto* as such. Now, the *Manifesto* as such used the name **D** as a generic name for any language that conformed to *Manifesto* ideas—for example, the very first of the *Manifesto*'s prescriptions reads, in part, "[The language] **D** shall provide facilities for users to define their own scalar types"— and so the 1998 book did the same. Here's another quote (this one is from Chapter 1 of the 1998 book but is very lightly edited here):

> No special significance attaches to our choice of the name **D**—we use it merely to refer generically to any language that conforms to the principles laid down in the *Manifesto*. There could be any number of distinct languages all qualifying as a valid **D**.[9] We define one such language in this book; we call it **Tutorial D**, and we use it as the basis for most of our examples.

In fact, of course, **Tutorial D** was expressly designed to be suitable as a vehicle for illustrating and teaching the ideas of the *Manifesto*. Subsequently, however, we as well as several other people have used it for a variety of related purposes too, including as a basis for various textbooks, live classes, and real applications—and I'll be using it in the present book as well, as already noted. *Note:* I should mention that an implementation of **Tutorial D** called *Rel*, by

---

[7] After all, the whole point about an object / relational system as far as users are concerned is simply that it allows attributes of relations to be of arbitrarily complex types. Thus, a proper object / relational system is really just a relational system with proper type support (including proper user defined type support in particular)—which just means it's a proper relational system, no more and no less. In particular, what some people are pleased to call "the object / relational model" is, likewise, really just the relational model, no more and no less.

[8] They still aren't, but that's another story.

[9] Sadly, SQL isn't one of them.

Dave Voorhis of the University of Derby, U.K., is available for free download at *dbappbuilder.sourceforge.net/Rel.html*.

To get back to the *Manifesto* as such: Two years later, we published a second edition of the *Manifesto* book:

■   C. J. Date and Hugh Darwen: *Foundation for Future Database Systems: The Third Manifesto*, 2nd ed. (Addison-Wesley, 2000)

Here's a quote from the preface to this edition:

The fact that the second edition of this book appears so hot on the heels of its predecessor clearly requires some explanation. In fact, there were several reasons why we felt it desirable to revise the book so soon, but the overriding one had to do with our model of type inheritance. To be specific, the version of the model described in the first edition has been so considerably—though, for the most part, compatibly—extended and improved that we now regard it as a part (albeit an optional part) of the *Manifesto* itself. In the first edition, it was presented merely as a set of somewhat tentative "proposals," with no very definite connection to the *Manifesto* proper; now, by contrast, we present it as a set of firm *prescriptions*, and we require a DBMS that supports the ideas of the *Manifesto*, if it supports type inheritance at all, to support our own inheritance model specifically.

Also, we've taken the opportunity to make a small but significant change to the book's overall title. The title of the first edition characterized the *Manifesto* as a "foundation for object / relational databases." While that characterization was accurate as far as it went, it did not really go far enough. Rather, we now regard (and in fact always did regard) the *Manifesto* as a foundation for future databases in general—including, for example, databases that contain temporal data and databases that are used in connection with the World Wide Web. Moreover, we also regard it as a good foundation on which to build *rule engines* (also known as *business logic servers*), which, as one of us has tried to show in another recent book,[10] are exactly what [we believe] the next generation of DBMSs really ought to be.

And a few years later we published yet another edition, again with a revised title:

---

[10] C. J. Date: *WHAT Not HOW: The Business Rules Approach to Application Development* (Addison-Wesley, 2000).

- C. J. Date and Hugh Darwen: *Databases, Types, and the Relational Model: The Third Manifesto*, 3rd ed. (Addison-Wesley, 2007)

This time the rewrite was motivated not so much by a change in what was described, but rather by a change in our intended audience. (The same goes for the change in title as well.) The first two editions were aimed primarily at database researchers and DBMS designers and developers. The new edition, by contrast, was aimed more at students and was meant to serve as more of a textbook. From the preface to that new edition:

> This is a textbook on database management. It's based on our earlier book *Foundation for Future Database Systems: The Third Manifesto* (Addison-Wesley, 2000), but it has been thoroughly revised—indeed, completely rewritten—from start to finish. Part of our reason for wanting to revise it was to make it more suitable as a textbook (the earlier book, by contrast, was quite terse and formal and not very easy to read); in particular, most chapters now include a set of exercises, answers to which can be found on the website *www.thethirdmanifesto.com*. However, we have naturally taken the opportunity to incorporate many other changes as well, including numerous clarifications, a certain amount of restructuring, many more examples, and—we regret to have to say—quite a few corrections also.

Throughout the remainder of the present book, references to "the *Manifesto* book" should be understood as referring to this third edition specifically (where it makes any difference, and unless the context demands otherwise).

Why "The Third" Manifesto?

As I've said, we wrote the original version of the *Manifesto* because we were concerned about certain trends we observed in the database industry at that time. In particular, we were concerned about certain well publicized but ill considered attempts to integrate object and relational technologies.

Of course, we weren't the first to address such matters. In fact, it was precisely one of our aims in writing our original *Manifesto* to respond to two earlier manifestos (hence that "Third" in our title):

1. Malcolm Atkinson, François Bancilhon, David DeWitt, Klaus Dittrich, David Maier, and Stanley Zdonik: "The Object-Oriented Database System Manifesto," Proc. 1st International Conference on Deductive and Object-Oriented Databases, Kyoto, Japan (1989)

2. Michael Stonebraker, Lawrence A. Rowe, Bruce G. Lindsay, James Gray, Michael Carey, Michael Brodie, Philip Bernstein, and David Beech: "Third Generation Database System Manifesto," *ACM SIGMOD Record 19*, No. 3 (September 1990)

Like our own *Manifesto*, both of these documents proposed a basis on which to build future DBMSs. However, it seemed to us that they both suffered from some very serious defects. Indeed, as we wrote at the time (this is a quote from the first edition of the *Manifesto* book):

- The first [*i.e., of those two earlier manifestos*] essentially ignored the relational model. In our opinion, this flaw was more than enough to rule it out as a serious contender. In any case, it seemed to us that it failed to give firm direction.

- The second did correctly embrace the relational model, but failed to emphasize (or indeed even mention) the hopelessness of continuing to follow a commonly accepted perversion of that model—namely, SQL—in pursuit of relational ideals. In other words, it simply assumed that SQL, with all its faults, was (and is) an adequate realization of the relational model and hence an adequate foundation on which to build.[11]

For interest, I include the *Manifesto*, plus some preliminary explanatory material, as an appendix to the present book.

DOMAINS vs. TYPES

In the introduction to this chapter, I said the following, more or less:

---

[11] By contrast, we feel (as we also stated in the *Manifesto* book) that any attempt to move forward, if it's to stand the test of time, must reject SQL unequivocally. To quote: "Our reasons for taking this position are too many and varied for us to spell them out in detail here; in any case, we've described them in depth in many other places" (and we went on to refer the reader to those other places for more specifics).

The relational model requires a supporting theory of types (or *domains*, as Codd called them). The requirement for such a theory arises most obviously from the fact that, in the relational model, every attribute of every relation is required to be of some type.

Indeed, Codd did use the term *domain*, not *type*. Some explanation on my part is clearly needed, therefore, and that's what this section is about.

Now, just why Codd chose the term *domain* isn't entirely clear—I can make an informed guess, but I don't particularly want to air that guess here—but almost certainly he was appealing to the mathematical theory of functions. So what's a function, mathematically speaking? In essence, it's just *a mapping from one set of values to another*. For example, we might define a function called TRIPLE, which takes as input a positive integer x and returns as output another positive integer y, computed as $3 \times x$. Here's a more precise definition:

Definition (mathematical function): Given two sets, not necessarily distinct, a rule—also known as a map or mapping—pairing each element x of the first set with exactly one element y of the second set; equivalently, the set of ordered pairs $\langle x,y \rangle$ that constitutes that pairing.

More terminology:

■ Given some particular function f, the first of the two sets involved in f is called the *domain* and the second is called the *codomain*.

■ The unique element y of the codomain corresponding to element x of the domain is the *image* of x under f, and the set of all such images is the *range* of f.

■ Note that (a) the range is a subset—a proper subset, in general—of the codomain, and (b) the function can be regarded as a directed relationship from the domain to the range.

For example, in the case of the functionTRIPLE:

■ The domain is the set {1,2,3,...} of all positive integers.

■ The codomain is the set {3,6,9,...} of all positive integers divisible by 3.

■ The range is the same as the codomain.

Alternatively, we might say the codomain is the same as the domain—i.e., it's the set {1,2,3,...} of all positive integers—in which case the range would be a proper subset of the codomain.

Now, you might be thinking at this point that a function is obviously just a binary relation. Certainly the following picture suggests as much:

```
TRIPLE
┌───┬───┐
│ X │ Y │
╞═══╪═══╡
│ 1 │ 3 │
│ 2 │ 6 │
│ 3 │ 9 │   ... etc.
└───┴───┘
```

However, the whole point about a function is that it's *directed* (it's a mapping *from* the domain *to* the codomain), whereas relations—at least, relations as understood in the relational model—aren't directed in that same sense. For example, if we interpret the picture just shown as representing not a function as such but rather as a binary relation, then it can be understood as both a mapping from X to Y *and also as a mapping from Y to X*—and in the latter case the roles of domain and codomain are reversed.

As the foregoing example suggests (indeed, I'd say it suggests very strongly), *domain* was never really the most appropriate term for the relational concept. In fact, I tend to think it was not much short of a disaster that Codd ever introduced it; in my opinion, it was that inappropriate term that led to an enormous amount of misunderstanding in the database world, misunderstanding that persists in some circles to this very day. The fact is, the appropriate term, the term I wish he'd used in the first place, is simply *type*. Because what Codd called a domain is indeed nothing but a type, as that term is understood—very well understood, I'd have to say—in the programming languages world. However, you don't have to take my word for it; I'll present detailed arguments in the next chapter in support of the position I'm taking here, viz., that domains and types are indeed the same thing.

SOME DEFINITIONS

Let me close this preliminary chapter by giving a few basic (and fairly formal) definitions for the record. The definitions in question are based on ones in *The Third Manifesto*. I'll be appealing to them, explicitly or implicitly, many times over in the chapters to come. *Note:* I suggest you try drawing a detailed picture of a relation as you read through these definitions, labeling the various components of your picture accordingly. I believe such an exercise can help get the terminology into your psyche, as it were, much better than just reading the formal text can.

> **Definition (type):** A named, and in practice finite, set of values; not to be confused with the internal or physical representation of the values in question, which is an implementation issue. Every value, every variable, every attribute, every read-only operator, every parameter, and every expression is of some type.[12] *Note:* Types are also referred to, in Codd's early writings in particular, as *domains*.

> **Definition (heading):** A heading H is a set, the elements of which are attributes. Let H have cardinality n;[13] then the value n is the degree of H. A heading of degree zero is nullary, a heading of degree one is unary, a heading of degree two is binary, ..., and more generally a heading of degree n is n-ary. Each attribute in H is of the form $<A_j,T_j>$ ($1 \leq j \leq n$), where A_j is the attribute name and T_j is the corresponding type name, and the attribute names A_j are all distinct.

> **Definition (tuple):** Let heading H be of degree n. For each attribute $<A_j,T_j>$ in H, define a component of the form $<A_j,T_j,V_j>$, where the attribute value V_j is a value of type T_j. The set—call it t—of all n components so defined is a tuple value (or just a tuple for short) over the attributes of H.

---

[12] Most of the terms mentioned in this sentence (value, variable, and so on) will be explained in later chapters; for now, I'm just going to assume you're familiar enough with them already. However, let me say something about the term *operator* in particular. Some people use that term to mean, more specifically, an operator that's (a) read-only and (b) denoted by some special symbol such as "+" instead of by an identifier such as PLUS—in which case other read-only operators (i.e., those denoted by such identifiers) are typically referred to as functions. However, this latter usage is misleading, and for that reason deprecated, because all read-only operators are (or at least should be) functions, strictly speaking.

[13] The cardinality of a set is the number n of elements it contains ($n \geq 0$). See the definition of *body* (next definition but one).

H is the tuple heading (or just the heading for short) for *t*; the degree and attributes of *H* are, respectively, the degree and attributes of *t*; and the type of *t* is TUPLE *H*.

Definition (body): Given a heading *H*, a body *B* conforming to *H* is a set of *m* tuples ($m \geq 0$), each with heading *H*. The value *m* is the cardinality of *B*.

Definition (relation): Let *H* be a heading, and let *B* be a body conforming to *H*. The pair <*H*,*B*>—call it *r*—is a relation value (or just a relation for short) over the attributes of *H*. *H* is the relation heading (or just the heading for short) for *r*; the degree and attributes of *H* and the cardinality of *B* are, respectively, the degree, attributes, and cardinality of *r*; and the type of *r* is RELATION *H*.

One final point of clarification: The foregoing definitions state among other things—fairly categorically, in fact—that the type of a given tuple is TUPLE *H* and the type of a given relation is RELATION *H* (where *H* is the pertinent heading in each case). However, let me elaborate on and clarify these statements. Here's a pertinent quote from the *Manifesto*:

> When we say "the name of [a certain tuple type] shall be ... TUPLE *H*," we do not mean to prescribe specific syntax. The *Manifesto* does not prescribe syntax. Rather, what we mean is that the type in question shall have a name that does both of the following, no more and no less: First, it shall specify that the type is indeed a tuple type; second, it shall specify the pertinent heading. Syntax of the form "TUPLE *H*" satisfies these requirements, and we therefore use it as a convenient shorthand; however, all [occurrences] of that syntax throughout this *Manifesto* are to be interpreted in the light of these remarks.

The same goes for RELATION *H* also, of course, mutatis mutandis.

EXERCISES

1. (*Try this exercise without looking back at the body of the chapter.*) What relvars does the suppliers and parts database contain? What attributes do they involve? What keys and foreign keys do they have?

Note: The point of this exercise is simply that it's worth making yourself as familiar as possible with the structure, at least in general terms, of the suppliers and parts example. It's not so important to remember the actual data values, though it wouldn't hurt if you did.

2. I showed in the body of the chapter how DELETE can be defined in terms of relational assignment (":=") and relational difference (MINUS). But what about INSERT? And (harder) what about UPDATE?

3. What's the difference between **D** and **Tutorial D**?

4. Is **Tutorial D** part of *The Third Manifesto*?

5. What do you understand by the term *object / relational*?

6. The picture of the suppliers and parts database in the body of the chapter shows sample values for the pertinent relvars, or in other words what some writers call the "state," or "current state," of the relvars in question. Moreover, that picture also shows certain attributes with double underlining, and that double underlining is intended to indicate that the attributes in question constitute a key for the corresponding relvar. But consider the following picture, which shows the result of restricting the current value of relvar S to just suppliers in Paris:

SNO	SNAME	STATUS	CITY
S2	Jones	10	Paris
S3	Blake	30	Paris

What this picture shows is just a relation as such, not a relation that happens to be the current value (or "current state") of some relvar. And relations as such don't have keys, relvars do.[14] So what do you think is an appropriate interpretation of that double underlining in pictures like this one?

---

[14] Why? Because to say something is a key is to say a certain integrity constraint is in effect—a certain uniqueness constraint, to be specific—and integrity constraints apply to variables, not values. (By definition, integrity constraints constrain updates, and updates apply to variables, not values. See the section "Values vs. Variables" in Chapter 2.)

7. In the body of the chapter, I described a certain assumption—viz., the assumption that the relational concept that most closely equated to the object *class* concept was the concept of a relation (or a relvar, rather)—as incorrect. So why do you think that assumption might have seemed attractive to some people?

8. Explain the logical difference between a binary relation and a function.

ANSWERS

For answers to Exercises 1, 3, and 5, please refer to the body of the chapter.

2. I'll answer this exercise in terms of a couple of simple examples. First, the **Tutorial D** INSERT statement

```
INSERT SP
       RELATION { TUPLE { SNO SNO('S5') ,
                          PNO PNO('P6') , QTY QTY(250) } } ;
```

(which effectively inserts just a single tuple into relvar SP) is shorthand for the following:

```
SP := SP
      UNION
      RELATION { TUPLE { SNO SNO('S5') ,
                         PNO PNO('P6') , QTY QTY(250) } } ;
```

Subsidiary exercise: What happens if the specified tuple already exists in the target relvar? What do you conclude?[15]

Aside: The expression

```
      RELATION { TUPLE { SNO SNO('S5') ,
                         PNO PNO('P6') , QTY QTY(250) } }
```

---

[15] *Answer:* The union of two sets *A* and *B* is the set of all elements *x* such that *x* is an element of *A* or *B* or both. It follows that nothing special will happen—in particular, no error will occur—if the specified tuple already exists in the target relvar. It follows further that it might be preferable *not* to define INSERT in terms of UNION as such, but rather instead of some kind of *disjoint* UNION that requires its operand sets not to have any elements in common. For further discussion, see, e.g., the book *SQL and Relational Theory*, 3rd ed. (O'Reilly, 2015).

—which appears in both of the code fragments above—is a *relation selector invocation*, and it denotes the relation that contains just the tuple to be inserted. (In fact, it's not just a relation selector invocation, it's a relation *literal*. See Chapter 4 for further explanation). Moreover, the subexpression TUPLE {...} within that relation literal is a *tuple* selector invocation, and indeed a tuple literal (again see Chapter 4). And the expression SNO('S5'), for example, which appears as a subexpression within that tuple literal, is a *scalar* selector invocation—and in fact a literal, too—and it denotes a specific supplier number (see Chapter 2 for further explanation). Likewise for the subexpressions PNO('P6') and QTY QTY(250), of course. *End of aside*.

Second, the **Tutorial D** UPDATE statement

```
UPDATE P WHERE CITY = 'Paris' :
          { CITY := 'Nice' , WEIGHT := 2 × WEIGHT } ;
```

—which effectively updates all parts in Paris, changing their city to Nice and doubling their weight—is shorthand for the following:

```
WITH ( t1 := P WHERE CITY = 'Paris' ,
       t2 := EXTEND t1 : { CITY := 'Nice' ,
                           WEIGHT := 2 × WEIGHT } ) :
P := ( P MINUS t1 ) UNION t2 ;
```

Note the use of a WITH specification in this example to introduce temporary names for the results of certain subexpressions. **Tutorial D**'s WITH construct can be very useful in general in simplifying the formulation of what otherwise might be very complicated expressions. For further explanation (also regarding the EXTEND operator used in lines 2 and 3), again I refer you to my book *SQL and Relational Theory*, 3rd ed. (O'Reilly, 2015).

4. No, it isn't—it's defined in the *Manifesto* book, but it's not part of the *Manifesto* as such.

6. Such pictures can always be regarded as showing a sample value for some relational expression *rx*, where *rx* is something other than a simple relvar

reference. (A relvar reference is just a relvar name, syntactically speaking.) Moreover, *rx* in turn can be regarded as defining a possible value for some relvar *R* (perhaps a view, for example) So the double underlining indicates that (a) a key *K* could in principle be declared for that relvar *R*, and (b) the pertinent attribute is part of *K*.

An alternative but equivalent way of saying the same thing is this: The relation depicted certainly doesn't "have" the indicated key—in fact, it would be logically incorrect to say the relation "has" that key—but it does satisfy the corresponding key or uniqueness constraint.

7. At least part of the reason, it seems to me, is that the terms *class* and *object* have no single, universally agreed meaning. Consider the following argument:

■ Over the years, there have been several books on object database design. Here are a couple of examples: (a) *Object-Oriented Modeling and Design for Database Applications*, by Michael Blaha and William Premerlani (Prentice-Hall, 1998); (b) *Object-Oriented Software Engineering*, by Ivar Jacobson (with Magnus Christerson, Patrik Jonsson, and Gunnar Övergaard), revised printing (Addison-Wesley, 1994).

■ Such books typically use (a) the terms *object* and *object modeling* to mean what the database community would more usually call an *entity* and *entity / relationship modeling*, respectively, and (b) the term *class* to mean a collection of such objects (or entities).

■ As a consequence, those books go on, in effect, to map those objects to tuples in relvars instead of values in domains (more precisely, they map classes to relvars instead of to domains).

■ Now, the foregoing isn't necessarily a problem, as far as it goes; the problem only arises when a change in context occurs and we move into the programming realm, where the terms *class* and *object* take on different meanings—*class* now being another term for *type*, and *object* now being another term for something that's of such a type.

In other words, what happens is that an equation ("class = relvar") that made sense with one interpretation of the pertinent terms gets carried over unchanged to a context where it doesn't make sense, because the meanings of the terms have changed. That's my guess, anyway.

8. A function *is* a binary relation, but it's a special case. Let *r* be a binary relation with attributes *X* and *Y*. Then *r* is a function from *X* to *Y* if and only if for one *X* value in *r* there's just one corresponding *Y* value in *r*, and it's a function from *Y* to *X* if and only if for one *Y* value in *r* there's just one corresponding *X* value in *r*. Note that it might be both—in which case the mapping is 1:1 in both directions, and if *r* is a value of some relvar, then {*X*} and {*Y*} will both be keys for that relvar

Chapter 2

Types and Domains:

The Basics

Data types, or just types for short, are fundamental to programming language theory in general. As a consequence, they're fundamental to relational theory in particular, because the relational model *is* a programming language—a fairly abstract one, agreed, since it doesn't prescribe any specific syntax, but a language neverthetheless. More specifically, the relational model requires a supporting theory of types because relations are defined over types; that is, every attribute of every relation is defined to be of some type (and the same is true of relvars too, of course). For example, attribute STATUS of the suppliers relvar S is defined to be of type INTEGER, and so every relation that's a possible value for relvar S must also have a STATUS attribute that's of type INTEGER—which means in turn that every tuple in such a relation must also have a STATUS attribute of type INTEGER, which means still further that the tuple in question must have a STATUS value that's an integer.

I'll be discussing these matters in detail later in this chapter. For now, let me just say that—with certain important exceptions, which I'll also be discussing later—a relational attribute (i.e., an attribute of a relation or relvar) can be *of any type whatsoever*, which means among other things that those types can be arbitrarily complex. In particular, they can be either system or user defined. In this chapter, however, I don't plan to say much about user defined types as such (though of course I will say something), because:

■ First, not many users will ever be faced with the job of defining a type. It's not the kind of thing that regular users generally need to get involved in.

■ Second, the whole point about user defined types—from the point of view of the user who's merely using them, that is, as opposed to the specialist user who has the job of defining them—is that they're supposed to behave as far as possible just like system defined types anyway.

From this point forward, therefore, you can take the term *type* to mean a system defined type specifically, barring explicit statements to the contrary. The relational model prescribes just one such, viz., type BOOLEAN (the most fundamental type of all). That type contains exactly two values: two truth values, to be precise, denoted by the literals TRUE and FALSE, respectively. However, real systems will support a variety of other system defined types as well, of course, and I'll assume for definiteness that the system defined types INT, or INTEGER (integers); RAT, or RATIONAL (rational numbers); and CHAR, or CHARACTER (character strings of arbitrary length), are among those supported.

Note: Perhaps I should explain before going any further exactly what I mean by the term *rational number*. By definition, such a number is one that can be expressed as the ratio of two integers, such as 3/8, 4/3, or 593/370 (and an irrational number is one that can't be so expressed, such as π or $\sqrt{2}$). Rational numbers fall into two broad categories:

a.   Those whose fractional part can be expressed by means of a possibly empty finite sequence of digits followed by an infinite sequence of zeros (e.g., 3/8 = 0.375000...). Of course, that infinite sequence of zeros can safely be ignored.

b.   Those whose fractional part can be expressed by means of a possibly empty finite sequence of digits followed by another finite sequence of such digits, the first of which is nonzero, that infinitely repeats (e.g., 593/370 = 1.60270270...).

By contrast, the fractional part of an irrational number consists of an infinite, nonrepeating sequence of digits (e.g., π = 3.14159..., $\sqrt{2}$ = 1.41421...).

Aside: Perhaps I should state for the record that although the foregoing examples are expressed in terms of decimal notation specifically, whether a number is rational or irrational has nothing to do with whatever radix happens to be in effect. It's true, however, that which of the foregoing categories, a. or b., a given rational number falls into does depend on the radix. For example, the number "one third" is in category b. in binary, but category a. in ternary. *End of aside.*

Now, many programming languages support a numeric type they call REAL. In mathematics, a real number is a number that's either rational or irrational. Computers, however, are finite, and what's more they're based on binary arithmetic (radix 2). As a consequence, the only real numbers they're capable of representing precisely are rational ones, and then only ones that, in binary, fall into category a. (e.g., decimal 3/8, which is 0.011 in binary). Hence **Tutorial D**'s choice of the keyword RATIONAL in preference to the more usual REAL.

Back to types in general. In the interest of historical accuracy, I must now remind you that when Codd originally defined the relational model, he said relations were defined over *domains*, not types. However, I claimed repeatedly in Chapter 1 that there aren't two concepts here but only one—domains and types are in fact the exact same thing. Now, you can take this claim as a position statement on my part, if you like, but I want to present a series of arguments in support of that position. My starting point will be the relational model as Codd originally defined it, and for that reason I'll use the term *domain*, not *type*, until further notice. In fact there are two major aspects to the original model that I want to discuss in this connection, and I'll devote a section to each in turn:

■ *Equality comparisons and "domain check override":* This part of the discussion I hope will convince you that domains really are types.

■ *Data value atomicity and first normal form:* And this part I hope will convince you that the types in question can be arbitrarily complex.

EQUALITY COMPARISONS

Despite what I said a little while back about ignoring user defined types (for the most part, anyway), let me now remind you that the relvar definitions in Chapter 1 do show the supplier number (SNO) attributes in relvars S and SP as being of a user defined type (sorry, domain), where the domain in question is named SNO as well for simplicity. They also show the part number (PNO) attributes in relvars P and SP as being of a user defined type (or domain), this one being called PNO. However, please understand that the fact that the domains in this example happen to be user defined isn't crucial to the argument I'm about to present; I just think it makes that argument a little more convincing, and perhaps easier to follow in places.

I'll start with the observation that—as "everyone knows"—in the relational model, two values can be tested for equality only if they come from the same domain. (Because if they come from different domains, they can't possibly be equal.) Thus, the following comparison, which might be part of the WHERE clause in some SQL query, is obviously valid:

```
SP.SNO = S.SNO      /* comparing like with like - OK      */
```

By contrast, this one obviously isn't:

```
SP.PNO = S.SNO      /* comparing like with unlike - not OK */
```

But why isn't it? *Answer:* Because part numbers and supplier numbers are different kinds of things—they're defined on different domains. So the general idea is that the DBMS should reject any attempt to perform a relational operation (join, union, whatever) that involves, either explicitly or implicitly, an equality comparison between values from different domains. For example, suppose some user wants to find suppliers who—like supplier S5 in our usual sample database value—currently supply no parts at all. Then the following might be an attempt to formulate the corresponding query in SQL:[1]

```
SELECT  S.SNO , S.SNAME , S.STATUS , S.CITY
FROM    S
WHERE   NOT EXISTS
      ( SELECT  *
        FROM    SP
        WHERE   SP.PNO = S.SNO )      /* not OK */
```

As the comment says, this attempt is not OK. Why not? Because in the last line, where the user presumably meant to say WHERE SP.SNO = S.SNO, he or she has actually said—probably by mistake, probably just a slip of the typing fingers—WHERE SP.***PNO*** = S.SNO instead. And, given that we're indeed talking about a simple typo (probably), it would be a friendly act on the part of the DBMS to interrupt the user at this point, highlight the error, and ask the user if he or she would like to correct it before proceeding.

Now, I really don't know whether any of today's SQL products will actually behave in the way I've just suggested. But if they don't, then, depending on exactly how you've defined the database, the query will either fail

---

[1] There's no terminating semicolon in this example because we're dealing with an expression (or would-be expression), not a statement. See Chapter 3, Exercise 6.)

or give the wrong answer. Well ... not exactly the wrong answer, perhaps, but the right answer to the wrong question. (Does that make you feel any better?)

To repeat, therefore, the DBMS should reject a comparison like SP.PNO = S.SNO, because it's not valid. However, Codd felt there should be a way in such a situation for the user to make the DBMS go ahead and do the comparison anyway, even though it's not valid, on the grounds that sometimes the user will know more than the DBMS does. Now, it's hard for me to do justice to this idea, because I frankly don't think it makes sense—but let me give it a try. Suppose it's your job to design a database involving, let's say, customers and suppliers; and you therefore decide to have a domain of customer numbers and a domain of supplier numbers; and you build your database that way, and open it up for general use, and everything works just fine for a year or two. Then, one day, one of your users comes along with a query you never thought of before—namely: "Are any of our customers also suppliers to us?" Observe that this is a perfectly reasonable query; observe too that it *might* involve a comparison between a customer number and a supplier number (a cross-domain comparison), to see if they're equal. And if it does, well, the system certainly mustn't prevent you from doing that comparison, because (of course!) the system certainly mustn't prevent you from posing a reasonable query.

On the basis of such arguments, Codd proposed what he called "semantic override" or "domain check override" (DCO) versions of some of his relational operators—though, interestingly, not all of them (*exercise for the reader*). A DCO version of join, for example, would perform the join even if the joining attributes were defined on different domains. In SQL terms, we might imagine this proposal being realized by means of a new clause, IGNORE DOMAIN CHECKS, that could be included in an SQL query as in the following hypothetical example:

```
SELECT ...
FROM   ...
WHERE  CNO = SNO    /* "CNO" is customer number */
IGNORE DOMAIN CHECKS
```

And this new clause would be separately authorizable—most users wouldn't be allowed to use it (perhaps only the DBA would be allowed to use it).

Before analyzing the DCO idea in detail, I want to look at a simpler example. Consider the following two SQL queries on the suppliers and parts database:

```
SELECT ...                         SELECT ...
FROM    P , SP                     FROM    P , SP
WHERE   P.WEIGHT = SP.QTY          WHERE   P.WEIGHT - SP.QTY = 0
```

Now, if you refer back to the database definition in Chapter 1, you'll see that weights and quantities are defined on different domains, and the query on the left is accordingly not valid. But what about the one on the right? According to Codd, that one's valid! In his book *The Relational Model for Database Management Version 2* (Addison-Wesley, 1990), page 47, he says that in such a situation "the DBMS [merely] checks that the basic data types are the same"; in the case at hand, those "basic data types" are presumably all just numbers (loosely speaking), and so that check succeeds.

To me, this conclusion is unacceptable. Clearly, the expressions

```
P.WEIGHT = SP.QTY
```

and

```
P.WEIGHT - SP.QTY = 0
```

both mean essentially the same thing. Surely, therefore, they must either both be valid or both not be valid; the idea that one might be valid and the other not surely makes no sense. So it seems to me there's something strange about Codd-style domain checking in the first place, before we even get to domain check override. (In essence, in fact, Codd-style domain checking applies only in the very special case where both comparands are specified by means of simple attribute names. Observe that the first of the foregoing examples falls into this category but the second one doesn't.)

Let's look at some even simpler examples. Consider the following three comparisons (each of which might appear as part of an SQL WHERE clause, for example):

```
S.SNO = 'X4'          P.PNO = 'X4'          S.SNO = P.PNO
```

Well, I hope you agree it's at least plausible that the first two of these could be valid (and evaluate successfully, and possibly even give TRUE), while the third isn't (and doesn't, and can't). But if so, then I hope you also agree there's something strange going on; apparently, we can have three values a, b, and c such that $a = c$ is true and $b = c$ is true, but as for $a = b$—well, we can't even do the comparison, let alone have it come out true! So what's going on?

I return now to the fact that attributes S.SNO and P.PNO are defined on domains SNO and PNO, respectively, and my claim that domains are actually types; as previously noted, in fact, I'm assuming for the sake of the present discussion that those particular domains SNO and PNO are actually *user defined* types. Now, it's possible (even likely) that those user defined types are both physically represented in terms of the system defined type CHAR; in fact, let's assume they are, just to be definite. However, those physical representations are part of the *implementation*, not part of the *model*—they're irrelevant to the user, and what's more they're supposed to be hidden as far as the user is concerned. In particular, therefore, the operators that apply to supplier numbers and part numbers are the operators defined in connection with types SNO and PNO, respectively, *not* the operators that happen to be defined in connection with type CHAR (see the section "What's a Type?" later in this chapter). For example, we can concatenate two character strings, but we probably can't concatenate two supplier numbers (we could do this latter only if concatenation were an operator defined in connection with type SNO).

As the foregoing paragraph suggests, however, when we define a type, we do also have to define the operators that can be used in connection with values and variables of the type in question. And one operator we *must* define is what's called a *selector* operator, which allows us to select, or specify, an arbitrary value of the type in question.[2] In the case of type SNO, for example, the selector—which in practice would probably also be called SNO—allows us to select the particular SNO value that has some specified CHAR representation. Here's an example:

```
SNO('S1')
```

This expression is an invocation of the SNO selector, and it returns a certain supplier number: namely, the one represented by the character string 'S1'. Likewise, the expression

```
PNO('P1')
```

---

[2] This observation is valid regardless of whether we're in an SQL context, as in the present discussion, or otherwise—but I should make it clear that selectors in SQL aren't as straightforward as they might be (see Chapter 5), and *selector* as such isn't an SQL term. I should also make it clear that selectors have nothing to do with the SQL SELECT operator. (Come to that, they also have nothing to do with the restrict operator of relational algebra, which is sometimes called "select.")

is an invocation of the PNO selector, and it returns a certain part number: namely, the one represented by the character string 'P1'. In other words, the SNO and PNO selectors effectively work by taking a certain CHAR value and converting it to a certain SNO value and a certain PNO value, respectively.[3]

Now let's get back to the comparison S.SNO = 'X4'. As you can see, the comparands here are of different types (types SNO and CHAR, to be specific; in fact, 'X4' is a character string literal). Since they're of different types, they certainly can't be equal (recall from the beginning of the present section that two values can be compared for equality "only if they come from the same domain"). But the system does at least know there's an operator—namely, the SNO selector—that effectively performs CHAR to SNO conversions. So it can invoke that operator, implicitly, to convert the CHAR comparand to a supplier number, thereby effectively replacing the original comparison by this one:

```
S.SNO = SNO('X4')
```

Now we're comparing two supplier numbers, which is legitimate.

In like fashion the system can effectively replace the comparison P.PNO = 'X4' by this one, which is also legitimate:

```
P.PNO = PNO('X4')
```

But in the case of the comparison S.SNO = P.PNO, there's no conversion operator known to the system—at least, let's assume there isn't—that will convert a supplier number to a part number or the other way around, and so the comparison fails on a *type error*: The comparands are of different types, and there's no way to make them be of the same type.

Note: Implicit type conversion as illustrated in the foregoing examples is often referred to more formally as *coercion*. Thus, in the first example, we can say the character string 'X4' is coerced to type SNO; in the second, we can say it's coerced to type PNO.

To continue with the example: Another operator we must define when we define a type like SNO or PNO is what's referred to, generically, as a THE_ operator, which—in the case at hand—effectively converts a given SNO or PNO value to the character string (or whatever else it might be) that's used to

---

[3] "Converting" a value of one type T_1 to some other type T_2 is indeed the way we usually talk about such matters, but such talk is really quite sloppy. What such a "conversion" really does is map a value v_1 of type T_1 to some corresponding value v_2 of type T_2. Nothing is done to the value v_1 as such—I mean, it remains unchanged after the "conversion" has been performed.

represent it.[4] Assume for the sake of discussion that the THE_ operators for types SNO and PNO are called THE_SC and THE_PC, respectively. Then, if we really did want to compare S.SNO and P.PNO for equality, the only sense I can make of that requirement is that we want to test whether the corresponding character string representations are the same, which we might do like this:

```
THE_SC ( S.SNO ) = THE_PC ( P.PNO )
```

In other words: Convert the supplier number to a string, convert the part number to a string, and compare the two strings.

Well, as I'm sure you can see, the mechanism I've been sketching here, involving selectors and THE_ operators, effectively provides both

a. The domain checking we want in the first place, and

b. A way of overriding that checking, when desired, in the second place.

Moreover, it does these things in a clean, fully orthogonal, non ad hoc manner.[5] By contrast, domain check override doesn't do the job, not properly; in fact, it doesn't really make sense at all, because it confuses types and their physical representations. (To repeat, types are a model concept, while physical representations are an implementation concept.)

Now, you might have realized that what I'm talking about here is what's known in programming language circles as *strong typing*. Different writers have slightly different definitions for this term, but basically what it means is that:

a. Everything—in particular, every value and every variable—has a type, and

b. Whenever we try to perform some operation, the system checks that the operands are of the right types for the operation in question (or, possibly, that they're coercible to those right types).

---

[4] Again this observation is valid regardless of whether we're in an SQL context or some other context—though (as with selectors, mutatis mutandis, and as we'll see in Chapter 5) THE_ operators in SQL aren't as straightforward as they might be, and "THE_ operator" as such isn't an SQL term.

[5] Orthogonality is a good general principle of programming language design. It can be stated loosely thus: *If features are logically unrelated, they should be unrelated in the language*. Here's a simple example of lack of orthogonality: In versions of SQL prior to SQL:1999, a value to be inserted via an INSERT statement had to be specified by either a literal or a simple variable reference, not by some more general expression.

Observe, moreover, that this mechanism applies to all operations, not just the equality comparisons I've been discussing; the emphasis on equality and other comparison operations, in discussions of domain checking in the literature, is sanctioned by historical usage but is in fact misplaced. For example, consider the following expressions:

```
P.WEIGHT × SP.QTY

P.WEIGHT + SP.QTY
```

The first of these is probably valid—it yields another weight: namely, the total weight of the pertinent shipment (assuming, of course, that the shipment in question is a shipment of the part in question). The second, by contrast, is probably not valid (what could it possibly mean to add a weight and a quantity?).

I'd like to close this section by stressing the absolutely fundamental role played—not just in type theory!—by the equality operator ("="). It wasn't an accident that the discussions above concentrated on the question of comparing two values for equality specifically. The fact is, equality truly is central, and the relational model requires it to be supported for every type. Indeed, since a type is basically a set of values (see the section "What's a Type?"), without the "=" operator we couldn't even say what values constitute the type in question! That is, given some type T and some value v, we couldn't say, absent that operator, whether or not v was one of the values in the set of values constituting type T.

What's more, the relational model doesn't just require support for the "=" operator, it specifies the corresponding semantics as well, thus:[6]

Let v_1 and v_2 be values of the same type. Then $v_1 = v_2$ evaluates to TRUE if v_1 and v_2 are the very same value and FALSE otherwise.

By contrast, if v_1 and v_2 are values of different types, then $v_1 = v_2$ has no meaning (it's not even a legal comparison) unless v_1 can be coerced to the type of v_2 or the other way around—in which case we aren't really talking about a comparison between v_1 and v_2 as such anyway.

---

[6] I'm appealing here, tacitly, to the relational model as defined in *The Third Manifesto*. I note in the interest of historical accuracy that Codd never did specify exactly what equality meant but rather just took that meaning for granted (and thereby fell into at least one serious logical trap, and arguably more than one).

DATA VALUE ATOMICITY

I hope the arguments in the previous section succeeded in convincing you that domains really are types, no more and no less. Now I want to turn to the issue of data value atomicity and the related notion of *first normal form*. A relation is said to be in first normal form (1NF for short) if and only every tuple in the relation in question contains just a single value (of the appropriate type, of course) in every attribute position—and it's usual to add that those "single values" must be "atomic." But this latter stipulation raises the obvious question: What does it mean for data to be atomic?

Now, on page 6 of that book of Codd's mentioned a couple of pages back (*The Relational Model for Database Management Version 2*), he defines atomic data to be "[data that] cannot be decomposed into smaller pieces by the DBMS (excluding certain special functions)." Even if we overlook that parenthetical exclusion, however, this definition is a trifle puzzling; at best, it's hardly very precise. For example, what about character strings? Are character strings atomic? Well, every database product I know of provides a variety of operators—LIKE, SUBSTRING, "| |" (concatenate), and so on—that rely by definition on the fact that character strings in general can be "decomposed into smaller pieces by the DBMS." So are such strings atomic? What do you think?

Here are a few more examples of values whose atomicity is at least open to question and yet we would surely want to allow as attribute values in tuples in relations:

■ Bit strings

■ Rational numbers (which might be regarded as being decomposable into integer and fractional parts)

■ Dates and times (which might be regarded as being decomposable into year / month / day and hour / minute / second components, respectively)

And so on.

Before drawing any conclusions from the discussion so far, I'd like to consider another example, one that some might regard as more startling, in a way. Consider the following figure:

R1

SNO	PNO
S2	P1
S2	P2
S3	P2
S4	P2
S4	P4
S4	P5

R2

SNO	PNO
S2	P1,P2
S3	P2
S4	P2,P4,P5

R3

SNO	PNO_SET
S2	{P1,P2}
S3	{P2}
S4	{P2,P4,P5}

Now, relation R1 in this figure is just a reduced version of the shipments relation from our usual running example—and as you can see, what it shows is simply that certain suppliers supply certain parts (thus, it contains one tuple for each pertinent {SNO,PNO} combination). Moreover, let's agree for the sake of the example that supplier numbers and part numbers are atomic values. Then we can presumably agree that R1, at least, is in 1NF.

Now suppose we replace R1 by R2, which shows that certain suppliers supply certain *groups* of parts: Attribute PNO in R2 is what some people would call *multivalued*, and values of that attribute are groups of part numbers. Well, most people would surely say that R2 is not in 1NF; in fact, it looks like a case of "repeating groups," and repeating groups are the one thing that just about everybody agrees 1NF is supposed to prohibit, because repeating groups are obviously not atomic (right?).

Well, let's agree for the sake of the argument that R2 isn't in 1NF. But suppose we now replace R2 by R3. Then I claim that, by contrast, R3 *is* in 1NF. For consider: First, note that I've renamed the attribute PNO_SET, and I've enclosed the groups of part numbers that are PNO_SET values in braces, to emphasize the fact that each such group is indeed a single value—a set value, to be sure, but a set is still, at a certain level of abstraction, a single value. Second (and regardless of what you might think of that first argument), the fact is that a set like {P2,P4,P5} is *no more and no less decomposable by the DBMS than a character string is*. Like character strings, sets do have some inner structure; as with character strings, however, it's convenient to ignore that structure for certain purposes. In other words, if character strings are compatible with the requirements of 1NF—that is, if character strings are considered to be atomic— then sets must be, too.[7]

---

[7] Observe that I don't claim that R3 is well designed—indeed, it probably isn't—but that's not the point at issue. I'm concerned here with what's legal, not with questions of good design. The design of R3 is legal.

The real point I'm getting at here is that the notion of atomicity *has no absolute meaning*; it just depends on what we want to do with the data. Sometimes we want to deal with an entire set of part numbers as a single thing; other times we want to deal with individual part numbers within that set—but then we're descending to a lower level of detail, or lower level of abstraction. The following analogy might help. In physics—which after all is where the terminology of atomicity comes from—the situation is exactly parallel: Sometimes we want to think about individual atoms as indivisible things, other times we want to think about the subatomic particles (the protons, neutrons, and electrons) that go to make up those atoms. What's more, protons and neutrons, at least, aren't really indivisible, either—they contain a variety of "subsubatomic" particles called quarks. And so on, possibly (?).

Let's return for a moment to relation R3. The original figure shows PNO_SET values in that relation just as sets. But it would be more useful in practice if they were, more specifically, relations (see R4 below, where I've changed the attribute name to PNO_REL).

R4

Why do I say R4 would be more useful than R3? Because relations, not general sets, are what the relational model is all about.[8] As a consequence, the full power of the relational algebra immediately becomes available for the relations in question—they can be restricted, projected, joined, and so on. By contrast, if we were to use general sets instead of relations, then we would need to introduce new set operators (set union, set intersection, and so on) for dealing with those sets ... Much better to get as much mileage as we can out of the operators we already have.

Terminology: Attribute PNO_REL of relation R4 is a *relation valued attribute* (RVA for short). (Of course, the underlying domain is relation valued too; that is, the values it contains are relations.) Now, you might not have encountered RVAs before, because SQL in particular doesn't support them—or rather, it doesn't support what would be its analog of RVAs, viz., *table valued columns*. Oddly enough, however, it does support columns whose values are arrays, and columns whose values are rows, and even columns whose values are "multisets of rows"—where a *multiset*, also known as a *bag*, is like a set except that it permits duplicates.[9] Columns whose values are multisets of rows thus do look a little bit like "table valued columns"; however, they aren't table valued columns, because the values they contain can't be operated upon by means of SQL's regular table operators and thus aren't regular SQL table values, by definition.

Now, I chose the foregoing example deliberately, for its shock value. After all, relations with RVAs do look rather like "relations with repeating groups," and you've probably always heard that repeating groups are a no-no in the relational world. But I could have used any number of different examples to make my point; I could have shown attributes (and therefore domains) that contained arrays; or bags (multisets); or lists; or photographs; or audio or video recordings; or X rays; or fingerprints; or XML documents; or any other kind of value, "atomic" or "nonatomic," you might care to think of. Attributes, and therefore domains, can contain *anything* (any *values*, that is).

Incidentally, you might recall my mentioning in Chapter 1 how we were hearing a great deal a few years back about so called "object / relational" systems. You might also recall my claim in that same chapter to the effect that a

---

[8] In case you're wondering, the difference is that sets in general can contain anything, but relations always contain tuples (and nothing but tuples). Note, however, that a relation certainly does resemble a general set inasmuch as it too can be regarded as a single value.

[9] The individual elements in an SQL multiset don't have to be rows but can be values of any available SQL type—for example, integers. See Chapter 3 for further discussion.

true object / relational system would be nothing more nor less than a true relational system—which is to say, a system that supports the relational model, with all that such support entails. Well, the preceding paragraph goes a long way toward explaining why such is the case. After all, the whole point about an object / relational system, from the user's point of view, is precisely that we can have attribute values in relations that are of arbitrary complexity. Or perhaps a better way to say it is: A proper object / relational system is just a relational system with proper type support (including proper user defined type support in particular)—which just means it's a proper relational system, no more and no less. As noted in Chapter 1, therefore (in footnote 7), what some people are pleased to call "the object / relational model" is in fact just the relational model, no more and no less.

WHAT'S A TYPE?

From this point forward, then, I'll favor the term *type* over the term *domain*. So what is a type, exactly? In essence, it's a named, finite set of values—all possible values of some specific kind: for example, all possible integers, or all possible character strings, or all possible supplier numbers, or all possible XML documents, or all possible relations with a certain heading (and so on). To elaborate briefly:

- The types we're interested in are (to repeat) always *named.* Types with different names are different types.

- The types we're interested in are also always *finite*, because we're dealing with computers, and (as pointed out in connection with type RATIONAL earlier in the chapter) computers are finite by definition.

Moreover:

- Every *value* is a value of some type—in fact, of exactly one type, except possibly if type inheritance is supported, a concept that's beyond the scope of this book.

  Aside: If every value is of exactly one type, then no value is of two or more types, and thus types are always disjoint (nonoverlapping).

However, perhaps I need to elaborate on this point, just for a moment. As one reviewer said, surely types *WarmBloodedAnimal* and *FourLeggedAnimal* overlap? Indeed they do; but it's my position that if types overlap, then for a variety of reasons we're getting into the realm of type inheritance—in fact, into the realm of what's called *multiple* inheritance. Since those reasons, and indeed the whole topic of inheritance as such, are at least partly independent of the context we're in (be it relational or something else), I'm not going to discuss such matters further in this book—at least, not in any depth. *End of aside.*

■ Every *variable*, every *attribute*, every *operator* that returns a result, and every *parameter* of every operator is defined, or declared, to be of some type.[10] And to say that, e.g., variable *V* is declared to be of type *T* means, precisely, that every value *v* that can be assigned to *V* is of type *T* in turn.

■ Every *expression* denotes some value and is therefore of some type—namely, the type of the value in question, which is to say the type of the value returned by the outermost operator in the expression (where by "outermost" I mean the operator that's executed last). For example, the type of the expression

```
( a / b ) × ( x − y )
```

is the type declared for the operator "×", whatever that happens to be.

The fact that parameters in particular are declared to be of some type touches on an issue that I've mentioned but haven't yet properly discussed: namely, the fact that *associated with every type there's a set of operators for operating on values and variables of the type in question*—where to say that operator *Op* is "associated with" type *T* essentially means just that operator *Op* has a parameter of type *T*.[11] For example, integers have the usual arithmetic

---

[10] Throughout this book I treat *defined* and *declared* as synonymous.

[11] The logical difference between type and representation is important here. To spell the matter out, the operators associated with type *T* are the operators associated with type *T* as such—*not* the operators associated with the representation of type *T*. For example, just because the representation for type SNO happens to be of type CHAR (say), it doesn't follow that we can concatenate two supplier numbers; we can do that only if concatenation is an operator that's defined for type SNO. (In fact I mentioned this very example in the section "Equality Comparisons" earlier, as you might recall.)

operators; dates and times have special calendar arithmetic operators; XML documents have what are called "XPath" and "XQuery" operators; relations have the operators of the relational algebra; and *every* type has the operators of assignment (":=") and equality comparison ("="). Thus, any system that provides proper type support—and "proper type support" here certainly includes the ability for users to define their own types—must provide a way for users to define their own operators too, because types without operators are useless. *Note:* User defined operators can be specified in association with system defined types as well as user defined ones (or a mixture, of course), as you would surely expect.

Observe now that, by definition, values and variables of a given type *T* can be operated upon *only* by means of the operators associated with that type *T*. For example, in the case of the system defined type INTEGER:

- The system provides an assignment operator ":=" for assigning integer values to integer variables.

- The system also provides a format for writing integer literals. However, it doesn't provide any more general integer selector operators, nor does it provide any corresponding THE_ operators, because—as should be obvious if you think about it—such operators aren't needed for a simple type like INTEGER. *Note:* I'll come back to this question of literals vs. selectors at the very end of the present section.

- It also provides comparison operators "=", "≠", "<", and so on, for comparing integer values.

- It also provides arithmetic operators "+", "×", and so on, for performing arithmetic on integer values.

- It does *not* provide string operators LIKE, SUBSTRING, "||" (concatenate), and so on, for performing string operations on integer values; in other words, string operations on integers aren't supported.

By contrast, in the case of the user defined type SNO, we'd certainly have to define the necessary selector and THE_ operators, and we'd also have to define assignment (":=") and comparison operators (certainly "=" and "≠", possibly "<" and so on as well). However, we probably wouldn't define operators "+", "×", and so on, which would mean that arithmetic on supplier numbers wouldn't be supported. (What could it possibly mean to add or multiply two supplier numbers?)

From everything I've said so far, then, it should be clear that defining a new type involves at least all of the following:

1. Defining a name for the type.

2. Defining the values that make up that type. I'll discuss this aspect in detail in Chapter 4.

3. Defining the hidden physical representation for values of that type. But this is an implementation issue, not a model issue, and I won't discuss it further in this book. At least, not much.

4. Defining at least one selector operator for selecting, or specifying, values of that type. *Note:* Regarding that "at least one," again I refer you to Chapter 4. By the way, here's as good a place as any to point out in the interest of accuracy that a selector for type *T* isn't "associated with" type *T* in the sense that it takes a parameter of type *T*; instead, it returns a result of type *T*.

5. Defining the operators, including in particular assignment (":="), equality comparison ("="), and THE_ operators, that apply to values and variables of that type (see below).

6. For those operators that return a result, defining the type of that result (again, see below).

Observe that points 4, 5, and 6 taken together imply that (a) the system knows precisely which expressions are legal, and (b) for those expressions that are legal it knows the type of the result as well.

By way of illustration, suppose we're given a user defined type called POINT, representing geometric points in two-dimensional space. Here then is the **Tutorial D** definition for an operator called REFLECT which, given a point PT with cartesian coordinates (x,y), returns the "reflected" or "inverse" point with cartesian coordinates $(-x,-y)$:

```
1. OPERATOR REFLECT ( PT POINT ) RETURNS POINT ;
2.    RETURN POINT ( - THE_X ( PT ) , - THE_Y ( PT ) ) ;
3. END OPERATOR ;
```

Explanation:

■ Line 1 shows that the operator (a) is called REFLECT, (b) takes a single parameter PT of type POINT, and (c) returns a result also of type POINT (so the type of the operator as such, also of any invocation of that operator, is POINT).

■ Line 2 is the operator implementation code. It consists of a single RETURN statement. The value to be returned is a point, and it's obtained by invoking the POINT selector. That invocation in turn has two arguments, corresponding to the X and Y coordinates of the point to be returned. Each of those arguments is defined by means of a THE_ operator invocation; those invocations yield the X and Y coordinates of the point argument corresponding to parameter PT, and negating those coordinates then produces the desired result.[12]

■ Line 3 marks the end of the definition.

Now, the discussions in this section so far have been framed in terms of user defined types, for the most part. But similar considerations apply to system defined types also, except that in this case at least some of the various definitions—certainly the required ones—will be provided by the system instead of by some user. For example, if INTEGER is a system defined type, then it's the system that defines the name, defines legal integer values, defines the hidden physical representation, defines a corresponding literal format, defines the corresponding operators ":=", "=", "+", and so on (though of course users can define additional operators if they want to).

One last item: I've mentioned selector operators several times. What I haven't said, though (at least, not explicitly), is that selectors—more precisely, selector invocations—are really just a generalization of the more familiar

---

[12] This paragraph touches on another important logical difference, incidentally: namely, that between arguments and parameters (see Exercise 5 at the end of the chapter). Note too that the POINT selector, unlike the SNO and PNO selectors discussed earlier, takes two arguments instead of one (because points are "possibly represented" by pairs of values, not just by a single value). See Chapter 4 for further discussion.

concept of a *literal*.[13]   What I mean by this remark is that all literals are selector invocations, but not all selector invocations are literals; in fact, a selector invocation is a literal if and only if its arguments are themselves all specified as literals in turn. For example, POINT(X,Y), POINT(X,2.5), and POINT(1.0,2.5) are all invocations of the POINT selector, but only the last is a POINT literal. It follows that every type has—*must* have—an associated format for writing literals. And for completeness I should add that every value of every type must be denotable by means of some literal of the type in question.

SCALAR vs. NONSCALAR TYPES

Types are often described as being either scalar or nonscalar. Loosely, a type is *scalar* if it has no user visible components and *nonscalar* otherwise—and values, variables, attributes, operators, parameters, and expressions of some type T are scalar or nonscalar according as type T itself is scalar or nonscalar. For example:

■   Type INTEGER is a scalar type; hence, values, variables, and so on of type INTEGER are also all scalar, meaning they have no user visible components.

■   Tuple and relation types are nonscalar—the pertinent user visible components being the corresponding attributes—and hence tuple and relation values, variables, and so on are also all nonscalar.

That said, I must now emphasize that these notions are quite informal. Indeed, we've already seen that the concept of data value atomicity has no absolute meaning; and "scalarness" is really just that same concept by another name. Thus, the relational model certainly doesn't rely on the scalar vs. nonscalar distinction in any formal sense. In this book, however, I do rely on it informally; I mean, I do find it intuitively useful on occasion. To be specific:

■   I'll use the term *scalar*, loosely, in connection with types that are neither tuple nor relation types.

---

[13] The concept might be familiar, but it's quite difficult to find a good definition for it in the literature! See Exercise 2 at the end of the chapter.

- I'll also use the term *nonscalar*, again loosely, in connection with types that *are* either tuple or relation types.

But I must make it clear that the foregoing characterizations are indeed loose, and only an approximation to the truth. A more accurate statement would be: Nongenerated types—see later in the present section—are always scalar; by contrast, generated types are typically nonscalar, but don't have to be. (An example of a scalar generated type is the SQL type CHAR (25), as we'll see in the next chapter.)

> *Aside:* Another term you'll sometimes hear used to mean "scalarness" is *encapsulation*. Be aware, however, that this term is also used, especially in object oriented contexts, to refer to the physical bundling, or packaging together, of code and data (or of operator definitions and data representation definitions, to be a little more precise about the matter). But to use the term in such a way is to mix model and implementation concerns; users shouldn't care, nor should they need to care, whether code and data are physically bundled together or kept separate. *End of aside.*

Let's look at an example. Here's a **Tutorial D** definition for the base relvar S ("suppliers")—but please note that this definition is a little different from the one I gave in Chapter 1, because now I'm defining the attributes all to be of some system defined type for simplicity:

```
1.  VAR S BASE   /* "suppliers relation variable" */
2.      RELATION
3.         { SNO CHAR , SNAME CHAR , STATUS INTEGER , CITY CHAR }
4.      KEY { SNO } ;
```

Explanation:

- In line 1, the keyword VAR means this is a variable definition; S is the name of that variable; and the keyword BASE means the variable is a base relvar specifically.

- Lines 2 and 3 specify the type of that variable. The keyword RELATION in line 2 means it's a relation type, and line 3 then specifies the set of attributes that make up the corresponding heading (where, as you'll recall from the previous chapter, an attribute is defined to be an *<attribute name, type name>* pair, and no two attributes in the same heading have the same attribute name). The relation type in question is, of course, a nonscalar type, because it has user visible components: viz., those attributes. No significance attaches to the order in which the attributes are specified.

■   Line 4 defines {SNO} to be a key for this relvar.

In fact, the example also illustrates another point: namely, that the type

```
RELATION
   { SNO CHAR , SNAME CHAR , STATUS INTEGER , CITY CHAR }
```

is a *generated* type. A generated type is a type that's obtained by invoking some *type generator* (the type generator in the example is, specifically, RELATION). You can think of a type generator as a special kind of operator; it's special because (a) it returns a type instead of a value, and (b) it's invoked at compile time instead of run time. For instance, most programming languages support a type generator called ARRAY, which lets users define a variety of specific array types. For present purposes, however, the only type generators we're interested in are TUPLE and RELATION. Here's an example involving the TUPLE type generator:

```
VAR STV  /* "supplier tuple variable" */
    TUPLE
    { STATUS INTEGER , SNO CHAR , CITY CHAR , SNAME CHAR } ;
```

The value of variable STV at any given time is a tuple with the same heading as that of relvar S[14] (I've deliberately specified the attributes in a different order, just to show the order doesn't matter). Thus, we might imagine a code fragment that (a) extracts a one-tuple restriction—perhaps the relation containing just the tuple for supplier S1—from the relation that's the current value of relvar S, then (b) extracts the single tuple from that one-tuple restriction, and finally (c) assigns that tuple to the tuple variable STV. In **Tutorial D:**

```
STV := TUPLE FROM ( S WHERE SNO = 'S1' ) ;
```

---

[14] Note that it does make sense to talk about the heading of a tuple—tuples have headings just as relations do, as the definitions in Chapter 1 make clear.

Important: I don't want you to misunderstand me here. While a variable like STV might certainly be needed in some application program that accesses the suppliers and parts database, I'm *not* saying such a variable can appear inside the database. A relational database contains variables of exactly one kind: namely, relation variables (relvars). Let me say that again in different words, because it's important: Relvars are the *only* kind of variable allowed in a relational database.

I note in passing that this latter fact—i.e., the fact that relvars are the only kind of variable allowed in a relational database—is sometimes referred to as *The Information Principle*.[15]

By the way, note carefully that, as the foregoing example suggests, there's a logical difference between a tuple *t* and the (unique) relation *r* that contains just that tuple *t*. In particular, they're of different types—*t* is of some tuple type and *r* is of some relation type (though the types in question do at least have to have the same heading, or in other words the same attributes and same degree).

Finally, a few miscellaneous points to close this section:

- Even though tuple and relation types do have user visible components (namely, their attributes), there's no suggestion that those components have to be physically stored as such, in the form in which they're seen by the user. In fact, the physical representation of tuples and relations should be hidden from the user, just as it should be for scalar values.

- Like scalar types, tuple and relation types certainly need associated selector operators (including literals as a special case). I'll defer the details to Chapter 4. They don't need THE_ operators, though; instead, they have operators that provide access to the corresponding attributes, and those operators play a role analogous to the role played by THE_ operators in connection with scalar types.

- Tuple and relation types also need assignment and equality comparison operators. I gave an example of tuple assignment earlier in the present section; I'll defer details of the other operators—relational assignment, and tuple and relational equality comparisons—to Chapter 4.

---

[15] Codd states it rather differently, though. Here's his wording: "All information in a relational database is represented explicitly at the logical level and in exactly one way—by values in tables."

TYPES AND THE RELATIONAL MODEL

It used to be a common misconception—maybe it still is—that the relational model deals only with rather simple types: numbers, strings, perhaps dates and times, and not much else. In this chapter, I've tried to show that this is indeed a misconception. Rather, relations can have attributes of *any type whatsoever* (other than as noted in just a moment); the relational model nowhere prescribes just what those types must be, and in fact they can be as complex as you like. They can even be relation types! In other words, the question as to what types are supported is orthogonal to the question of support for the relational model as such. Or, less precisely but more catchily: *Types are orthogonal to tables.*

I also remind you that the foregoing state of affairs in no way violates the requirements of first normal form. First normal form just means that every tuple in every relation contains a single value, of the appropriate type, in every attribute position. Now we know that those types can be (almost) anything, we also know that all relations are in first normal form by definition.

In closing, let me come back to the fact that there are certain important exceptions to the rule that relational attributes can be of any type whatsoever. In fact, there are two such, both of which I'll simplify just slightly for present purposes:

- The first is that if relation r is of type T, then no attribute of r is itself allowed to be of type T (think about it!).

- The second is that if relation r is a relation in the database, then no attribute of r is allowed to be of any pointer type.

Let me elaborate briefly on the second exception. The fact is, prerelational databases were full of pointers, and access to such databases thus involved a lot of pointer chasing, a state of affairs that (a) made application programming error prone and (b) made direct end user access to those databases virtually impossible. (These aren't the only problems with pointers, but they're among the more obvious ones.) Codd wanted to get away from such problems with his relational model, and of course he succeeded.

EXERCISES

1. What's a type? What's the difference between a domain and a type?

2. What do you understand by the term *selector?* And what exactly is a literal?

3. What's a THE_ operator?

4. Physical representations are always hidden from the user: true or false?

5. The present chapter and its predecessor have touched on several logical differences (see Chapter 1 if you need to refresh your memory regarding this important notion), including:

database	vs.	DBMS
foreign key	vs.	pointer
generated type	vs.	nongenerated type
parameter	vs.	argument
relation	vs.	type
type	vs.	representation
user defined type	vs.	system defined type
user defined operator	vs.	system defined operator

What exactly is the logical difference in each case?

6. Explain in your own words the difference between the concepts *scalar* and *nonscalar*.

7. What do you understand by the term *coercion?* Why is coercion a bad idea?

8. Why doesn't domain check override make sense?

9. What's a type generator?

10. Define *first normal form.* Why do you think it's so called?

11. Let X be an expression. What's the type of X? What's the significance of the fact that X is of some type?

12. Using the definition of the REFLECT operator in the body of the chapter (section "What's a Type?") as a template, define a **Tutorial D** operator that, given an integer, returns the cube of that integer.

13. Let LENGTH be a user defined type, with the obvious semantics. Use **Tutorial D** to define an operator that, given the length of two adjacent sides of a rectangle, returns the corresponding area.

14. Give an example of a relation type. Distinguish between relation types, relation values, and relation variables.

15. It's sometimes suggested that types are really variables, in a sense. For example, employee numbers might grow from three digits to four as a business expands, so we might need to update "the set of all possible employee numbers." Discuss.

16. Here are sample values for a certain database concerning departments and employees:

DEPT

DNO	DNAME	BUDGET	LOCATION
D1	Marketing	10M	Cairo
D2	Development	12M	La Paz
D3	Research	5M	Cairo

EMP

ENO	ENAME	DNO	SALARY
E1	Lopez	D1	40K
E2	Cheng	D1	35K
E3	Finzi	D2	30K
E4	Saito	D2	35K

Suppose the attributes are of the following user defined types:

```
DNO      : DNO
DNAME    : NAME
BUDGET   : MONEY
LOCATION : CITY
ENO      : ENO
ENAME    : NAME
SALARY   : MONEY
```

Which of the following scalar expressions (or would-be expressions) are valid? For those that are, state the type of the result; for the others, give an expression that will achieve what appears to be the desired effect.

    a.   `LOCATION = 'London'`

    b.   `ENAME = DNAME`

    c.   `SALARY × 5`

    d.   `BUDGET + 50000`

    e.   `ENO > 'E2'`

    f.   `ENAME || DNAME`

    g.   `LOCATION || 'burg'`

17. A type is a set of values and the empty set is a legitimate set; thus, we might define an *empty type* to be a type where the set in question is empty. Can you think of any uses for such a type?

18. Why are pointers excluded from the relational model?

19. Do you think that types "belong to" databases, in the same sense that relvars do?

20. Explain as carefully as you can the logical difference between a relation with a relation valued attribute (RVA) and a "relation with a repeating group."

ANSWERS

1. A type is a named, and in practice finite, set of values—all possible values of some specific kind: for example, all possible integers, or all possible character strings, or all possible supplier numbers, or all possible XML documents, or all possible relations with a certain heading (etc., etc.). There's no difference between a domain and a type.[16]

---

[16] This is true, but be aware that both Codd and SQL attempt—mistakenly, confusingly, and most unfortunately—to draw a distinction between them (actually, different distinctions in the two cases, Codd vs. SQL). I mentioned Codd's attempt in the preface. Regarding SQL's attempt, see Chapter 3.

2. A selector is an operator that allows us to select, or specify, an arbitrary value of the type in question. Every type has at least one associated selector. Let *T* be a type and let *S* be a selector for *T*. Then every value of type *T* must be returned by some successful invocation of *S*, and every successful invocation of *S* must return some value of type *T*. For further discussion, see Chapter 4.

Note: Selectors are provided "automatically" in **Tutorial D**, since they're required by the relational model, at least implicitly. The picture is rather more complicated in SQL, however. In fact, although the selector concept does necessarily exist, SQL doesn't really have a term for it; certainly *selector* as such isn't an SQL term. For further discussion, see Chapters 3 and 5.

Turning now to literals: A literal—sometimes called "a self defining symbol"—is a special case of a selector invocation; to be specific, it's a selector invocation all of whose arguments are themselves specified as literals in turn (implying in particular that a selector invocation with no arguments at all, such as the INTEGER selector invocation "4", is a literal by definition). Thus, a literal is a symbol that denotes a value that's fixed and determined by the symbol in question, and thus in particular is known at compile time (implying that the type of that value is also fixed and determined by the symbol in question and known at compile time). Every value of every type, tuple and relation types included, must be denotable by means of some literal. Here are some **Tutorial D** examples:

```
4                        /* a literal of type INTEGER  */
'XYZ'                    /* a literal of type CHAR     */
FALSE                    /* a literal of type BOOLEAN  */
2.5                      /* a literal of type RATIONAL */
POINT ( 5.0 , 2.5 )      /* a literal of type POINT    */
```

Note: The last of these is a literal of the user defined type POINT from the body of the chapter.

Of course, the foregoing examples are all scalar. Here by contrast is an example of a tuple literal:

```
TUPLE { SNO 'S1' , STATUS 33 }
```

As for examples of relation literals, see either Chapter 4 or the answer to Exercise 2 in Chapter 1.

3. A THE_ operator is an operator that provides access to some component of some "possible representation," or *possrep*, of some specific scalar value (meaning, by definition, some specific value of some specific scalar type). For further discussion of these matters, especially regarding "possreps" as such (which weren't mentioned—at least, not by that name—in the body of the chapter), see Chapter 4.

Note: THE_ operators are effectively provided "automatically" in both **Tutorial D** and SQL, to a first approximation. However, although the THE_ operator concept necessarily exists, SQL doesn't exactly have a term for it; certainly "THE_ operator" isn't an SQL term. For further discussion, see Chapter 5.

4. True in principle; might not be completely true in practice (but to the extent it isn't, we're talking about a confusion over model vs. implementation). The following quote, which I used as one of the epigraphs to this book, is pertinent:

> A major purpose of type systems is to avoid embarrassing questions about representations, and to forbid situations in which these questions might come up.

In other words, types are a good idea because they *raise the level of abstraction* (without a proper type system, everything would be nothing but tedious—and error prone—bit twiddling). Here's another nice quote to emphasize the point further (this one's from Andrew Wright, "On Sapphire and Type-Safe Languages," *CACM 46*, No. 4, April 2003):

> [Types make] program development and debugging easier by making program behavior more understandable.

5. A *database* is a repository for data. (In the relational world, we might say, a little more specifically, that a database is a container for *relvars*, though more precise definitions are of course possible.) A *DBMS* is a software system for managing databases; it provides data storage, recovery, concurrency, integrity, query/update, and other services. Be aware, however, that many people very confusingly use the term *database* to mean either (a) some DBMS product or

(b) the specific instance of such a product that's installed on some specific computer. This practice is deprecated.

A *foreign key* is a subset of the heading of some relvar, values of which must be equal to values of some "target" key in some other relvar (or possibly in the same relvar). A *pointer*—meaning, more specifically, a pointer value—is basically just an address. Pointer data requires certain special operators, usually known as referencing and dereferencing, a brief explanation of which can be found in the section "Row and Table Types" in Chapter 3, and a rather longer one in Chapter 5. *Note:* A much more extensive discussion of the logical difference between foreign keys and pointers in general can be found in my book *Keys, Foreign Keys, and Relational Theory* (Technics, 2023).

A *generated* type is a type obtained by executing some type generator such as ARRAY or RELATION; specific array and relation types are thus generated types (see Chapter 4 for further discussion). A *nongenerated* type is a type that's not a generated type. *Note:* User defined scalar types produced by executing a TYPE statement in **Tutorial D** (again see Chapter 4) or a CREATE TYPE statement in SQL (see Chapter 5) might also be regarded as generated types, in a sense, but I won't normally do so in this book.

A *parameter* is a formal operand in terms of which some operator is defined. An *argument* is an actual operand that's substituted for some parameter in some invocation of the operator in question. Be aware, however, that people often use these two terms as if they were interchangeable; much confusion is caused that way, and you need to be on the lookout for it.

By the way, there's also a logical difference between an argument as such and the expression that's used to specify it. For example, consider the expression $(2 + 3) - 1$, which represents an invocation of the arithmetic operator "$-$". The first argument to that invocation is the value five, but that argument is specified by the expression $2 + 3$, which represents an invocation of the arithmetic operator "$+$". In fact, of course, *every* expression represents some operator invocation. Even a simple variable reference can be be regarded as representing an invocation of a certain operator: namely, the operator that simply returns the current value of the specified variable. Similarly for a literal.

A *relation* is a value; it has a type—a relation type, of course—but it isn't itself a type. A *type* is a named, and in practice finite, set of values: viz., all possible values of some particular kind.

Type is a model concept; types have semantics that must be understood by the user. *Representation* is an implementation concept; representations are supposed to be hidden from the user. In particular, if *X* is a value or variable of type *T*, then the operators that apply to *X* are the operators defined for values and variables of type *T*, not the operators defined for some representation that happens to be in use, or might happen to be in use, for values and variables of type *T*. For example, just because the representation for type ENO ("employee numbers") happens to be CHAR, say, it doesn't follow that we can concatenate two employee numbers; we can do that only if concatenation is an operator that's been defined for values of type ENO.

A *system defined* (or *built in*) type is a type that's available for use as soon as the system is installed (it "comes in the same box the system comes in"). A *user defined* type is a type whose definition and implementation are provided by some suitably skilled user after the system is installed. (To the user of such a type, however—as opposed to the user who actually defines that type—that type should look and feel just like a system defined type.)

A *system defined* (or *built in*) operator is an operator that's available for use as soon as the system is installed (it comes in the same box the system comes in). A *user defined* operator is an operator whose definition and implementation are provided by some suitably skilled user after the system is installed. (To the user of such an operator, however—as opposed to the user who designs and implements that operator—that operator should look and feel just like a system defined operator.) User defined operators can take arguments of either user or system defined types (or a mixture), but system defined operators can obviously take arguments of system defined types only.

6. A scalar type is a type that has no user visible components; a nonscalar type is a type that's not a scalar type. Values, variables, and read-only operators (etc.) are scalar or nonscalar according as their type is scalar or nonscalar. Be aware, however, that in the final analysis these terms are neither very formal nor very precise, and neither the relational model nor the theory of types described in the present book rely on them in any way.

7. Coercion is implicit type conversion. It's deprecated because it can lead to errors that are hard to detect (but note that this is primarily a pragmatic issue;

whether or not coercions are allowed has little or nothing to do with type theory as such, nor with the relational model as such).

Note: Coercion is also a bad idea because the rules controlling the way the implicit conversions are done might not be obvious. A notorious illustration of this point is provided by the language PL/I. In PL/I, it's possible to find three values *a*, *b*, and *c* such that—thanks to PL/I's coercion rules—the comparisons $a > b$, $b > c$, and $c > a$ all evaluate to TRUE (!). If you're familiar with PL/I, you might like to try to find such a set of values.

8. Because it muddles types and representations.

9. A type generator is an operator that's invoked at compile time instead of run time and returns a type, not a value. The relational model requires support for two such, viz., TUPLE and RELATION. Points arising:

■ Types generated by the TUPLE and RELATION type generators are nonscalar, but there's no reason in principle why generated types have to be nonscalar. As we'll see in the next chapter, SQL in particular supports several scalar type generators, CHAR and NUMERIC among them.

■ Type generators are known by many different names in the literature, including *type constructors* (the SQL term); *parameterized types*; *polymorphic types*; *type templates*; and *generic types*.

10. A relation is in first normal form (1NF) if and only if every tuple in that relation contains a single value, of the appropriate type, in every attribute position. Note, therefore, that *every* relation is in first normal form, by definition. Of course, given this fact—i.e., that every relation is in 1NF—you might be forgiven for wondering why we even bother to talk about the concept at all (and in particular why it's called "first"). The reason, though (as you probably know), is that (a) we can extend the concept to apply to relvars as well as relations, and then (b) we can define a series of "higher" normal forms (2NF, 3NF, etc.) for relvars—not relations—and those normal forms turn out to be important in database design. In other words, 1NF is the base on which those higher normal forms build. But it really isn't all that important as a notion in itself.

To repeat, however, do note that those higher normal forms apply specifically to relvars, not to relations as such. They also apply specifically to design theory, not to the relational model as such; the relational model as such doesn't care, and doesn't need to care, which particular normal form any given relvar happens to be in. See my book *Database Design and Relational Theory*, 2nd ed. (Apress, 2019) for further discussion.

Perhaps I should add that 1NF is one of those concepts whose definition has evolved somewhat over the years. It used to be defined to mean that every tuple of the relation in question had to contain a single "atomic" value in every attribute position. As we've come to realize, however (and as I've tried to show in the body of this chapter), the concept of data value atomicity actually has no objective meaning. An extensive discussion of such matters can be found in Chapter 8 ("What First Normal Form Really Means") of my book *Date on Database: Writings 2000-2006* (Apress, 2006).

11. The type of *X* is the type, *T* say, of the operator—"the outermost operator"—that's executed last (at any rate conceptually) when *X* is evaluated. That type is significant because it means *X* can be used in exactly (that is, in all and only) those positions where a literal of type *T* can appear.

12.
```
OPERATOR CUBE ( I INTEGER ) RETURNS INTEGER ;
    RETURN I × I × I ;
END OPERATOR ;
```

Subsidiary exercise: What would be involved in modifying the foregoing definition so that the operator returns, not the cube, but the *N*th power for arbitrary *N*?

13.
```
OPERATOR AREA_OF_R ( H LENGTH , W LENGTH ) RETURNS AREA ;
    RETURN H × W ;
END OPERATOR ;
```

I'm assuming here, not unreasonably, that (a) it's legal to multiply ("×") a value of type LENGTH by another such value, and (b) the result of such a multiplication is a value of type AREA (another user defined type).

14. The following relation type is the type of the suppliers relvar S:[17]

```
RELATION { SNO SNO , SNAME NAME ,
                   STATUS INTEGER , CITY CHAR }
```

The suppliers relvar S itself is a variable of this type. And every legal value of that variable—the value shown in Chapter 1 in particular, of course—is a value of this type.

15. Such an operation—i.e., growing employee numbers from three digits to four—logically means replacing one type by another, not "updating a type" (after all, types aren't variables and hence can't be updated, by definition).[18] To elaborate:

■ First of all, the operation of defining a type doesn't actually create the corresponding set of values; conceptually, those values already exist, and always will exist (think of type INTEGER, for example). Thus, all the "define type" operation—i.e., the TYPE statement, in the case of **Tutorial D**—really does is introduce a name by which that set of values can be referenced.

■ Likewise, dropping a type doesn't actually drop the corresponding values, it just drops the name that was introduced by the corresponding "define type" operation.

■ It follows that "updating a type" really means dropping the type name and then reintroducing that very same name to refer to a presumably different set of values.

Of course, nothing in what I've just said precludes support for some kind of pragmatic "alter type" shorthand to simplify matters (and SQL does in fact provide such a shorthand, as you probably know); but invoking such a shorthand shouldn't be thought of as "updating the type."

---

[17] The type as given in Chapter 1, that is, not the simplified version defined in the body of the present chapter.

[18] Actually, growing employee numbers from three digits to four is a fairly simple change, and it *might* be possible to handle it by merely revising the pertinent type constraint (see Chapter 4). But I'm skeptical.

By the way, here's a question for you to ponder: If despite everything I've said you still think a type is a variable, then what type is that variable?

16. I assume throughout the following that any given scalar type *T* always has a selector with the same name *T*. See Chapter 4 for further discussion.

   a. Not valid; LOCATION = CITY ('London').

   b. Valid; BOOLEAN.

   c. Presumably valid; MONEY. I'm assuming that multiplying a money value by an integer returns another money value. *Note:* A similar remark applies to d.-g. below.

   d. Not valid; BUDGET + MONEY (50000).

   e. Not valid; ENO > ENO ('E2').

   f. Not valid; NAME (THE_C (ENAME) || THE_C (DNAME)). I'm assuming that type NAME has a single possrep component—see Chapter 4—and that component is called C and is of type CHAR.

   g. Not valid; CITY (THE_C (LOCATION) || 'burg'). I'm assuming that type CITY has a single possrep component and that component is called C and is of type CHAR. Again see Chapter 4.

17. The (unique!) empty scalar type is certainly a valid type; however, it wouldn't make much sense to define a variable to be of that type, because no value could ever be assigned to such a variable. Perhaps surprisingly, however, the empty scalar type turns out to be crucially important in connection with type inheritance—but that's a topic that's beyond the scope of the present book. Suffice it to say simply that the empty scalar type is a subtype of every scalar type by definition, and thus always exists, at least conceptually. Refer to my book *Type Inheritance and Relational Theory* (O'Reilly, 2016), if you want to know more.

18. Because (a) they're logically unnecessary; (b) they're error prone; (c) end users can't readily use them, and in fact might not be able to use them at all;

(d) they're clumsy (in particular, they have a directionality to them, which other values don't); and (e) they undermine type inheritance. (Details of this last point are beyond the scope of this book.) There could be other reasons too.

19. In general, no, they don't. (Which database does type INTEGER belong to?) In an important sense, the whole business of types and type management is orthogonal to the business of databases and database management. We might even imagine the need for a "type administrator," whose job it would be to look after types in a manner analogous to that in which the database administrator looks after databases.

20. An RVA is an attribute whose type is some relation type, and whose values are therefore relations of that type. A repeating group is an "attribute" of some type *T* whose values aren't values of type *T*—note the contradiction here!—but, rather, are bags (or sets, or sequences, or some other kind of "collection") of values of type *T*.

Note: In the "repeating group" case type *T* is often a tuple type (or something approximating a tuple type), not just a simple scalar type. For example, in a system that supports files with repeating groups—I deliberately switch here to the more conventional terminology of files, records, and fields— a file might be such that each record consists of an ENO field (employee number), an ENAME field (employee name), and a repeating group JOBHIST, in which each entry consists of a JOB field (job title), a FROM field, and a TO field (where FROM and TO are dates). Fields ENO, ENAME, JOB, FROM, and TO are all scalar.

To get back to RVAs as such: Clearly, we need to be able to map between relations with such attributes and relations without them, and **Tutorial D** provides two operators, GROUP and UNGROUP, for that purpose. For example, wiith reference to relations R1 and R4 as shown in the body of the chapter (pages 34 and 35, respectively), the expression

```
R1 GROUP { PNO } AS PNO_REL
```

will produce R4, and the expression

```
R4 UNGROUP PNO_REL
```

will produce R1. *Note:* For the record, the type of relation R4 is:

```
RELATION { SNO CHAR , PNO_REL RELATION { PNO CHAR } }
```

(assuming for simplicity once again that supplier numbers are of the system defined CHAR, and likewise for part numbers).

By the way, I should point out that GROUP and UNGROUP aren't exact inverses of one another. Let Z1 and Z2 be relations of the same type as R1 and R4, respectively. Then grouping Z1 and then ungrouping the result is guaranteed to bring us back to Z1, but ungrouping Z2 and grouping the result is *not* guaranteed to bring us back to Z2 (assuming the groupings and ungroupings are all done in terms of part numbers, as in the previous paragraph). Why not? Because, first, Z2 might contain a tuple in which the PNO_REL value is an empty relation (and if it does, that tuple will contribute nothing to the UNGROUP result); second, grouping a relation can never produce a result that contains such a tuple. I'll leave development of sample values to illustrate these points as a subsidiary exercise.

Chapter 3

Types and Domains in SQL:

The Basics

I turn now to SQL. Let me start by stressing the fact that what follows isn't just a revised version of the previous chapter, edited where appropriate to talk in terms of SQL instead of the relational model. Rather, it addresses a number of issues that have to do with SQL specifically, issues that in most cases don't have an exact counterpart in the relational context. But of course I do assume you've read that previous chapter and taken its general message on board.

Let me remind you from the preface that by SQL I mean, throughout this book, the standard version of that language (barring explicit statements to the contrary, of course). The version of the standard I'm mostly working from is SQL:2011. Here's the reference:

International Organization for Standardization (ISO): *Database Language SQL*, Document ISO/IEC 9075:2008 (2011)

You might also find the following book helpful (it's a comprehensive tutorial and guide to the standard as of 1997):

C. J. Date and Hugh Darwen: *A Guide to the SQL Standard*, 4th ed. (Addison-Wesley, 1997)

Although this book is by now fairly old as these things go, just about everything it has to say is still both valid and applicable—where by "applicable" I mean applicable to the discussions in the present chapter in particular.

THE SUPPLIERS AND PARTS DATABASE

Here for purposes of reference is an SQL definition for our running example, the suppliers and parts database:

```
CREATE TABLE S
  ( SNO    CHAR(5) ,
    SNAME  VARCHAR(20) ,
    STATUS INTEGER ,
    CITY   VARCHAR(25) ,
    UNIQUE ( SNO ) ) ;

CREATE TABLE P
  ( PNO    CHAR(6) ,
    PNAME  VARCHAR(12) ,
    COLOR  VARCHAR(10) ,
    WEIGHT DECIMAL(4,1) ,
    CITY   VARCHAR(25) ,
    UNIQUE ( PNO ) ) ;

CREATE TABLE SP
  ( SNO CHAR(5) ,
    PNO CHAR(6) ,
    QTY INTEGER ,
    UNIQUE ( SNO , PNO ) ,
    FOREIGN KEY ( SNO ) REFERENCES S ( SNO ) ,
    FOREIGN KEY ( PNO ) REFERENCES P ( PNO ) ) ;
```

Note: I continue to assume as I did throughout most of the previous chapter that the data types we have to deal with, in connection with the suppliers and parts database in particular, are all system defined—or "predefined," rather, to use the not very appropriate but official SQL term. I'll discuss the broader issue of user defined types in the next two chapters (in general terms in Chapter 4, and in SQL in particular in Chapter 5).

SCALAR TYPES

SQL supports a number of more or less self-explanatory system defined (i.e., built-in, or "predefined") scalar types, the following among them:

```
BOOLEAN      INTEGER           CHARACTER(n)
             SMALLINT          CHARACTER VARYING(n)
             BIGINT            CHARACTER LARGE OBJECT(n)
             NUMERIC(p,q)      BINARY(n)
             DECIMAL(p,q)      BINARY VARYING(n)
             FLOAT(p)          BINARY LARGE OBJECT(n)
```

Points arising:

■ The foregoing list is deliberately incomplete. Other types include an "XML document" type (XML); a variety of "national character string types" (NATIONAL CHARACTER, etc.); and several datetime types (DATE, TIME, TIMESTAMP, INTERVAL). But the specifics of these additional types are beyond the scope of this book.

■ A number of defaults, abbreviations, and alternative spellings are supported, the following among them:

INT **for** INTEGER

NUMERIC(p) **for** NUMERIC($p,0$)

NUMERIC **for** NUMERIC(p)   —p implementation defined

DEC **for** DECIMAL

DECIMAL(p) **for** DECIMAL($p,0$)

DECIMAL **for** DECIMAL(p)   —p implementation defined

FLOAT **for** FLOAT(p)   —p implementation defined

REAL **for** FLOAT(p)   —p implementation defined

DOUBLE PRECISION **for** FLOAT(p)   —p implementation defined

CHAR **for** CHARACTER

VARCHAR **for** CHARACTER VARYING **or** CHAR VARYING

CLOB **for** CHARACTER LARGE OBJECT **or** CHAR LARGE OBJECT

VARBINARY **for** BINARY VARYING

BLOB **for** BINARY LARGE OBJECT

- Types SMALLINT, INTEGER, and BIGINT are all integer types, of course. The corresponding precisions are implementation defined, but that of SMALLINT can't be more than that of INTEGER, which in turn can't be more than that of BIGINT.

- The keyword BINARY in the various "binary" type names doesn't mean binary numbers. It doesn't even mean bit strings! Instead, it means *byte* strings, and the associated parenthesized length specification "(*n*)" gives the corresponding length not in bits but in 8-bit bytes or *octets*.[1]

- Types CLOB and BLOB are subject to numerous limitations. For example, "<" and ">" aren't supported, and so it's not possible to compare two CLOB values, or two BLOB values, to see if one is less than another. I'll ignore these types too from this point forward, except just to note that:

  a. The keyword OBJECT in the unabbreviated type names has nothing to do with objects in the OO sense. In fact, CLOB and BLOB values—CLOBs and BLOBs for short—are basically just strings, usually very long ones.

  b. The main (or only?) difference as far as I can see between CLOBs and BLOBs is that CLOBs are constrained to contain characters from some specified character set—see later—whereas BLOBs are uncontrained (i.e., each octet in a given BLOB can have any of 256 different values).

- Like types CLOB and BLOB, types CHAR and VARCHAR have an associated length specification. I'll have more to say in this connection in the section "Types vs. Type Generators," later.

- The p in NUMERIC, DECIMAL, and FLOAT is the associated *precision* ($p > 0$), and the q in NUMERIC and DECIMAL is the associated *scale*

---

[1] Actually the history here is a little complicated. SQL:1992 supported two types called BIT and BIT VARYING, whose values *were* bit strings and whose length specifications were indeed given in terms of bits. Subsequently, however, those types were replaced by types BINARY and BINARY VARYING, respectively, whose values were byte strings and whose length specifications were therefore given in terms of octets.

factor ($q \geq 0$, $p \geq q$). Thus, e.g., the specification DECIMAL (5,2) denotes decimal numbers in the range −999.99 to +999.99, inclusive.

Note: SQL actually calls q just the *scale*, but there are good reasons to prefer the term *scale factor*.

■ Literals of more or less conventional format are supported for these various types (but see the subsection "A Remark on Numeric Types" below for further remarks regarding numeric literals in particular).

■ Explicit scalar assignments are supported. The syntax is:

```
SET <scalar variable ref> = <scalar exp> ;
```

Scalar assignments are also performed implicitly when various other operations (e.g., FETCH) are executed.

Note: Here and elsewhere in this book, in formal syntax definitions like the one just shown, I use *ref* and *exp* as convenient abbreviations for *reference* and *expression*, respectively.

■ Explicit scalar equality comparisons are supported. The syntax is:

```
<scalar exp> = <scalar exp>
```

Scalar equality comparisons are also performed implicitly when numerous other operations (e.g., joins and unions, grouping and duplicate elimination operations, and many others) are executed.

Note: SQL's support for equality is unfortunately severely flawed, however. To elaborate:

a. First of all, SQL supports coercions, with the consequence that "=" can give TRUE even when the comparands are of different types and thus clearly distinct. See the section "Type Checking and Coercion," later.

b. Second, in the case of character string types, it's possible for "=" to give TRUE even when the comparands are of the same type but, again, clearly distinct. See the section "Collations," later.

c. It's also possible—for all types, not just character string types—for "=" not to give TRUE even when the comparands aren't distinguishable. This happens in particular when (but not only when) the comparands are both null.

d. For certain types not discussed in detail in this book (e.g., XML), "=" isn't defined at all! (The same is true for certain user defined types also. See Chapter 5.)

Moreover, the foregoing list of flaws is *not* complete. You can find further specifics, and a more detailed explanation, if you're interested, in Chapter 1 ("Equality") of my book *Stating the Obvious, and Other Database Writings* (Technics, 2020).

■ Regarding type BOOLEAN in particular, I note that although it was added to the standard in 1999, not all SQL systems support it. Of course, boolean expressions can (and always could) appear in WHERE and HAVING clauses, even without support for type BOOLEAN as such; but if a system fails to support that type—support it explicitly, I mean—then no table can have a column of type BOOLEAN, and no variable can be declared to be of type BOOLEAN.[2] As a consequence, various workarounds (e.g., "yes/no columns") might sometimes be needed.

A Remark on Numeric Types

I claimed above that SQL's support for its various system defined types included support for "literals of more or less conventional format." Now, however, I need to modify that claim somewhat, because the support in question isn't quite as obvious or self-explanatory as you might reasonably have expected. In particular—and I trust you find this as surprising as I do—although SQL does support various NUMERIC and DECIMAL types, as we've seen, what it *doesn't* do is support any corresponding NUMERIC or DECIMAL literals! For example, the literal

```
123.45
```

---

[2] I have to say that the idea that a language might support expressions that return a value of a type not known in that language strikes me as bizarre in the extreme. But that's certainly the way SQL was when it was first defined and first implemented, and it appears to still be the case with certain SQL products to this day.

—which I assure you is certainly a valid literal, in SQL—is *not* considered to be of type NUMERIC (*p,q*), nor of type DECIMAL (*p,q*), for any *p* and *q* whatsoever. Rather, it's considered to be of a type for which no specific SQL keyword exists: namely, "exact numeric." So are NUMERIC and DECIMAL really types at all, in SQL?[3]

Similar remarks apply to floating point numbers. For example, the valid SQL literal

```
5.0E2
```

—i.e., 5.0×10^2, or in other words 500.0—is considered to be of type, not FLOAT (*p*) for some *p*, but rather another type for which no specific SQL keyword exists: namely, "approximate numeric."

To get back to "exact numeric" for a moment: For the record, I note that the difference between NUMERIC (*p,q*) and DECIMAL (*p,q*), where $p > 0$, $q \geq 0$, and $p \geq q$, is that the former has precision *exactly p* decimal digits and the latter has precision *at least p* decimal digits. According to the standard, moreover, "digits" here means *significant* digits in both cases, which is rather surprising if true—it would surely seem more reasonable to say NUMERIC (*p,q*) has *at most p* significant digits and DECIMAL (*p,q*) has *at most r* significant digits for some $r \geq p$. For otherwise, 3.0, for example, wouldn't be a value of either type NUMERIC (5,1) or type DECIMAL (5,1).[4]

DOMAINS

In addition to the scalar types discussed, or at least touched on, above, SQL supports something it calls domains. However, SQL's domains aren't true relational domains; I mean, they're not types, they're just a kind of factored out "common column definition," with a number of rather strange properties that are well beyond the scope of this book. You can use them if you like, but don't make the mistake of thinking they're true relational domains, or types.

---

[3] *Answer:* No, they're not—despite what the standard itself has to say on the matter!—as we'll see in the section "Types vs. Type Generators," later.

[4] On the other hand, I suppose that 3.0 is at least coercible to both of those types, so perhaps it's coercion that saves the day here. *Exercise:* What exactly does the standard have to say in this connection?

I really don't want to say much more about SQL's domains here; you can find a tutorial description of them, if you want to know more, in the book by Hugh Darwen and myself mentioned near the beginning of this chapter, viz., *A Guide to the SQL Standard*, 4th ed. (Addison-Wesley, 1997). However, I do want to note for the record that one thing SQL's domains most definitely don't do is constrain comparisons. For example, let columns S.CITY and P.CITY be defined on SQL domains SCD and PCD, respectively. Then you might expect the comparison S.CITY = P.CITY to fail. However, it won't, not necessarily; rather, it'll fail if and only if *the data types underlying those domains* fail to satisfy the requirements for such comparisons as outlined in the section "Type Checking and Coercion," later. In SQL, in other words, such comparisons are legal if and only if the columns involved have what might be called "compatible" data types—see below—regardless of whether they're defined on the same SQL domain, and regardless even of whether any SQL domains as such are involved at all.

Analogous remarks apply to assignment also, as you'd probably expect.

As for that notion of "type compatibility," well, here are the rules as far as SQL's system defined types are concerned:

1. The boolean type is compatible with itself.

2. All numeric types are compatible with one another. I remind you, though, that the "binary"—actually byte string—types aren't numeric types (see point 4 below).

3. All character string types are compatible with one another. (At least to a first approximation. Further details are beyond the scope of the present discussion, but I'll come back to them in the next section, and later in the chapter as well.)

4. All "binary"—actually byte string—types are compatible with one anotherf.

5. There are no other instances of compatibility (other than ones having to do with types that I've already said are beyond the scope of this book, such as datetime types).

As indicated, I'll have more to say about this issue of type compatibility in the section immediately following, as well as in the section "Type Checking and Coercion," later.

TYPES vs. TYPE GENERATORS

Let me now focus for a moment, just to be definite, on fixed length character string types specifically—i.e., CHARACTER or CHAR types, not CHARACTER VARYING or VARCHAR types. Observe now that, strictly speaking, CHARACTER (or CHAR) isn't a type as such; instead, it's a type *generator* (or type *constructor*, to use the SQL term). By contrast, CHAR (25), for example, *is* a type as such, and it's obtained by invoking that type generator with the value 25 as the sole argument to that invocation.

Now, what I've just said is *not* the way that SQL itself talks about these matters—at least, not consistently. For example, here's a quote from the standard:

> The ... types CHARACTER, CHARACTER VARYING, and CHARACTER LARGE OBJECT are collectively referred to as *character string types*.

So according to this quote CHARACTER is a type. But if we look for the BNF production rule for the syntax category *<character string type>*, then—simplifying just slightly—this is what we find:

```
<character string type> ::=
      CHARACTER [ ( <length> ) ]
    | CHAR [ ( <length> ) ]
    | CHARACTER VARYING ( <length> )
    | CHAR VARYING ( <length> )
    | VARCHAR ( <length> )
    | <character large object type>
```

(I omit further details of *<character large object type>* for simplicity.) So now it's, e.g., CHAR (25), not just CHAR, that's the type. *Note:* It's true that the production rule does allow just CHAR, unqualified, as a *<character string type>* type, without an explicit length specification. However, such a specification is defined to be just shorthand for CHAR (1); so there's still a length specification, albeit an implicit one, even in that case.

To reinforce the point, I invite you to consider the types CHAR (25) and CHAR (26). These two types are utterly different!—in fact, no value of either one is a value of the other, and the set of values constituting type CHAR (25) and the set of values constituting type CHAR (26) are disjoint sets. Or to spell it out in different words: No string of 25 characters is a string of 26 characters, and no string of 26 characters is a string of 25 characters.

> *Aside:* If the types under discussion had been VARCHAR (25) vs. VARCHAR (26) instead of CHAR (25) vs. CHAR (26), matters would have been somewhat different. To be specific, types VARCHAR (25) and VARCHAR (26), unlike types CHAR (25) and CHAR (26), are *not* disjoint; in fact, every value of type VARCHAR (25) is also a value of type VARCHAR (26),[5] though the converse is false. Of course, the reason for the difference is that the length specification in VARCHAR is a *maximum* length. In CHAR, by contrast, it's an *actual* length. *End of aside.*

Remarks analogous to the foregoing apply to other system defined "scalar types" (so called) from the list I gave earlier in this chapter. For example, consider the following sample values:

```
581.0

581.
```

The first of these values is of type NUMERIC (4,1), the second is of type NUMERIC (3,0). Of course, they do both denote the same measure (for want of a better word), but there's certainly a logical difference between them; to be specific, the first is accurate to one decimal place and the second isn't. Logically, therefore, if we want them to "compare equal," we'll need to convert one of them to the type of the other before we're allowed to do the comparison. Now, that conversion process might be implicit and "silent"—in fact, in most programming languages it probably would be, as indeed it is, effectively, in SQL in particular—but the fact remains that it's logically required nonetheless.

To return now to the case of types CHAR (25) and CHAR (26): Similar considerations apply here also. To be specific, a value *v25* of type CHAR (25)

---

[5] As a consequence, it would be perfectly legitimate—in fact natural—to regard the former as a subtype of the latter. Perversely, though, SQL doesn't do so. (Why doesn't that surprise me?) To quote the standard once again: "Every predefined data type is a subtype of itself and of no other data types."

and a value *v26* of type CHAR (26) might be forced to "compare equal" by appending a single space character at the end of the *v25* value before doing the comparison. Furthermore, that appending might be done implicitly and silently—but once again it's logically required. See the section "Collations," later, for further discussion of such matters.

All of that being said, let me now say that I'll often overlook the point in what follows—the point, that is, that many SQL "types" aren't really types as such at all, but rather type generators—and for simplicity I'll refer to CHAR and the rest as if they were indeed types as such, much as SQL itself does. Though I can't help adding that it goes very much against the grain to do so ... The fact is, the "simplicity" that results (or allegedly results) from such a manner of speaking is spurious. Certainly SQL manages to get itself into all kinds of knots in connection with such matters, as we'll see, precisely because it isn't clear as to whether, e.g., CHAR (25) and CHAR (26) are one type or two. But I'll leave it at that for now.

> *Aside:* Well, maybe I won't, not quite. Let me at least say a word about how **Tutorial D** addresses these issues. Basically, **Tutorial D** has just one type for character strings (CHAR); one type for rational numbers (RAT); and one type for integers (INT). Thus, the question of converting, say, a character string of length 25 to one of length 26 doesn't arise. By contrast, the question of converting, say, an integer to a rational number certainly does arise, and **Tutorial D** provides an explicit operator (CAST) for precisely that purpose. *End of aside*.

IMPLEMENTATION DEFINED vs. IMPLEMENTATION DEPENDENT

You probably noticed, when I listed all of those system defined types near the beginning of the chapter, that certain aspects of those types—specifically, the actual precision for SMALLINT, INTEGER, and BIGINT, and the default precision for NUMERIC, DECIMAL, FLOAT, REAL, and DOUBLE PRECISION—were characterized as "implementation defined." That term and its companion "implementation dependent" are both used heavily in the SQL standard, and you need to understand their significance. Here then are the definitions:

Definition (implementation defined): An SQL feature is said to be implementation defined if its semantics can vary from one implementation to another but do at least have to be specified for the implementation in question. In other words, the implementation in question is free to decide how it will implement the feature in question, but the result of that decision must be documented. An example is the maximum length of a character string.

Definition (implementation dependent): An SQL feature is said to be implementation dependent if its semantics can vary from one implementation to another and don't even have to be specified for the implementation in question. In other words, the term effectively means *undefined*; the implementation in question is free to decide how it will implement the feature in question, and the result of that decision doesn't even have to be documented (it might vary from release to release, or even more frequently). An example is the full effect of an ORDER BY clause, if the specifications in that clause specify an ordering that's not total.

Let's take a closer look at ORDER BY in particular as an example of a feature whose semantics are "implementation dependent." Consider the following SQL expression:

```
SELECT  *
FROM    S
ORDER   BY CITY
```

Column CITY of table S is defined to be of type VARCHAR (25), and "ORDER BY CITY" thus basically just means alphabetical ordering. Assuming our usual sample value for table S, then, the foregoing expression can return any of four distinct results, corresponding to the following sequences (I'll show just the supplier numbers, for simplicity):

- S5 , S1 , S4 , S2 , S3

- S5 , S4 , S1 , S2 , S3

- S5 , S1 , S4 , S3 , S2

- S5 , S4 , S1 , S3 , S2

None of these sequences is more correct than any other, and which one we get on any particular occasion is, in general, unpredictable.

I'll have more to say about the matter of unpredictable results in general in the section "Collations," later in this chapter.

TYPE CHECKING AND COERCION

SQL supports only a weak form of strong typing (if you see what I mean).[6] To be specific (this is partly a repeat—but only partly, and in different words—of something I said in the section "Domains" earlier in this chapter):

- Boolean values can be assigned only to boolean variables and compared only with boolean values.

- Numeric values can be assigned only to numeric variables and compared only with numeric values (where "numeric" means types INTEGER, SMALLINT, BIGINT, NUMERIC, DECIMAL, FLOAT, REAL, and DOUBLE PRECISION).

- Character string values can be assigned only to character string variables and compared only with character string values (where "character string" means types CHAR, VARCHAR, and CLOB).

- Byte string values can be assigned only to byte string variables and compared only with byte string values (where "byte string" means types BINARY, VARBINARY, and BLOB).

Thus, for example, an attempt to compare a number and a character string is illegal. However, an attempt to compare (say) two numbers is always legal, even if the numbers in question are of different types—say INTEGER and FLOAT, respectively (in this example, the INTEGER value will be coerced to type FLOAT before the comparison is done). Which brings us back to the issue, already discussed briefly in Chapter 2, of type coercion.

---

[6] See the section "Equality Comparisons" in Chapter 2 if you need to refresh your memory regarding the concept of strong typing.

Now, it's a widely accepted principle in computing that coercions are generally best avoided, because they're error prone (in particular, they can give rise to errors that are hard to detect). In SQL in particular, one bizarre consequence of permitting coercions is that certain union, intersection, and difference operations can yield a result with rows that don't appear in either operand! By way of example, consider the SQL tables T1 and T2 shown below:

```
T1                        T2

┌───┬─────┐               ┌─────┬───┐
│ X │  Y  │               │  X  │ Y │
╞═══╪═════╡               ╞═════╪═══╡
│ 0 │ 1.0 │               │ 0.0 │ 0 │
│ 0 │ 2.0 │               │ 0.0 │ 1 │
└───┴─────┘               │ 1.0 │ 2 │
                          └─────┴───┘
```

I'm assuming here that (a) column X is of type INTEGER in table T1 but NUMERIC (2,1) in table T2, and (b) column Y is of type NUMERIC (2,1) in table T1 but INTEGER in table T2. Now consider the following SQL expression:

```
SELECT X , Y FROM T1
UNION
SELECT X , Y FROM T2
```

Here's the result (T3):

```
T3

┌─────┬─────┐
│  X  │  Y  │
╞═════╪═════╡
│ 0.0 │ 1.0 │
│ 0.0 │ 2.0 │
│ 0.0 │ 0.0 │
│ 1.0 │ 2.0 │
└─────┴─────┘
```

As this picture suggests, columns X and Y in T3 are both of type NUMERIC (2,1), and every individual value in each of those columns is obtained, in effect, by coercing some INTEGER value to type NUMERIC (2,1). Thus, the result consists exclusively of rows that appear in neither T1 nor T2!—a very strange kind of union, you might be forgiven for thinking. (Note too that the T1 row (0,1.0) and the T2 row (0.0,1)—which are clearly distinct from one another—have been treated as duplicates in that union process.)

Aside: One reviewer suggested that the "strangeness" of the union in this example might not matter in practice, since at least no information is lost in the process. Well, that observation might be valid, in this particular example; I don't want to argue the point. But if the SQL language designers want to define an operator that manifestly doesn't behave like the union operator of the relational model (or the union operator of set theory, come to that), then it seems to me that, first, it doesn't help the cause of understanding to call that operator "union"; second, and rather more important, it isn't up to me to show that such a "union" can sometimes cause problems—rather, it's up to those language designers to show that it can't. *End of aside.*

Strong recommendations: Do your best to avoid coercions wherever possible. (My own clear preference would be to do away with them entirely, regardless of whether we're in the SQL context or any other context.) In the SQL context in particular, I recommend that at least you ensure that *columns with the same name are always of the same type*; this discipline will go a long way toward ensuring that type conversions in general are avoided, be they implicit or explicit. And when they can't be avoided, I recommend doing them explicitly, using CAST or some CAST equivalent, as in the following revised version of the foregoing UNION example:

```
SELECT CAST ( X AS NUMERIC(2,1) ) AS X , Y FROM T1
UNION
SELECT X , CAST ( Y AS NUMERIC(2,1) ) AS Y FROM T2
```

For completeness, however, I need to add that, unfortunately, certain coercions are built into the very fabric of SQL and are thus very difficult to avoid 100%. To be specific:

■ If a table expression *tx* in parentheses is used as a *row subquery*, then the table *t* denoted by *tx* is supposed to have just one row *r*, and—assuming it does—that table *t* is coerced to that row *r*.

■ If a table expression *tx* in parentheses is used as a *scalar subquery*, then the table *t* denoted by *tx* is supposed to have just one column and just one row and hence to contain just one value *v*, and—assuming it does—that table *t* is doubly coerced to that value *v*.

To elaborate briefly:

■ (*Subqueries in general*) First, as I'm sure you know, the term *subquery* occurs ubiquitously in SQL contexts. Speaking a trifle loosely, what it refers to is just a SELECT expression enclosed in parentheses. For example, consider the following SQL expression:

```
SELECT  S.SNO , S.SNAME , S.STATUS , S.CITY
FROM    S
WHERE   SNO IN
      ( SELECT  SNO
        FROM    SP )
```

This expression represents the query "Get full details for suppliers who supply at least one part," and the subexpression "(SELECT SNO FROM SP)" following the keyword IN is a subquery; in fact, it's an example of what SQL calls a *table* subquery, because a table as such is what it denotes and evaluates to.

■ (*Row subqueries*) Let *sq* be a subquery. By definition, the expression *tx* within the parentheses in *sq* evaluates to a table (see the previous bullet item). In some contexts, however, SQL will allow *sq* to be used as a *row* expression—i.e., to appear in a position where a row value, not a table value, is required. For example:

```
SELECT  S.SNO
FROM    S
WHERE   ROW ( STATUS , CITY ) =
            ( SELECT  STATUS , CITY
              FROM    S
              WHERE   SNO ='S1' )
```

("Get supplier numbers for suppliers with the same status and city as supplier S1"). The subquery here—i.e., the expression in parentheses following the "=" sign—denotes a table containing just one row, and that table then gets coerced to the single row it contains.[7]

---

[7] It's an error if that table contains more than one row. However, I'm sorry to say that if instead it contains no rows at all, then that's *not* an error—instead, that empty table gets coerced to a table containing just one row, viz., a row with a null in every column position, and that one-row table then gets coerced in turn to the single row it contains (i.e., a row of all nulls).

■ (*Scalar subqueries*) Again let *sq* be a subquery. To say it again, the expression *tx* within the parentheses in *sq* evaluates to a table, by definition. In some contexts, however, SQL will allow *sq* to be used as a *scalar* expression—i.e., to appear in a position where a scalar value, not a table value, is required. For example:

```
SELECT  S.SNO
FROM    S
WHERE   STATUS =
      ( SELECT  STATUS
        FROM    S
        WHERE   SNO ='S1' )
```

("Get supplier numbers for suppliers with the same status as supplier S1"). The subquery here—i.e., the expression in parentheses following the "=" sign—denotes a table containing just one row and one column; that table gets coerced to the single row it contains, and that row then gets coerced to the single column value it contains.[8]

Finally, be aware that SQL also uses the term *coercion* in a very special sense in connection with character strings. The details are beyond the scope of this book; if you want to know more, please refer to Chapter 1 ("Equality") of my book *Stating the Obvious, and Other Database Writings* (Technics, 2020).

COLLATIONS

SQL's rules regarding type checking and coercion, in the case of character strings in particular, are (sadly) rather more complex than I've been pretending so far, and I need to elaborate somewhat. Actually it's impossible in a book of this nature to do more than just scratch the surface of the matter, but the basic idea is that any given character string

a. Consists of characters from one associated *character set*, and

b. Has one associated *collation*.

---

[8] The previous footnote applies here also, mutatis mutandis.

Now, I'm going to assume for the purposes of this book that the concept of a character set is well understood. (Actually there's quite a lot that could be said about that concept, but this isn't the place for such a discussion; for more information, I refer you to the book *A Guide to the SQL Standard*, 4th ed., Addison-Wesley, 1997, by Hugh Darwen and myself.) However, I do want to say a little more about collations.

A *collation*, also known as a *collating sequence*, is a rule that's associated with a specific character set and governs the comparison of strings of characters from that character set. Let C be a collation for character set S, and let a and b be any two characters from S (not necessarily distinct) Then C must be such that, according to C, exactly one of the comparisons $a < b$, $a = b$, and $a > b$ evaluates to TRUE and the other two to FALSE.[9]

Lack of Determinacy

So much for the basic collation idea. However, there are complications.

■ One such arises from the fact that any given collation can—or, rather, must—have either PAD SPACE or NO PAD defined for it. Suppose the character strings 'AB' and 'AB ' (note the trailing space in the latter) have the same character set and the same collation. Then those two strings are clearly distinct, and yet they're considered to "compare equal" if PAD SPACE applies.[10]

Note, however, that the choice (i.e., between PAD SPACE and NO PAD) affects comparisons only—it makes no difference to assignments. **Recommendation:** Don't use PAD SPACE; always use NO PAD instead, if possible.

■ Another complication arises from the fact that the comparison $a = b$ might evaluate to TRUE under a given collation, even if the characters a and b are distinct. For example, we might define a collation CASE_INSENSITIVE,

---

[9] *Historical note:* Early versions of SQL supported just one character set, that character set had just one collation, and that collation was based on the numerical order of the binary codes used to represent the characters in that character set. But there's no intrinsic reason why collating sequences in general should have to depend on internal coding schemes, and there are good practical reasons why they shouldn't.

[10] *Historical note:* The original (i.e., IBM) version of SQL supported PAD SPACE only, and did that only implicitly. The reason for this state of affairs was a desire on the part of the SQL language designers in IBM to conform to the corresponding rules for PL/I.

according to which any given lowercase letter and its uppercase counterpart are defined to "compare equal." As a consequence, again, strings that are clearly distinct will sometimes compare equal.

We see, therefore, that if c_1 and c_2 are character strings, then the comparison $c_1 = c_2$ can give TRUE in SQL even if c_1 and c_2 are distinct (possibly even if they're of different types, thanks to SQL's support for coercions). I'll use the term "distinct, considered equal" to refer to such pairs of values. Now, equality comparisons are performed, often implicitly, in numerous contexts— examples include MATCH, LIKE, UNIQUE, UNION, and JOIN—and the kind of equality involved in all such cases is indeed such that "distinct, considered equal" values are treated as equal. For example:

- Let collation CASE_INSENSITIVE be as defined above.

- Let PAD SPACE apply to that collation.

- Let the PNO columns of tables P and SP both use that collation.

- Let 'P2' and 'p2   ' (i.e., p2 followed by three spaces) be PNO values in, respectively, some row of P and some row of SP.

- Then those two rows will be regarded as satisfying the foreign key constraint from SP to P, despite the lowercase p and trailing spaces in the foreign key value.

What's more, when evaluating expressions involving operators such as UNION, INTERSECT, JOIN, GROUP BY, DISTINCT (and so on), the system sometimes has to decide which of several "distinct, considered equal" values is to be chosen as the value of some column in some result row. Unfortunately, SQL fails to give complete guidance in such situations. As a consequence, certain table expressions are *indeterminate*—the SQL term is "possibly nondeterministic"—in the sense that SQL doesn't fully specify how they should be evaluated; indeed, they might quite legitimately give different results on different occasions. For example, if collation CASE_INSENSITIVE applies to column C in table T, then SELECT MAX (C) FROM T might legitimately return 'ZZZ' on one occasion and 'zzz' on another, even if T hasn't changed in the interim.

I won't give SQL's rules here for when a given expression is "possibly nondeterministic," but the answer to Exercise 5 at the end of the chapter goes into a little more detail. However, I will at least point out the following, because it's important:

- First, possibly nondeterministic expressions aren't allowed in integrity constraints (presumably because they could cause updates to succeed or fail unpredictably).

- Second, it's a direct consequence of the previous point—a consequence, though, that I strongly suspect wasn't foreseen when the "possibly nondeterministic" concept was originally invented—that SQL table expressions (even simple SELECT expressions, sometimes) will often not be allowed in constraints, if they—the table expressions in question, that is—involve a column of some character string type!

What makes matters even weirder, though, is this: Although as just noted possibly nondeterministic expressions aren't allowed in constraints, they *are* allowed in queries and updates, where they can surely do just as much damage. Why?

Of course, if such expressions weren't allowed to appear in queries and updates either, they wouldn't be allowed to appear anywhere at all—a state of affairs that does make one wonder what on earth the SQL language designers could have been thinking when they first came up with the concept.

Lack of Determinacy bis

I pointed out earlier, in the section "Implementation Defined vs. Implementation Dependent," that the ORDER BY operator could legitimately but unpredictably produce different outputs from the same input. So I suppose we might say that ORDER BY too is "possibly nondeterministic," in general. But a more conventional way of saying the same thing would be to say simply that ORDER BY isn't a *function*, mathematically speaking. Recall the following definition from Chapter 1:

> **Definition (mathematical function):** Given two sets, not necessarily distinct, a rule—also known as a map or mapping—pairing each element *x*

of the first set with exactly one element y of the second set; equivalently, the set of ordered pairs $<x,y>$ that constitutes that pairing.

The crucial point here is that, given any particular input, a function has exactly one corresponding output. So ORDER BY is indeed not a function. Note carefully that, by contrast, the usual operators of the relational algebra as such—union, restriction, projection, join, etc.—*are* all functions, according to the definition.[11]

Now, the reason I mention this point is the following: Although the usual operators of the relational algebra are indeed functions as I've just said, *most of them have counterparts in SQL that aren't*. And this state of affairs is a direct consequence of the fact that, as explained earlier in this section, SQL sometimes defines the result of the comparison $c_1 = c_2$ to be TRUE even when c_1 and c_2 are distinct. To illustrate:

- Consider the character strings 'Paris' and 'Paris ', respectively (note the trailing space in the second of these). These values are clearly distinct—for one thing, they're of different lengths—and yet SQL sometimes regards them as equal, as we've seen.

- Now consider this SQL expression:

```
SELECT DISTINCT CITY
FROM S
```

If one supplier has CITY 'Paris' and another has CITY 'Paris ', then the result will include either 'Paris' or 'Paris ' (or possibly both), but which result we get might not be defined; indeed, it *isn't* defined, at least as far as SQL is concerned. We could even legitimately get one result on one day and another on another, even if the database hasn't changed at all in the interim. You might like to meditate on some of the implications of this state of affairs.

Strong recommendation: Avoid possibly nondeterministic expressions as much as you can.

---

[11] Just to spell the point out for the record: ORDER BY is *not* "an operator of the relational algebra as such" (though statements to the opposite effect aren't exactly unknown in the literature). Why isn't it? *Answer:* Because its result isn't a relation—instead, it's an ordered list.

ROW AND TABLE TYPES

So far in this chapter we've been concerned with scalar types specifically, but now it's time to say something about SQL's row and table types. First rows. Of course, rows are SQL's analogs of tuples in the relational world, so I'll begin with an example of a tuple variable definition (the example is repeated from Chapter 2, except that now I give the attributes in their more familiar sequence):

```
VAR STV  /* "supplier tuple variable" */
    TUPLE
    { SNO CHAR , SNAME CHAR , STATUS INTEGER , CITY CHAR } ;
```

The expression TUPLE {...} here is, as you'll recall, an invocation of the TUPLE type generator. And SQL, as you'd expect, has a corresponding ROW type generator (though it calls it a type *constructor*). Here's an SQL analog of the foregoing **Tutorial D** example:

```
DECLARE SRV  /* SQL row variable */
        ROW ( SNO    VARCHAR(5) ,
              SNAME  VARCHAR(25) ,
              STATUS INTEGER ,
              CITY   VARCHAR(25) ) ;
```

Now, in SQL, if row *r* is part of table *t*, the components of *r* are referred to as *columns* (the columns in question being, of course, precisely the columns of *t*). But if instead row *r* is a value of some row type *R* that's defined by means of the ROW type generator—also in the case of that row type *R* itself, also of variables of that type, such as SRV in the example—the components are referred to in SQL not as columns but as *fields*. It is not known why this is. However, it does mean in the case at hand that SNO, SNAME, STATUS, and CITY are "fields" of the row variable SRV, and "fields" of every possible value of that variable also.

Next, rows in SQL, no matter whether their components are called columns or fields, differ from tuples in that those components are ordered, left to right; in other words, the sequence in which the components are defined has significance, and different sequences correspond to different row types. So if there are four components (as there are in the foregoing example, of course), then there are actually $4! = 4 \times 3 \times 2 \times 1 = 24$ row types, all of them consisting of the same four components but every one of them different from all the rest. *Note:* The expression *n*!—which can be read as either "*n* factorial" or "factorial *n*" and is often pronounced "*n* bang"—is defined as the product $n \times (n-1) \times ... \times 2 \times 1$.

SQL also supports row assignment. Recall this **Tutorial D** tuple assignment from the section "Scalar vs. Nonscalar Types" in Chapter 2:

```
STV := TUPLE FROM ( S WHERE SNO = 'S1' ) ;
```

Here's an SQL row assignment analog:

```
SET SRV = ( S WHERE SNO = 'S1' ) ;
```

The expression on the right side here is a *row subquery*—i.e., it's a table expression, syntactically speaking, but it's a table expression that's being used as a row expression, as explained in the section "Type Checking and Coercion," earlier in this chapter. Just to remind you, what happens here is this:

- First, the table expression S WHERE SNO = 'S1' is evaluated, to yield a table that happens to contain exactly one row.

- Second, that table is coerced to the single row it contains. (SQL has no explicit counterpart to **Tutorial D**'s TUPLE FROM operator—hence the need for coercion.)

- Third, that row is then assigned to the row variable SRV.

Row assignments are also involved, implicitly, in SQL UPDATE statements.

Turning now to tables: Interestingly, SQL doesn't really have a TABLE type generator (or type constructor, as SQL would probably call it) at all!—i.e., it has nothing directly analogous to the RELATION type generator described in the previous chapter. Of course, it does have a mechanism, CREATE TABLE, for defining what by rights should be called table variables[12]—but the keyword TABLE in CREATE TABLE, unlike the keyword ROW in DECLARE ROW as discussed above does *not* denote a table type generator. Let me elaborate. First of all, recall this **Tutorial D** definition from the previous chapter:

---

[12] *Base* table variables, to be more precise. It also supports a mechanism, CREATE VIEW, for defining virtual table variables or views (which, like base tables, ought by rights to be considered to be of some table type). But I don't have much to say about views in this book.

```
VAR S BASE
    RELATION
      { SNO CHAR , SNAME CHAR , STATUS INTEGER , CITY CHAR }
    KEY { SNO } ;
```

Here's an SQL analog:

```
CREATE  TABLE  S
      ( SNO    VARCHAR(5)  NOT NULL ,
        SNAME  VARCHAR(25) NOT NULL ,
        STATUS INTEGER     NOT NULL ,
        CITY   VARCHAR(25) NOT NULL ,
        UNIQUE ( SNO ) ) ;
```

Observe now that there's nothing—no sequence of linguistic tokens—in this CREATE TABLE statement that can logically be labeled "an invocation of the TABLE type generator." (The truth of this observation might become more apparent when you realize that the specification UNIQUE (SNO), which defines a certain integrity constraint on suppliers, doesn't have to come after the column definitions but can appear almost anywhere—e.g., between the definitions of columns SNAME and STATUS. Not to mention the NOT NULL specifications on the individual column definitions, which also define certain integrity constraints.) In fact, to the extent that the variable S can be regarded, in SQL, as having any type at all, that type is nothing more than *bag of rows*, where the rows in question are of the following row type:

```
ROW ( SNO VARCHAR(5) , SNAME VARCHAR(25) ,
                       STATUS INTEGER , CITY VARCHAR(25) )
```

In case you're not convinced, let me repeat something I said in Chapter 2, albeit in considerably different words. To be specific: If SQL really did support a TABLE type generator (or constructor), then tables would be what some people like to call "first class objects," and they'd be usable everywhere in the language that made logical sense (orthogonality!). And one thing we'd be able to do in particular is this: We'd be able to define "tables that contain tables"—i.e., tables with columns of some table type, meaning columns containing values that are themselves tables in turn. But SQL doesn't let us do that. It does let us define columns whose values are bags of rows; but a bag of rows isn't a table, because it can't be operated upon by means of SQL's regular table operators.

So there's no TABLE type generator in SQL, and as a consequence there aren't any table types either. That said, however, I need to say too that SQL does nevertheless support something it calls "typed tables"![13] I don't want to get into a lot of detail on this topic at this juncture (I'll examine it in detail in Chapter 5); here I'll just note that the term is hardly very appropriate, because if *TT* is a "typed table" that has been defined to be "of type *T*," then *TT* is *not* of type *T*, and neither are its rows! More important, I think you should avoid "typed tables" anyway, because they're inextricably intertwined with SQL's support for *pointers*, and of course pointers are explicitly prohibited in the relational model.

> *Aside:* Perhaps I should elaborate briefly on what I mean by the term *pointer*. A pointer is a value (an address, essentially) for which certain special operators—notably certain *referencing* and *dereferencing* operators—are, and in fact must be, defined.[14] Here are rough definitions:
>
> a. Given a variable *V*, the referencing operator applied to *V* returns the address of *V*.
>
> b. Given a value *v* of type pointer (an address, in other words), the dereferencing operator applied to *v* returns the variable that *v* points to (i.e., the variable located at the given address).
>
> Note in particular that the dereferencing operator returns a *variable*, a fact that makes it quite unusual—operators in general return values, not variables (if they return anything at all, that is). *End of aside.*

To repeat, pointers are explicitly prohibited in the relational model. Thus, if some table *T* has a column whose values are pointers to rows in some "target" table *T'*, then that table *T* can't possibly represent a relation in the relational model sense. (As a matter of fact, the target table *T'* can't either.) As I've indicated, however, tables like table *T* (and *T'*) unfortunately are permitted in SQL; the pointers are called *reference values*, and the columns that contain them

---

[13] Of course, that term in and of itself implies rather strongly that most tables *don't* have types, in SQL.

[14] I say "must be defined," but in fact SQL manages to get away with defining just one of these two operators (viz., dereferencing). For further explanation I refer you to Chapter 5.

are said to be of some *REF type*. Quite frankly, it's not clear why these features are included in SQL at all; certainly there seems to be no useful functionality that can be achieved with them that can't equally well—in fact, better—be achieved without them. **Strong recommendation:** Don't use them, nor any features related to them.

> *Aside:* To avoid a possible confusion, I should add that SQL actually uses the terminology of "references" and "referencing" in two quite different senses. One is as sketched above. The other, and older, sense has to do with foreign keys; a foreign key value in one row is said to "reference" the row that contains the corresponding target key value. Note, however, that foreign keys most certainly aren't pointers!—there are many logical differences between the two concepts, including in particular the fact that foreign keys refer to rows, which are values, whereas pointers are addresses and therefore, by definition, refer to variables. (After all, it's variables, not values, that "have location." Values, having no location, certainly don't have addresses.) *End of aside.*

EXERCISES

1. This chapter has touched on several further logical differences, including:

CHAR (25)	vs.	VARCHAR (25)
implementation defined	vs.	implementation dependent
NUMERIC (p,q)	vs.	DECIMAL (p,q)
PAD SPACE	vs.	NO PAD
reference	vs.	expression
relational domain	vs.	SQL domain
type	vs.	type generator

What exactly is the logical difference in each case?

2. In the relational world, the equality operator "=" applies to every type. SQL, by contrast, doesn't require "=" to apply to every type, nor does it fully define the semantics in all of the cases where it does apply. What are the implications of this state of affairs?

3. Following on from the previous exercise, we can say that, in the relational world, if v_1 and v_2 are values such that $v_1 = v_2$ evaluates to TRUE, then executing some operator *Op* on v_1 and executing that same operator *Op* on v_2 always has exactly the same effect, for all possible operators *Op*. But this is another precept that SQL violates. Can you think of any examples of such violation? What are the implications?

4. *The Assignment Principle*—which is very simple, but fundamental—states that immediately after assignment of the value *v* to the variable *V*, the comparison $V = v$ evaluates to TRUE. Yet again, however, this is a precept that SQL violates (fairly ubiquitously, in fact). Can you think of any examples of such violation? What are the implications?

5. What do you understand by the term *possibly nondeterministic*?

6. In the previous chapter I gave an example—actually an incorrect example, but that's not the point at issue here—of an SQL SELECT expression where I pointed out that there was no terminating semicolon because the expression was indeed an expression and not a statement. But what's the difference?

7. What's a subquery?

8. In SQL, does the equality operator "=" apply to type BOOLEAN? To row types? To table types?

9. Consider the following, all of which are legitimate SQL concepts, or constructs: (a) NUMERIC; (b) NUMERIC (4,1); (c) exact numeric. SQL does seem to be terribly muddled over which if any of these are types and which if any are something else. Do you think the muddle could possibly stem from a confusion over the logical difference between types and representations?

ANSWERS

1. CHAR (25) and VARCHAR (25) are both SQL character string types—CHAR (25) consists of character strings of length exactly 25 characters, VARCHAR (25) consists of character strings of length at most 25 characters. (By the way, CHAR

values always contain at least one character. Whether the same is true of VARCHAR is unclear; the standard seems to contradict itself on the issue.)

For the logical difference between the SQL concepts *implementation defined* and *implementation dependent*, see the body of the chapter.

The difference between NUMERIC (*p,q*) and DECIMAL (*p,q*) is a little subtle. It's also hard to remember! Anyway, NUMERIC (*p,q*) means the precision must be *exactly p* digits, whereas DECIMAL (*p,q*) means it must be *at least p* digits but is otherwise implementation defined.[15] Thus, e.g., the implementation might represent both NUMERIC and DECIMAL values internally as packed decimal; and if it did, then, e.g., a NUMERIC (2,1) value and a DECIMAL (2,1) value could each be represented in two bytes. But since—in IBM System/360 packed decimal, at any rate—a two-byte packed decimal field can actually hold three decimal digits (with a four-bit sign), the DECIMAL items could be allowed to have values in the range –99.9 to +99.9, whereas the NUMERIC items would have to be constrained to values in the range –9.9 to +9.9. In other words, the range of NUMERIC values is strictly defined, for maximum portability, whereas the range of DECIMAL values adjusts to the implementation, for maximum exploitation of the capabilities of that implementation. (Do you think this is a good idea?)

For the logical difference between PAD SPACE and NO PAD, see the body of the chapter.

A *reference*—in the programming language sense, at least—is just the name of a variable, used to denote either the variable as such or the value of that variable, as the context demands. Note that such a reference definitely denotes the variable as such if it's used to specify a target for some update operation (in particular, if it appears on the left side of an assignment). If on the other hand it denotes the value of the variable, then it can be regarded as an invocation of a read-only operator (and hence as an expression, q.v.), where the read-only operator in question is essentially "Return the current value of the specified variable." Like all expressions, therefore, it can appear wherever a literal of the appropriate type can appear. An *expression*—again in the programming language sense—is a read-only operator invocation; in other

---

[15] If you need to remember which is "exactly *p* digits" and which is "at least *p* digits," then the fact that both types are considered to be "exact numeric" doesn't help very much. (I nearly wrote "desn't *exactly* help," but decided against it.)

words, it's a construct that denotes a value (in effect, it's a rule for computing the value in question). Every expression is of some type: namely, the type of the value it denotes.

In the relational world, a *domain* is a type. In the SQL world ... Well, it's a little hard to say exactly what a domain is, in SQL. For further discussion, see the body of the chapter.

A *type* is a named, and in practice finite, set of values; not to be confused with the internal or physical representation of the values in question, which is an implementation issue. (To say that something is "of" type *T* is to say that every value of the something in question must be a value from the set of values constituting *T*.) A *type generator* is an operator that's invoked at compile time instead of run time and returns a type instead of a value. As explained in the body of the chapter, SQL unfortunately fails, sometimes, to make a clear distinction between these concepts.

2. Let *T* be an SQL type for which "=" isn't defined at all, and let *C* be a column of type *T*. Then *C* can't be any part of a key or foreign key, nor can it be any part of the argument to DISTINCT or GROUP BY or ORDER BY, nor can restrictions or joins or unions or intersections or differences be defined in terms of it. And what about implementation constructs such as indexes? There are probably other implications as well.

Second, let *T* be an SQL type for which the semantics of "=" are defined, but not fully defined, in the language (a situation that can certainly arise if, but not only if, *T* is a user defined type), and let *C* be a column of type *T*. Then the effects of making *C* part of a key or foreign key or applying DISTINCT or GROUP BY (etc., etc.) to it will be less than fully defined as well. *Note:* Presumably for this very reason, the standard doesn't actually allow such a column *C* to be used in all of the contexts just mentioned—and possibly not in any of them (?). The specifics of exactly what's allowed in this connection are baroque in the extreme, however; so if you want to know more, I'm afraid I'm going to have to refer you to the standard itself.

3. Here's a trivial example of such violation. Let v_1 be the character string 'AB ' (note the trailing space), let v_2 be the character string 'AB', and let PAD SPACE apply to the pertinent collation. Then the comparison $v_1 = v_2$ gives TRUE, and yet the operator invocations CHAR_LENGTH(v_1) and CHAR_LENGTH(v_2) give 3

and 2, respectively. (Note too that even though the comparison $v_1 = v_2$ gives TRUE, the comparisons $v_1||v_1 = v_2||v_2$ and $v_1||v_2 = v_2||v_1$ most certainly don't!) I leave the detailed implications for you to think about, but it should be clear that problems are likely to surface in connection with DISTINCT, GROUP BY, and ORDER BY operations among others (as well as in connection with keys, foreign keys, and certain implementation constructs, such as indexes).

4. One answer has to do with nulls; if we "set X to null" (which isn't really assigning a value to X, because nulls aren't values, but never mind), the comparison X = NULL certainly doesn't give TRUE. There are many other examples too, not involving reliance on nulls. E.g., let X be a variable of type CHAR (3), let Y be the character string 'AB' (no trailing space), and let NO PAD apply to the pertinent collation. Then assigning Y to X will actually set X to the string 'AB ' (one trailing space), and after that assignment the comparison X = Y will give FALSE. Again I leave it to you to think about possible further implications.

5. The following answer consists of an extended extract, though lightly edited here, from my book *SQL and Relational Theory*, 3rd ed. (O'Reilly, 2015).
    First of all, a given SQL table expression is said to be "possibly nondeterministic" if it might give different results on different evaluations, even if the database hasn't changed in the interim. Here's the standard's own definition:

> A *<query expression>* or *<query specification>* is *possibly nondeterministic* if an implementation might, at two different times where the state of the SQL-data is the same, produce results that differ by more than the order of the rows due to General Rules that specify implementation dependent behavior.[16]

Actually this definition is a trifle odd, inasmuch as tables—which is what *<query expression>*s and *<query specification>*s are supposed to evaluate to— aren't supposed to have an ordering to their rows anyway. But let's overlook that detail; the important point is that, as noted in the body of the chapter,

---

[16] The difference between *<query expression>*s and *<query specification>*s as far as the standard is concerned is basically just that the former can involve union, intersection, and difference operations and the latter can't.

possibly nondeterministic expressions aren't allowed in integrity constraints,[17] a state of affairs that could have serious practical implications if true.

The standard's rules for labeling a given table expression "possibly nondeterministic" are quite complex, and full details are beyond the scope of this book. However, a given table expression *tx* is certainly considered to be "possibly nondeterministic" if any of the following is true:[18]

- *tx* is a union, intersection, or difference, and some column of the operand tables is of type character string.

- *tx* is a SELECT expression, the SELECT item commalist[19] in that SELECT expression contains an item (*C* say) of type character string, and at least one of the following is true:

    a. The SELECT item commalist is preceded by the keyword DISTINCT.

    b. *C* involves a MAX or MIN invocation.

    c. *tx* includes a GROUP BY clause and *C* is one of the grouping columns.

- *tx* is a SELECT expression that includes a HAVING clause and the boolean expression in that HAVING clause contains either (a) a reference to a grouping column of type character string or (b) a MAX or MIN invocation in which the argument is of type character string.

- *tx* is a JOIN expression and at least one of the operand expressions is possibly nondeterministic.

---

[17] Nor in view definitions, if WITH CHECK OPTION is specified.

[18] What follows represents my own understanding and paraphrasing of the pertinent text from SQL:1992 (except that I've also taken into account certain minor revisions made in subsequent versions of the standard). More important, I follow SQL:1992 here in talking about character string types only. The rules have since been extended to include as "possibly nondeterministic" (a) expressions involving data of certain user defined types and (b) expressions involving invocations of certain user defined operators (or *routines*, to use the standard's term). Further specifics are beyond the scope of this book.

[19] The term *commalist* is explained in Chapter 4.

Note, however, that these rules are certainly stronger than they need be. For example, suppose that (a) NO PAD applies to the pertinent collation and (b) no two characters from the pertinent character set are "distinct, considered equal" according to that collation. Then, e.g., SELECT MAX (*C*) FROM *T*, where column *C* of table *T* is of the character string type in question, is surely well defined.

6. (Another logical difference here!) An *expression* represents an operator invocation, and it denotes a value; it can be thought of as a rule for computing the value in question. Note that the arguments to that operator invocation are themselves specified as expressions in turn—though the expressions in question might just be simple literals or simple variable references. By contrast, a *statement* doesn't denote a value; instead, it causes some action to occur, such as assigning a value to some variable or changing the flow of control. In SQL, for example,

```
X + Y
```

is an expression, but

```
SET Z = X + Y ;
```

is a statement.

7 "Subquery" is an SQL term meaning, loosely, a SELECT expression enclosed in parentheses. For more specifics, see the body of the chapter.

8. Regarding the SQL type BOOLEAN, yes, "=" does apply; TRUE is equal to TRUE and FALSE is equal to FALSE, as I presume you'd expect. Perhaps surprisingly, though, "<" applies as well!—FALSE is considered to be less than TRUE (i.e., the comparison "FALSE < TRUE" returns TRUE, in SQL).

Next: The foregoing paragraph is correct, but it doesn't tell the whole story. As I'm sure know, the SQL type BOOLEAN actually has three values, not two. (So do you think the name "BOOLEAN" is appropriate?) The three values are TRUE, FALSE, and UNKNOWN—and yes, UNKNOWN is equal to UNKNOWN (i.e., "UNKNOWN = UNKNOWN" does correctly return TRUE, not, as you might have expected, UNKNOWN, because unlike null UNKNOWN is a *value*—it's "the third truth value"). What's more, UNKNOWN is considered as being "between" FALSE and TRUE; that is, "FALSE < UNKNOWN" and "UNKNOWN < TRUE" both return TRUE.

At the risk of confusing you, let me now point out that if B is an SQL variable of type BOOLEAN, then—like other SQL variables—B might "be null," meaning its value is unknown. If so, then the comparison "B = B" will return, not TRUE, but UNKNOWN. Note carefully, therefore that unknown isn't equal to UNKNOWN. In fact, of course, unknown isn't equal to anything at all!—not even itself. (Note the violation of what's called *The First Axiom of Equality* here: viz., that *x* = *x* for all *x*.)

Row types: Again, yes, "=" does apply—and in SQL, though not in the relational model, "<" applies as well. (The reason "<" doesn't apply in the relational case is that rows—or tuples, rather—in the relational model are *sets*, and "<" doesn't make sense for sets.[20] In SQL, though, rows aren't sets, they're *sequences*, because rows in SQL have a left to right ordering to their components.)

Here then for the record is an accurate statement of the rules regarding row comparisons in SQL.[21] Let the comparand rows be *Left* and *Right,* respectively. *Left* and *Right* must be of the same degree; i.e., they must both contain the same number of components, *n* say. Let *i* range from 1 to *n*, and let the *i*th components of *Left* and *Right* be L_i and R_i, respectively. The data type of L_i must be compatible with that of R_i (see the body of the chapter for a discussion of data type compatibility in SQL). Then the result of the comparison condition overall is defined as follows:

- ■ "*Left* = *Right*" is true if and only if for all *i*, "$L_i = R_i$" is true.

- ■ "*Left* <> *Right*" is true if and only if there exists some *j* such that "$L_j <> R_j$" is true.[22]

---

[20] On the other hand, "⊆" (set inclusion) does make sense.

[21] The statement is indeed accurate as claimed. Despite its length, however, it's still not complete. For a complete statement, I'm afraid I'll have to refer you to the standard itself once again.

[22] In SQL, the symbol "<>" denotes "not equals" (more usually written "≠", of course).

■ *"Left < Right"* is true if and only if there exists some j such that *"L_j < R_j"* is true and for all $i < j$, *"$L_i = R_i$"* is true.

■ *"Left > Right"* is true if and only if there exists some j such that *"L_j > R_j"* is true and for all $i < j$, *"$L_i = R_i$"* is true.

■ *"Left <= Right"* is true if and only if *"Left < Right"* is true or *"Left = Right"* is true.

■ *"Left >= Right"* is true if and only if *"Left > Right"* is true or *"Left = Right"* is true.

■ *"Left = Right"* is false if and only if *"Left <> Right"* is true.

■ *"Left <> Right"* is false if and only if *"Left = Right"* is true.

■ *"Left < Right"* is false if and only if *"Left >= Right"* is true.

■ *"Left > Right"* is false if and only if *"Left <= Right"* is true.

■ *"Left <= Right"* is false if and only if *"Left > Right"* is true.

■ *"Left >= Right"* is false if and only if *"Left < Right"* is true.

Finally, let *op* be any of =, <>, <, <=, >, >=. Then:

■ *"Left op Right"* is unknown if and only if it is not true and not false.

Here for interest (and by way of contrast) are the comparison rules—in their entirety!—for tuples in the relational model:

■ Tuples t_1 and t_2 are equal if and only if they're the very same tuple.

Table types: Well, first of all, there *are* no table types in SQL, and so there's certainly no "=" operator for tables. Nevertheless, it's still possible to do table comparisons in SQL, albeit only in roundabout ways. For example, consider the following **Tutorial D** expression:

```
S { CITY } = P { CITY }
```

This expression denotes an equality comparison between the projection of the current value of the suppliers relvar S on {CITY} and the projection of the current value of the parts relvar P on {CITY}. Here then is an SQL analog:[23]

```
NOT EXISTS ( SELECT CITY FROM S
             EXCEPT
             SELECT CITY FROM P )
AND
NOT EXISTS ( SELECT CITY FROM P
             EXCEPT
             SELECT CITY FROM S )
```

Here's another example. First of all, consider the following **Tutorial D** expression:

```
S { SNO } ⊃ SP { SNO }
```

Meaning: The projection of the current value of relvar S on {SNO} is a proper superset of the projection of the current value of relvar SP on {SNO}. And here's an SQL analog:

```
EXISTS ( SELECT SNO FROM S
         EXCEPT
         SELECT SNO FROM SP )
AND
NOT EXISTS ( SELECT SNO FROM SP
             EXCEPT
             SELECT SNO FROM S )
```

Now, I claimed above that SQL has no direct support for table equality comparisons, and that's true. As a consequence, the following putative SQL analog of the **Tutorial D** comparison S{CITY} = P{CITY}—

```
( SELECT DISTINCT CITY FROM S ) =
( SELECT DISTINCT CITY FROM P )
```

---

[23] "EXCEPT" is the way SQL spells the difference operator MINUS.

—is illegal. But the odd thing is, SQL does have direct support for equality comparisons on *bags*, including as a special case bags of rows in particular. To elaborate:

■ First of all, I remind you that a *bag* (also known as a *multiset*) is like a set, except that it permits duplicate elements.[24] As explained in the body of the chapter, therefore, SQL tables contain, in general, bags, not sets, of rows—though SQL typically uses the multiset terminology.

■ Next, regarding bag (or multiset) equality in SQL, here's the pertinent quote from the standard:

> Two multisets *A* and *B* are distinct if there exists a value *V* in the element type of *A* and *B*, including the null value,[25] such that the number of elements in *A* that are not distinct from *V* does not equal the number of elements in *B* that are not distinct from *V*.

I hope that's perfectly clear! Note that the extract quoted does indeed define what it means for two bags to be equal, because—simplifying considerably—if *A* and *B* aren't "distinct" according to SQL, then they must be equal (again, according to SQL).

■ Finally, SQL provides an operator for converting a table to a bag of rows.

So we can do the desired equality comparison by converting the tables in question to bags of rows and then comparing those bags.[26] So far so good ... Believe it or not, however, the operator that converts a table to a bag of rows is

---

[24] An extensive discussion of bags and bag theory in general can be found in Chapter 15 ("The Theory of Bags: An Investigative Tutorial") of my book *Logic and Relational Theory* (Technics, 2020).

[25] Of course, the phrase "null value" is a contradiction in terms, since the whole point about null is that it's not a value, but that phrase appears ubiquitously throughout the SQLstandard nevertheless (374 times, in my copy of SQL:2011). *Note:* I'm afraid the same phrase also appears in various early writings of my own, a state of affairs I regret and hereby apologize for.

[26] Note care fully, however, that although an SQL table does indeed contain a bag of rows, an SQL table *isn't* a bag of rows, precisely because it can't be operated upon by means of SQL's bag operators (nor can a bag of rows be operated upon by SQL's table operators).

called *TABLE* (!). Thus, the desired comparison can legitimately be formulated in SQL as follows:

```
TABLE ( SELECT DISTINCT CITY FROM S ) =
TABLE ( SELECT DISTINCT CITY FROM P )
```

But this trick only works for equality comparisons—SQL has no direct support for "⊃" etc. (certainly not for tables, and not for bags of rows either). And there's another complication, too: Believe it or not, the standard doesn't actually guarantee that the single column, in each of those two bags of rows resulting from the two TABLE invocations in the example, has any prescribed name; in particular, it doesn't guarantee that the column name in question is CITY! Of course, this lack of specificity probably doesn't matter in the present context, but it could easily matter very much indeed in other contexts.

9. Only you can answer this question definitively—but speaking for myself, yes, I do think the muddle arises over a confusion between types and representations. To be a little more specific:

■ I think "exact numeric" is a type, and I think NUMERIC (4,1) is just one of many possible representations for values of that type. Other such "possreps" include NUMERIC (*p*,*q*) for other values of *p* and *q*, and DECIMAL (*p*,*q*) likewise.

■ As for NUMERIC, it's a type generator, but the corresponding generated types are, or should be, *representation* types (and the same goes for DECIMAL). But of course the picture is muddied, considerably, because both those type generators and the corresponding generated types are exposed to the user, in SQL.

Chapter 4

Types:

A Closer Look

In this chapter I want to revisit and elaborate on some of the basic material on type theory from Chapter 2, and I want to take a much closer look at user defined types in particular. Of course, "revisiting and elaborating" does mean there'll be a small amount of repetition in what follows of material from that earlier chapter—but I don't think there's all that much, and what little there is I hope you won't find too annoying.

As a point of departure, I remind you that:

■ First of all, relational theory actually requires a supporting theory of types, because relations are defined over them—every attribute of every relation, and every attribute of every relvar, is of some type. But to put it like that is to put the cart before the horse, in a way. The more fundamental point is that *every* value is of some type, and *every* variable is declared to be of some type—and this observation applies to relation values and variables (relvars) in particular, and to tuple values and variables ("tuplevars") as well. Though of course there aren't any tuplevars as such, nor are there any free floating tuples, in a true relational database.

As for attributes, attributes of relations and tuples are likewise all of some type, and attributes of relvars and tuplevars are all declared to be of some type.

■ That said, there are certain limitations that apply to attribute types in particular:

a. First, no attribute of any relvar in a relational database is allowed to be of any pointer type.

b.   Second, no type can be defined, either directly or indirectly, in terms of itself ("recursively defined"). In particular, therefore, no attribute of any relvar or tuplevar can have the same heading as the relvar or tuplevar in question.

But apart from these exceptions, attributes in general can be of any type whatsoever (and it's important to realize as much)—which implies among other things that the types in question can be arbitrarily complex. Importantly, they can even be relation or tuple types in turn (see the answer to Exercise 5 at the end of the chapter for examples).

Note: Since this chapter is mostly about user defined types specifically, I revert in my examples to the original version of the suppliers and parts database as defined in Chapter 1, in which several though not all of the attributes are of some user defined type.

VALUES vs. VARIABLES

Values vs. variables is one of the great logical differences. Of course, I've appealed to this particular logical difference over and over again in previous chapters—in fact, I've stressed the point repeatedly that there's a logical difference between *relation* values and variables in particular—but I've never really pinned down, in general terms, just what that difference is. So now I will.

Before I get into details, though, let me say this: You might be thinking that what I'm about to say is so obvious it doesn't need saying at all; I mean, you might find it hard to believe that people could get confused over a distinction as basic and straightforward as the one between values and variables. If so, then I apologize. But the fact is, although the point is indeed very simple, it's also one over which there's a great deal of confusion in the field at large. Here by way of illustration is an extract from a tutorial on object databases[1] (the italicized portions in brackets are comments by myself):

We distinguish the declared type of a variable from ... the type of the object that is the current value of the variable [*so an object is a value*] ... We distinguish objects from values [*so an object isn't a value after all*] ... [A] mutator [is an operator

---

[1] Stanley B. Zdonik and David Maier, "Fundamentals of Object-Oriented Databases," in Zdonik and Maier (eds.), *Readings in Object-Oriented Database Systems* (Morgan Kaufmann, 1990).

such that it's] possible to observe its effect on some object [*so in fact an object is a variable*].

So in just a few lines we go from an object being a value, to an object not being a value, to an object being a variable. So what is it? Is it a value? Is it a variable? Or is it something else entirely? If so, what?[2]

Well, it's my belief that values and variables, at least, do have precise and widely agreed definitions, even if those definitions are sometimes not fully appreciated or adhered to; indeed, I believe values and variables have been pretty well understood, in some circles if not all, ever since programming languages first came on the scene. Here then as a basis for further discussion are such precise definitions, deliberately spelled out in considerable detail (they're based on ones in my book *The New Relational Database Dictionary*, O'Reilly, 2016):

Definition (value): An "individual constant"; for example, the individual constant denoted by the integer literal 3. Values can be of arbitrary complexity; in particular, they can be either scalar or nonscalar (note in particular that tuples and relations are values—nonscalar values, in fact). Values have no location in time or space. However, they can be represented in memory by means of some encoding, and those representations do have location in time and space; indeed, distinct occurrences of the same value can appear at any number of distinct locations in time and space, meaning, loosely, that the same value can occur as the current value of any number of distinct variables, and/or as any number of attribute values within the current value of any number of distinct tuplevars and/or relvars, at the same time or different times. Note that, by definition, a value can't be updated; for if it could, then after such an update it would no longer be that value. Note too that every value is of some type—in fact, of exactly one type (and types are thus disjoint), except possibly if type inheritance is supported. Note finally that a value isn't a type, nor is it a variable.

Definition (variable): A holder for a representation of a value. Unlike values, variables do have location in time and space, and they can be

---

[2] This lack of clarity as to exactly what an object is accounts for the total lack of mention of objects as such anywhere in *The Third Manifesto*. Indeed, we—meaning Hugh Darwen and I, the authors of the *Manifesto*—found we could formulate everything we wanted to say in terms of values and variables alone, without ever having to appeal to any kind of "object" notion at all.

updated (that is, the current value of the variable can be replaced by another value, probably different). Indeed, to be a variable is to be updatable, and to be updatable is to be a variable; equivalently, to be a variable is to be assignable to, and to be assignable to is to be a variable. Every variable is declared to be of some type. Note finally that a variable isn't a type, nor is it a value.

As you can see, these definitions are fairly detailed!—but I'd still like to elaborate on them somewhat.

■ First of all, regarding values specifically: Please understand that it isn't just simple things like the example mentioned in the definition, the integer 3, that are legitimate values. On the contrary, values can be arbitrarily complex. For example, as noted in Chapter 2 (albeit in slightly different words), a value might be a supplier number; or a geometric point; or a rectangle; or an X ray; or an XML document; or a fingerprint; or an array; or a relation (and on and on).

Analogous remarks apply to variables too, of course—or rather, and more fundamentally, they apply to types, as we'll see later.

■ To repeat, values vs. variables is one of the great logical differences. But there's also a logical difference between a value as such, on the one hand, and an appearance, or occurrence, of the value in question in some context (for example, as the current value of some variable), on the other. As the definition says, the very same value can occur in many different contexts (in particular, it can occur as the current value of many different variables), all at the same time. Each of those occurrences consists internally of some encoding, or physical representation, of the value in question. Moreover, those encodings aren't necessarily all the same. For example, the integer value 3 exists exactly once in the set of all integers—there's exactly one integer 3 "in the universe," as it were—but any number of variables might simultaneously contain an occurrence of that integer as their current value. What's more, some of those occurrences might be physically represented by means of, say, a decimal encoding, and others by means of a binary encoding, of the integer in question. Thus, there's also a logical difference between an occurrence of a value, on the one hand, and the internal encoding or physical representation of that occurrence on the other. And there might even be a logical difference between the encodings used for different occurrences of the same value, at the same time or different times.

■ All of that being said, for obvious reasons it's usual to abbreviate *encoding of an occurrence of a value* to just *occurrence of a value*, or (more often) just *value*, so long as there's no risk of ambiguity. Note, however, that *occurrence of a value* is a model concept, while *encoding of an occurrence* is an implementation concept. For example, users certainly might need to know whether two distinct variables contain occurrences of the same value (i.e., to know whether those variables "compare equal"); but they don't need to know whether those two occurrences are represented by means of the same physical encoding.

To illustrate this last point, let variables N1 and N2 both be declared to be of type INTEGER. After the following assignments, then, N1 and N2 will both contain an occurrence of the integer value 3 and will thus "compare equal" (and of course the user certainly needs to understand that these things are so):

```
N1 := 3 ;
N2 := 3 ;
```

As for the corresponding physical representations, however, they might or might not be the same (for example, N1 might use a decimal representation and N2 a binary representation). Either way, however, it's of no concern to the user.

TYPES

With that preliminary discussion of values and variables out of the way, I can now move on to discuss types as such. Basically, of course, a type is just a named set of values (all possible values of some particular kind). Here, however, is a more precise definition, based like those in the previous section on one in my book *The New Relational Database Dictionary* (O'Reilly, 2016):

Definition (type): A named, and in practice finite, set of values; not to be confused with the internal or physical representation of the values in question, which is an implementation issue. Every value, every variable, every attribute, every read-only operator, every parameter, and every expression is of some type. Types can be either scalar or nonscalar (in particular, they can be tuple or relation types); as a consequence, attributes of relations in particular can also be either scalar or nonscalar. Types can also be either system defined (i.e., built in) or user defined. They can also be generated. Note finally that a type isn't a value, nor is it a variable.

To elaborate:

- First of all, a given type can be either system defined (i.e., built in) or user defined.[3] The relational model prescribes just one system defined type, viz., type BOOLEAN (the most fundamental type of all). That type contains exactly two values: two truth values, to be precise, denoted by the literals TRUE and FALSE, respectively. However, real systems will of course support a variety of other system defined types as well, and I'll continue to assume as I did in Chapter 2 that types INT or INTEGER (integers), RAT or RATIONAL (rational numbers),[4] and CHAR or CHARACTER (character strings of arbitrary length) are all available as system defined types in addition to type BOOLEAN.

  Of course, the whole point about a user defined type—from the point of view of a user who is merely using it, that is, as opposed to the user who has the responsibility for defining it—is that it's supposed to behave just like a system defined type anyway. In most contexts, in other words, the question of whether a particular type is system or user defined is largely irrelevant.

- Second, types are always named (and types with different names are different types, so that, e.g., types INTEGER and RATIONAL are different types). Thus, every type has exactly one name.

  Aside: Does the foregoing imply that (e.g.) INTEGER and INT must therefore be different types? No, it doesn't; the type in question still has just one name as such (which I'll assume is INTEGER, just to be

---

[3] I'm making a tacit assumption here that the type in question isn't a generated type (the question of whether a given type is system or user defined doesn't really have meaning for generated types). See the section "Type Generators," later, for further explanation.

[4] I'll also assume, just in order to be definite, that the rational numbers in question—meaning values of type RATIONAL—are accurate to one decimal place, barring explicit statements to the contrary.

definite), but that name has an abbreviated form or *synonym*, INT. In other words, scalar types in general do always have exactly one name, but they can optionally and additionally have a synonym, or possibly even several such. For further details see Chapter 3 ("The Naming of Types") in the book *Database Explorations*, by Hugh Darwen and myself (Trafford, 2010), available free online at the website *www.thethirdmanifesto.com*. *End of aside.*

■ Third, I note in the interest of accuracy that, instead of saying (e.g.) that type INTEGER is the set of *all possible* integers, I should say rather that it's the set of all integers *that are capable of representation in the computer system under consideration.* Obviously, there'll always be some integers that are beyond the representational capability of any given system. In other words, the types we have to deal with in practice are always finite, precisely because we're dealing with computers, which are of course finite in turn.

So much for what types are; I turn now to the question of what they're for. The following quote, which I used as one of the epigraphs to this book, is pertinent here (I mean, it provides a good answer to that question):

> A major purpose of type systems is to avoid embarrassing questions about representations, and to forbid situations in which these questions might come up.

However, a full appreciation of the significance of this answer requires a lot more by way of background understanding, so let me continue with my explanations. The next point is that, in a properly typed system, just about everything *has*, or is *of*, some type. Again let me elaborate:

■ First and foremost, every *value* is certainly of some type. In other words, if *v* is a value, then *v* can be thought of as carrying around with it a kind of flag that announces "I'm an integer" or "I'm a supplier number" or "I'm a rectangle" or "I'm an XML document" (etc., etc.). Points arising:

  a. Since tuples and relations are values, these remarks apply to tuples and relations in particular. In these cases, however, the functionality of what I've just referred to as "a kind of flag" is provided by the pertinent *heading.* See the section "Type Generators," later, where I'll have a lot more to say about tuples and relations as such.

b. By definition, any given value always has exactly one type (except possibly if type inheritance is supported, which as far as this book is concerned it isn't), and that type never changes.

c. If every value is of exactly one type, then no value is of two or more types, and distinct types are thus disjoint (assuming, again, that inheritance isn't supported). However, please note that I'll have a little more to say on this particular issue in the answer to Exercise 2 at the end of the chapter.

■ Next, every variable, every attribute of every relvar,[5] every operator that returns a result, every parameter to every operator, and more generally every expression, has what's called a *declared* type.[6] To be specific:

a. Every *variable* is explicitly declared to be of some type, meaning that every possible value of the variable in question is a value of the type in question.

b. Every *attribute* of every relvar is explicitly declared to be of some type, meaning that every possible value of the attribute in question is a value of the type in question.

c. Every *operator* that returns a result is explicitly declared to be of some type, meaning that every possible result that can be returned by an invocation of the operator in question is a value of the type in question.
    Note: Operators in general are of two kinds:

---

[5] Or tuplevar—but for simplicity I'll ignore tuplevars from now on, until further notice.

[6] The difference between declared types and other types is important—very important!—if we're in an inheritance context, but not so otherwise. That is, the declared type of some item reduces to just the type of the item concerned, in the sense in which that term *type* is usually understood, so long as the possibility of inheritance is ignored. Nevertheless, I'll often include that qualifier *declared* in what follows, for emphasis.

    i.   Read-only operators,[7] which return a result and thus have a declared type as just explained, and

   ii.   Update operators, which return no result and thus have no declared type.

The section "Operators," later, goes into more detail on the difference between these two kinds. Here let me just note that if *Op* is an update operator and *P* is a parameter to *Op* that's "subject to update," then the argument *A* corresponding to *P* in any given invocation of *Op* must be a variable specifically (why?).

  d.   Every *parameter* to every operator is explicitly declared to be of some type, meaning that every possible argument that can be substituted for the parameter in question is a value of the type in question (or a variable of the type in question, if the operator in question is an update operator and might update the argument in question—see point c. above).

  e.   More generally, every *expression* denotes some value and is thus implicitly declared to be of some type: namely, the type of the value in question, which is to say the type of the result returned by the outermost operator in the expression (where by "outermost" I mean the one that's executed last). For example, the type of the expression

```
( a / b ) × ( x - y )
```

is the type declared for the operator "×", whatever that happens to be. Note in particular that variable references and literals are both considered to be expressions—the operator to be invoked in each case being effectively just "Return the value of"—and thus certainly do have a declared type.

Aside: To repeat, variables, attributes, etc., all have a declared type. By contrast, *values* as such aren't declared at all, and thus can't properly be

---

[7] The qualifier *read-only* derives from the fact that such operators simply "read" their arguments and don't update them (in fact they aren't allowed to update anything at all, with the possible exception of variables that are purely local to their own implementation code).

described as having a declared type as such. That being said, though, the only way a value can be referenced is by means of some expression— possibly just a literal—and such expressions do have a declared type, as we've just seen. So sometimes we have to be rather careful over the logical difference between a value as such, on the one hand, and the expression that's being used to denote that value in some particular context, on the other. *End of aside.*

Now, the fact that parameters in particular are declared to be of some type raises an issue that I've touched on but haven't yet properly discussed—namely, that:

> Associated with every type there's a set of operators for operating on values and variables of the type in question[8]—where to say that operator *Op* is "associated with" type *T* basically just means that operator *Op* has a parameter of type *T*.

For example, as noted in Chapter 2, integers have the usual arithmetic operators; dates and times have special calendar arithmetic operators; XML documents have what are called "XPath" and "XQuery" operators; relations have the operators of the relational algebra; and *every* type has the operators of assignment (":=") and equality comparison ("="). But I need to elaborate briefly on these last two:

- ■ (*Assignment*) All assignments are required to abide by *The Assignment Principle*, which as you'll recall from Exercise 4 in the previous chapter simply states that immediately after assignment of value *v* to variable *V*, the equality comparison *v* = *V* must evaluate to TRUE. (Of course, this principle—which applies to assignments of all kinds, please note, including relational assignments in particular—is really nothing but a slightly formal definition of the semantics of assignment.)

  > *Aside:* In fact, as the *Manifesto* book explains, the database itself is really a variable—a database variable or "dbvar"—and database

---

[8] It follows that any system that provides proper type support—and "proper type support" here certainly includes the ability for users to define their own types—must also provide a way for users to define their own operators, because (as I put it in Chapter 2) types without operators are useless. See the section "Operators," later.

updates are really just assignments to that variable. Thus, it follows from *The Assignment Principle* that such updates must do exactly what they say, no more and no less; in other words, they mustn't have any side effects (by which I mean effects that aren't explicitly defined somehow but are nevertheless visible to the user). But now I'm beginning to stray into an area that's a long way beyond the principal topic of this book, so I'll leave it at that. Further discussion of such matters can be found, if you're interested, in my book *View Updating and Relational Theory* (O'Reilly, 2013). *End of aside.*

■ (*Equality*) I think the following paragraph, excerpted from *The Third Manifesto* but edited somewhat here, summarizes very well what's required of this operator:

> The equality comparison operator "=" shall be supported for every type. Let v_1 and v_2 be values of the same type; then (and only then) $v_1 = v_2$ shall be a valid equality comparison, and it shall return TRUE if and only if v_1 and v_2 are the very same value.

As mentioned a few pages back, I'll have much more to say about operators in general in the section "Operators," later.

Scalar vs. Nonscalar Types

Note: This subsection is included primarily just as a reminder. It has little to say that hasn't already been said in Chapter 2.

It can be convenient, sometimes, to draw a distinction between scalar and nonscalar types. Loosely, a type is said to be *scalar* if it has no user visible components and *nonscalar* otherwise; and then values, variables, attributes, operators, parameters, and expressions of some type T are said to be scalar or nonscalar according as type T itself is scalar or nonscalar. For example:

■ Type INTEGER is a scalar type; hence, values, variables, and so on of type INTEGER are also all said to be scalar.

■ Tuple and relation types are nonscalar—the pertinent user visible components being the corresponding attributes—and hence tuple and relation values, variables, and so on are also all said to be nonscalar.

That said, I must emphasize that these notions are quite informal. Indeed, I explained in Chapter 2 that the concept, frequently appealed to when relational databases are under discussion, of *data value atomicity* has no absolute meaning, and "scalarness" is really just that same concept by another name. So the relational model in particular certainly doesn't rely on the scalar vs. nonscalar distinction in any formal sense. In this book, however, I do rely on it informally; I mean, I do find it intuitively useful, on occasion. To be specific:

■ I use the term *nonscalar* to refer to tuple and relation types considered jointly. Of course, there are other nonscalar types in addition to these two—array types are an obvious example—but tuple and relation types are the ones most relevant to the present book.

■ I use the term *scalar*, loosely, to refer to types that aren't nonscalar in the foregoing sense—especially to types that are neither tuple nor relation types in particular.

I also use the unqualified term *scalar* as a noun, very occasionally, to mean a scalar value specifically.

TYPES vs. REPRESENTATIONS

To repeat from the section "Values vs. Variables," earlier, there's a logical difference between a type as such, on the one hand, and the physical representation of values of that type inside the system on the other. In fact, types are a model issue, while physical representations are an implementation issue. For example, supplier numbers might be physically represented as character strings, but it doesn't follow that we can perform character string operations such as "| |" (concatenate) on supplier numbers; we can do such things only if the operator in question has been defined for the type in question. And the operators we define for a given type will naturally depend on the intended use and meaning of the type in question, not on the way values of that type happen to be physically represented; indeed, those physical representations are, or should be, hidden from the user. In other words, the distinction we draw between types and physical representations is one important aspect of the notion, very familiar from the world of databases in general, of *data independence*.

Let *T* be a scalar type. Then the physical representation of values of type *T* can be as complex as you like; as explained above, however, that physical representation is supposed to be hidden from the user. But *The Third Manifesto* does require that values of type *T* additionally have at least one "possible" representation.[9] Such possible representations are explicitly declared as part of the definition of type *T*, and they're *not* hidden from the user. Moreover, if *PR* is a possible representation for type *T*, then *PR*, unlike *T* as such, does have a set of components, and those components too are visible to the user. Please understand, however, that the components in question aren't components of type *T* as such—rather, they're components of possible representation *PR* (type *T* as such is still scalar in the sense defined in the previous section, and thus has no user visible components). For example, consider the user defined type QTY ("quantities"), whose definition in **Tutorial D** might look like this:

```
TYPE QTY POSSREP QPR ( Q INTEGER ) ;
```

This definition says, in effect, that quantities—i.e., values of type QTY—can possibly be represented by integers. More precisely, it says that:

a. Type QTY has just one declared possible representation ("possrep" for short).

b. That possrep is called QPR.

c. QPR has user visible components—in fact, it has exactly one such, called Q, of declared type INTEGER.

What it carefully *doesn't* say is that quantities as such are physically represented as integers; nor does it say that quantities as such have user visible components, and in fact they don't.

Important: To repeat, the fact that quantities can possibly be represented by integers doesn't mean they physically are. They might be; on the other hand, they might be physically represented by rational numbers, or character strings, or

---

[9] Unless *T* is what's called a dummy type. But dummy types occur and have relevance only in the context of type inheritance, a topic that's beyond the scope of this book, and so we can ignore them here.

anything else you might care to think of. Indeed, distinct QTY values might be physically represented in different ways. Even different occurrences of the *same* QTY value might be physically represented in different ways! In other words, there's a logical difference between possible representations and physical representations. (I'd like to say there's a big logical difference, but all logical differences are big differences by definition.)

Now, I introduced the possrep name QPR in the foregoing example in order to stress the fact that types and possreps are indeed logically distinct constructs. In **Tutorial D** in particular, however, explicit possrep names can be (and often are) omitted, thanks to the following syntax rule:

If a possrep is declared for type *T* but has no explicitly declared name, then that possrep is named *T* by default.

Here by way of illustration is a simpler definition for type QTY:

```
TYPE QTY POSSREP ( Q INTEGER ) ;
```

In effect, this definition is shorthand for the following:

```
TYPE QTY POSSREP QTY ( Q INTEGER ) ;
```

I turn now to a more complicated example:

```
TYPE POINT  /* geometric points in two-dimensional space */
     POSSREP CARTESIAN ( X RATIONAL , Y RATIONAL )
     POSSREP POLAR ( RHO RATIONAL , THETA RATIONAL ) ;
```

POINT here is a user defined type with two distinct possible representations, CARTESIAN and POLAR, reflecting the fact that points in two-dimensional space can indeed "possibly be represented" by either cartesian or polar coordinates. Each of those possible representations in turn has two components (both of which are of the same type, RATIONAL, as it happens). Note carefully, however, that—to say it again—the type as such is still scalar: It has no user visible components.

Selectors and THE_ Operators

Let *PR* be a possrep for scalar type *T*. Then the declaration of *PR*—which is in fact part of the declaration of *T*, as we've seen—causes "automatic" definition of the following more or less self-explanatory operators:

a. A *selector* operator, which allows the user to specify or "select" an arbitrary value of type *T* by supplying a value for each component of possrep *PR*, and

b. A set of *THE_* operators, one for each component of possrep *PR*, which allow the user to access the corresponding *PR* components for an arbitrary value of type *T*.

The selector has declared type *T*, and each THE_ operator has declared type the same as that of the corresponding *PR* component.

   Note: When I say the declaration of *PR* causes "automatic definition" of these operators, what I mean is that whatever agency—possibly the system, possibly some human user—is responsible for defining type *T* is also responsible for providing implementation code for the operators in question. I'll come back to this matter in the next section ("The TYPE Statement"). Meanwhile, here are some sample selector and THE_ operator invocations for type POINT, expressed as usual in **Tutorial D**:

```
CARTESIAN ( 5.0 , -2.5 )
/* returns the point with x = 5.0, y = -2.5 */

CARTESIAN ( X1 , Y1 )
/* returns the point with x = X1, y = Y1, where */
/* X1 and Y1 are variables of type RATIONAL    */

POLAR ( 2.7 , 1.0 )
/* returns the point with ρ (rho) = 2.7, θ (theta) = 1.0 */

THE_X ( PT )
/* returns the x coordinate of the point in PT, */
/* where PT is a variable of type POINT        */

THE_RHO ( PT )
/* returns the rho coordinate of the point in PT */

THE_Y ( exp )
/* returns the y coordinate of the point denoted by */
/* the expression exp (which must be of type POINT) */
```

```
THE_THETA ( exp )
/* returns the theta coordinate of the point denoted by */
/* the expression exp (which must be of type POINT)      */
```

Note that, in **Tutorial D** at any rate, (a) selectors have the same name as the corresponding possrep, and (b) THE_ operators have names of the form THE_*C*, where *C* is the name of the corresponding component of the corresponding possrep. Note too that selectors—more precisely, selector *invocations*—are a generalization of the more familiar concept of a literal. What I mean by this remark is that all literals are selector invocations, but "most" selector invocations aren't literals. To be precise, a selector invocation is a literal if and only if all of its arguments are themselves specified as literals in turn. For example, the following expressions—

```
CARTESIAN (  X1 ,   Y1 )

CARTESIAN (  X1 , 0.0 )

CARTESIAN ( 1.0 , 0.0 )
```

—are all invocations of the CARTESIAN selector, but only the last one is a literal.

Let *PR* be a possrep for scalar type *T*. Then (as the foregoing discussion suggests):

■ *PR* provides—*must* provide—an associated format for denoting literal values of type *T*.

■ Every value of type *T* must be denotable by means of some literal of the format in question.

Of course, all of the concepts discussed so far in the present subsection apply to simpler types as well[10]—for example, type QTY. Here are some sample QTY selector invocations:

---

[10] Including system defined types in particular, though for historical reasons the corresponding selectors and THE_ operators might deviate somewhat from the syntax and other rules as described in the present section. See the *Manifesto* book for further discussion.

```
QTY ( 100 )

QTY ( N )

QTY ( N1 - N2 )
```

And here are some sample THE_ operator invocations:

```
THE_Q ( Q1 )

THE_Q ( Q1 - Q2 )

THE_Q ( QTY ( 100 ) )
```

Note: I'm assuming for the sake of these examples that (a) N, N1, and N2 are variables of type INTEGER, (b) Q, Q1, and Q2 are variables of type QTY, and (c) "−" is a *polymorphic* operator—it applies to both integers and quantities.[11]

Discussion of the QTY selector raises another point, however. Consider attribute QTY of relvar SP ("shipments") in the suppliers and parts database, which is of declared type QTY (yes, the attribute and the type have the same name in this example). Because the attribute in question *is* of declared type QTY, it's strictly incorrect to say, for example, that the quantity for a certain shipment is 100. A quantity is a value of type QTY, not a value of type INTEGER! For the shipment in question, therefore, we should more properly say the quantity is QTY(100), not just 100 as such. In informal contexts, however, we usually don't bother to be quite so precise, thus using (e.g.) 100 as a convenient shorthand for QTY(100). Note in particular that I used such shorthands ubiquitously in my picture of the suppliers and parts database in Chapter 1.

Here's one further example of a type definition:

```
TYPE LINESEG POSSREP ( BEGIN POINT , END POINT ) ;
```

Type LINESEG denotes line segments. What the example shows is that a possrep can (of course) be defined in terms of user defined types, not just in terms of system defined types as in all of the examples we've seen previously. In other words, user defined types are indeed types, and other types can be defined in terms of them.

---

[11] But what kind of polymorphism is it? *Answer: Overloading* polymorphism. I'll have more to say about the different kinds of polymorphism in the section "Operators," later.

THE TYPE STATEMENT

Defining a new type in **Tutorial D** can be done either by means of the TYPE statement, as already illustrated in several examples in the previous section, or by means of some type generator. I'll defer discussion of the latter possibility to the section "Type Generators," later; in the present section, I'll focus on the TYPE statement specifically. Here by way of example is a definition for the user defined type WEIGHT (a type that was used, as you'll recall, in the definition of the parts relvar P in the suppliers and parts database):

```
TYPE WEIGHT POSSREP ( L RATIONAL )
          CONSTRAINT L > 0.0 AND L < 500.0 ;
```

Explanation: Weights can possibly be represented by rational numbers, where the rational number in question (here denoted L, for reasons that should become clear in a little while) is such that $0.0 < L < 500.0$.

Now, the preceding sentence represents, in its entirety, an informal statement of the *type constraint* for type WEIGHT. In general, the type constraint for any given type is simply a definition of the set of values that constitute the type in question. In the example, the type constraint says, in effect, that WEIGHT values are, precisely, all and only those values that can possibly be represented by a rational number L such that $0.0 < L < 500.0$. (If a given POSSREP declaration contains no explicit CONSTRAINT specification, then CONSTRAINT TRUE is assumed by default. In the WEIGHT example, therefore, omitting the CONSTRAINT specification would simply mean that anything that can be represented by a rational number—negative values included!—would be a valid weight, and nothing else would be.)

Before going any further, I should warn you that the term "type constraint" is perhaps a little misleading. Constraints in general constrain update operations. But if *T* is a type and *TC* is the type constraint for *T*, *TC* doesn't constrain updates on type *T* as such, it constrains updates on *variables* of type *T*—or, in the case of relation (or tuple) variables, on variables with an attribute of type *T*. (In fact, of course, *T can't* be updated. It's variables, not types, that are subject to update.)

So when are type constraints checked? *Answer:* Whenever some selector is invoked. Assume again that values of type WEIGHT are such that they must be capable of representation as rational numbers L such that $0.0 < L < 500.0$.

Then the expression WEIGHT (250.0) is an invocation of the WEIGHT selector, and it succeeds. By contrast, the expression WEIGHT (600.0) is also such an invocation, but it fails. Indeed, it should surely be obvious that we can never tolerate an expression that's supposed to denote a value of some type T but in fact doesn't; after all, "a value of type T that's not a value of type T" is a contradiction in terms. Since, ultimately, the only way any expression can ever yield a value of type T is via some invocation of some selector for type T, it follows that no variable can ever be assigned a value that's not of the right type.

The WEIGHT example raises another point, however. In Chapter 1, I said part weights were given in pounds. In practice, however, it's probably not a good idea to bundle the type notion as such with the somewhat separate notion of units of measure. Indeed, we could allow users to think of weights as being measured either in pounds or in (say) grams by providing two separate possreps, one for pounds and one for grams, like this:

```
TYPE WEIGHT
     POSSREP LBS ( L RATIONAL ) /* pounds */
     POSSREP GMS ( G RATIONAL ) /* grams  */
     CONSTRAINT L > 0.0 AND L < 500.0 AND G = 454 × L ;
```

Note the extended CONSTRAINT specification, which effectively constrains, or specifies, both the set of L values and the set of G values that correspond to legitimate WEIGHT values. (Legal L values are 0.1, 0.2, ..., 4999.9, and I'm assuming for simplicity that there are 454 grams to the pound;[12] thus, legal G values are 45.4, 90.8, ..., 226954.6.) Now:

■ If *wx* is an expression of type WEIGHT, then THE_L (*wx*) will return a rational number *lbs* denoting the corresponding weight in pounds, while THE_G (*wx*) will return a rational number *gms* denoting that same weight in grams (and *gms* will be equal to 454 × *lbs*).

■ If *zx* is an expression of type RATIONAL, then the expressions LBS (*zx*) and GMS (454 × *zx*) will both return the same WEIGHT value.

By way of another example, let's go back to type POINT, with its cartesian and polar possible representations. Here again is the corresponding TYPE statement, but now shown with an appropriate type constraint (I assume for the

---

[12] More precisely, there are 453.592 grams to the pound. I use the figure 454 in the example merely to simplify the discussion.

sake of the example that operators SIN and COS are available and have the obvious semantics):

```
TYPE POINT  /* geometric points in two-dimensional space */
    POSSREP CARTESIAN ( X RATIONAL , Y RATIONAL )
    POSSREP POLAR ( RHO RATIONAL , THETA RATIONAL )
    CONSTRAINT X = RHO × COS ( THETA )
           AND Y = RHO × SIN ( THETA ) ;
```

Suppose now for the sake of discussion that the physical representation of points is in fact cartesian coordinates (though as noted earlier there's no need in general for a physical representation to be identical to any of the declared possible ones). Then the system will provide certain highly privileged and protected operators, denoted in what follows by *italic pseudocode*, that effectively expose that physical representation, and those privileged operators can then be used to implement the necessary selectors. (Obviously, whoever is responsible for providing those implementations—perhaps the DBA—must be an exception to the rule that users in general aren't aware of physical representations.) For example (using a kind of pidgin form of **Tutorial D**):

```
OPERATOR CARTESIAN ( X RATIONAL , Y RATIONAL )
                                    RETURNS POINT ;
    VAR PT POINT ;
    X component of physical representation of PT := X ;
    Y component of physical representation of PT := Y ;
    RETURN ( PT ) ;
END OPERATOR ;

OPERATOR POLAR ( RHO RATIONAL , THETA RATIONAL )
                                    RETURNS POINT ;
    RETURN ( CARTESIAN ( RHO × COS ( THETA ) ,
                         RHO × SIN ( THETA ) ) ) ;
END OPERATOR ;
```

Observe that the CARTESIAN implementation as here defined makes use of those "highly privileged and protected operators" that expose the physical representation, and the POLAR implementation then makes use of the CARTESIAN selector. Alternatively, the POLAR selector could use those privileged operators directly, like this:

```
OPERATOR POLAR ( RHO RATIONAL , THETA RATIONAL )
                                        RETURNS POINT ;
   VAR PT POINT ;
   X component of physical representation of PT
                            := RHO × COS ( THETA ) ;
   Y component of physical representation of PT
                            := RHO × SIN ( THETA ) ;
   RETURN ( PT ) ;
END OPERATOR ;
```

Those same privileged operators can also be used to implement the necessary THE_ operators, like this (the caret symbol "^"—see the definition of THE_RHO—denotes exponentiation):

```
OPERATOR THE_X ( PT POINT ) RETURNS RATIONAL ;
   RETURN ( X̄ component of physical representation of PT ) ;
END OPERATOR ;

OPERATOR THE_Y ( PT POINT ) RETURNS RATIONAL ;
   RETURN ( Ȳ component of physical representation of PT ) ;
END OPERATOR ;

OPERATOR THE_RHO ( PT POINT ) RETURNS RATIONAL ;
   RETURN ( S̄QRT ( THE_X ( PT ) ^ 2 + THE_Y ( PT ) ^ 2 ) ) ;
END OPERATOR ;

OPERATOR THE_THETA ( PT POINT ) RETURNS RATIONAL ;
   RETURN ( ĀRCTAN ( THE_Y ( PT ) / THE_X ( PT ) ) ) ;
END OPERATOR ;
```

Observe that the definitions of THE_RHO and THE_THETA make use of THE_X and THE_Y (I assume for the sake of the example that operators SQRT and ARCTAN are available and have the obvious semantics). Alternatively, of course, THE_RHO and THE_THETA could be defined directly in terms of the privileged operators.

Finally, please note the following: I've been using type POINT to illustrate the idea that a given scalar type can have two different possreps (or maybe more than two), and I've called the possreps in that particular case CARTESIAN and POLAR, respectively. For simplicity, however, I'm going to assume for the remainder of this book that the CARTESIAN possrep for points has been renamed POINT, implying that, e.g., POINT (5.0,−2.5) is a valid point selector invocation.

A BNF Grammar

Here for purposes of reference is an abbreviated BNF grammar for scalar type definitions in **Tutorial D** without inheritance. *Note:* When I say the grammar is abbreviated, what I mean is that there are still some issues to be discussed later in this chapter that will have the effect of extending it, though only in comparatively minor ways. Also, when I say the grammar is for scalar type definitions, of course I'm referring to user defined types specifically (which are always scalar by definition, in **Tutorial D**).

```
<scalar type def>
    ::=    TYPE <scalar type name> <possrep def list>
                              [ <possrep constraint def> ]

<possrep def>
    ::=    POSSREP [ <possrep name> ]
                    ( <possrep component def commalist> )

<possrep component def>
    ::=    <possrep component name> <type name>

<possrep constraint def>
    ::=    CONSTRAINT <bool exp>
```

Explanation:

1. Brackets "[" and "]" indicate that the material they enclose is optional, as is usual with BNF notation.

2. By contrast, braces "{" and "}" stand for themselves; i.e., they're symbols in the language being defined, not, as they more usually are, symbols of the metalanguage.
   Note: Actually there aren't any braces in the abbreviated grammar shown above anyway. In general, however, **Tutorial D** uses braces to enclose a commalist of items (see the next point below) whenever the commalist in question denotes the elements of a set—or occasionally a bag—of some kind.

3. The grammar makes use of both "lists" and "commalists." The term *commalist* can be defined as follows. Let *xyz* be some syntactic construct (for example, *<attribute name>*; note, however, that this particular syntactic construct isn't one that's mentioned in the foregoing grammar). Then the

term *xyz commalist* denotes a sequence of zero or more *xyz*'s in which each pair of adjacent *xyz*'s is separated by a comma (spaces appearing immediately before or immediately after any comma are ignored). For example, if *A*, *B*, and *C* are all *<attribute name>*s, then the following are all *<attribute name commalist>*s:

```
A , B , C

C , A , B , A

B

A , C
```

So too is the empty sequence of attribute names.

In addition, when some commalist is intended to denote the elements of some set and is therefore enclosed in braces, then (a) spaces appearing immediately after the opening brace or immediately before the closing brace are ignored; (b) the order in which the elements appear within the commalist is immaterial, because sets have no ordering to their elements; and (c) if an element appears more than once, it's treated as if it appeared just once, because sets don't contain duplicate elements.

The term *list* is defined analogously, the only difference being that the separating commas are replaced by spaces (at least one such in each case).

4. The *<possrep def list>* mustn't be empty.

5. Omitting the *<possrep name>* from a *<possrep def>* is equivalent to specifying a *<possrep name>* equal to the *<scalar type name>* of the containing *<scalar type def>*.

6. No two distinct *<possrep def>*s in the same *<possrep def list>* can have the same *<possrep name>*.

7. The *<possrep component def commalist>* will usually not be empty (but see the last part of the answer to Exercise 5 at the end of the chapter).

8. No two distinct *<possrep component def>*s in the same *<possrep def list>* can have the same *<possrep component name>*.

9. Omitting the *<possrep constraint def>* is equivalent to specifying
    CONSTRAINT TRUE.

10. In general, a *<bool exp>* ("boolean expression") is any expression that
    denotes a truth value. In the context at hand, though, the *<bool exp>*
    mustn't mention any variables; however, *<possrep component name>*s
    from the associated *<possrep def list>* can be used to refer to the indicated
    components of the corresponding possible representations of an arbitrary
    value of the scalar type being defined (see earlier in this section for
    examples).

    Observe that *<scalar type def>*s quite rightly have nothing to say about
physical representations. Observe too that possrep components are defined to
have an associated type, but the type in question is specified by means of a *<type
name>*, not a *<scalar type name>*; in other words, the components of a possrep
PR for some scalar type *T* don't necessarily have to be scalar themselves (again
see the answer to Exercise 5 at the end of the chapter).
    Here now for future reference are definitions, in outline, for the user
defined scalar types used in the definition of the suppliers and parts database
(apart from types QTY and WEIGHT, which have already been discussed).
CONSTRAINT specifications are omitted for simplicity, as are explicit possrep
names.

```
TYPE SNO   POSSREP ( SC CHAR ) ... ;
TYPE NAME  POSSREP ( NC CHAR ) ... ;
TYPE PNO   POSSREP ( PC CHAR ) ... ;
TYPE COLOR POSSREP ( CC CHAR ) ... ;
```

(Recall from Chapter 1 that, by contrast, the supplier STATUS attribute and the
supplier and part CITY attributes are defined in terms of system defined types—
viz., INTEGER and CHAR, respectively—so no type definitions are shown here
corresponding to these attributes.)
    Of course, it must be possible to get rid of a scalar type if we have no
further use for it:

```
DROP TYPE <scalar type name> ;
```

    The *<scalar type name>* must identify a user defined type, not a system
defined one. After this operation has been executed, the specified type will no
longer be known to the system and will thus no longer be available for use.

OPERATORS

So far in this chapter, the only operators for which I've shown definitions have been either selectors or THE_ operators. It's time to look at some more general examples. Here first is a user defined operator, ABS, that applies to values of the system defined type RATIONAL:[13]

```
OPERATOR ABS ( X RATIONAL ) RETURNS RATIONAL ;
   RETURN ( IF X ≥ 0.0 THEN +X ELSE -X END IF ) ;
END OPERATOR ;
```

Operator ABS ("absolute value") is defined in terms of just one parameter, X, of declared type RATIONAL, and it returns a result of that same type (note the RETURNS specification). By definition, therefore, (a) that operator has declared type RATIONAL, and (b) an invocation of that operator, such as ABS (A + B), is an expression of declared type RATIONAL as well.

The next example, DIST ("distance between"), takes two parameters both of the same user defined type (POINT) and returns a result of another user defined type (LENGTH):

```
OPERATOR DIST ( PT1 POINT , PT2 POINT ) RETURNS LENGTH ;
   RETURN ( WITH ( X1 := THE_X ( PT1 ) ,
                   Y1 := THE_Y ( PT1 ) ,
                   X2 := THE_X ( PT2 ) ,
                   Y2 := THE_Y ( PT2 ) ) :
           LENGTH ( SQRT ( ( X1 - X2 ) ^ 2 +
                           ( Y1 - Y2 ) ^ 2 ) ) ) ;
END OPERATOR ;
```

I omit the definition of type LENGTH for simplicity, but I'm assuming, reasonably enough, that:

a. The corresponding selector is also called LENGTH.

b. The LENGTH selector takes an argument of type RATIONAL.

---

[13] User defined operators can of course be defined in connection with system defined types as well as user defined ones (or indeed a mixture of both).

c.   The SQRT operator takes an argument of type RATIONAL (nonnegative) and returns a result of that same type (also nonnegative).

Also, note the use of a WITH specification to introduce names for the results of certain subexpressions. We've met this construct before (see the answer to Exercise 3 in Chapter 1); in general, it can be very useful in simplifying the formulation of expressions, especially ones that involve repeated use of the same subexpression (though such is not the case in this particular example). For further discussion, see my book *SQL and Relational Theory*, 3rd ed. (O'Reilly, 2015).

Here's another example—a definition for the required equality comparison operator (let's call it EQP, just for the moment) for type POINT:

```
OPERATOR EQP ( PT1 POINT , PT2 POINT ) RETURNS BOOLEAN ;
   RETURN ( THE_X ( PT1 ) = THE_X ( PT2 ) AND
            THE_Y ( PT1 ) = THE_Y ( PT2 ) ) ;
END OPERATOR ;
```

Observe that the expression in the RETURN statement here makes use of the system defined equality operator ("=") operator for type RATIONAL. For simplicity, I'm going to assume from this point forward that the usual infix notation "=" can be used for the equality operator for all types, including type POINT in particular. I omit consideration here of how such infix notation might be specified in practice, since it's basically just a matter of syntax.[14]

Here's another example—the (presumably required) "<" operator for type QTY:

```
OPERATOR LTQ ( Q1 QTY , Q2 QTY ) RETURNS BOOLEAN ;
   RETURN ( THE_Q ( Q1 ) < THE_Q ( Q2 ) ) ;
END OPERATOR ;
```

The expression in the RETURN statement here makes use of the system defined "<" operator for type INTEGER. I've shown the operator name as LTQ, but again I'm going to assume from this point forward that the usual infix notation "<" can be used—for all "ordered types," that is, not just for type QTY in particular. See the section "Miscellaneous Issues," later, for a discussion of ordered types in general.

---

[14] In any case, the definition and implementation code for "=", as well as for ":=" (and for certain other operators too, such as "<", where applicable—see the next example), can and surely will be provided automatically. I show explicit code in the example purely for illustrative purposes.

Here finally is an example of an update operator definition (all of the previous examples have been of read-only operators, which merely "read" their arguments and don't update them). The operator is called REFLECT (it's an update version of the read-only operator of the same name from Chapter 2). What it does, in effect, is move the point with cartesian coordinates (x,y) to the inverse position $(-x,-y)$, and it does this not by returning a result as such, but rather by updating its point argument appropriately. Note, therefore, that the definition includes an UPDATES specification in place of a RETURNS specification.

```
OPERATOR REFLECT ( PT POINT ) UPDATES { PT } ;
   THE_X ( PT ) := - THE_X ( PT ) ;
   THE_Y ( PT ) := - THE_Y ( PT ) ;
   RETURN ;
END OPERATOR ;
```

Points arising:

1. The operator has just one parameter PT, of declared type POINT, and—as indicated by the UPDATES specification—that parameter is subject to update, meaning that when the operator is invoked it will update the argument corresponding to that parameter.

2. Since it's going to be updated, the argument in question must be a variable specifically.

3. Since the operator doesn't return anything, it has no declared type, and an invocation doesn't constitute an expression. In particular, therefore, such an invocation can't be used as a subexpression, meaning an expression nested inside some other expression.[15] Instead, such an invocation has to be done by means of an explicit CALL statement, as here:

```
CALL REFLECT ( ZPT ) ;
```

The CALL statement will fail on a syntax error—at compile time, please note, not at run time—if the expression denoting an argument that's to be updated is anything other than a simple variable reference.

---

[15] Read-only operator invocations, by contrast, *can* be used as expressions nested inside other expressions. In fact, the terms *expression* and *read-only operator invocation* are effectively synonymous.

4. The RETURN statement has no argument, because update operators don't return a value when they're invoked. *Note:* Such a RETURN statement will be executed implicitly when the END OPERATOR statement is reached (if it ever is). In the example, therefore, the RETURN statement could have been omitted if desired.

Finally, it must be possible to get rid of an operator if we have no further use for it. **Tutorial D** provides an operator called DROP OPERATOR for this purpose. The operator to be dropped must be user defined, not built in.

THE_ Pseudovariables

The foregoing REFLECT operator definition also serves to illustrate another important notion, *THE_ pseudovariables*. In essence, a THE_ pseudovariable reference is a THE_ operator invocation appearing on the left side of an assignment. Such an invocation actually designates, instead of merely returning the value of, the specified possrep component of the specified argument. Within the REFLECT definition, for instance, the assignment

```
THE_X ( PT ) := ... ;
```

assigns a value to the X component of the cartesian possrep of the argument variable corresponding to the parameter PT. (Of course, to repeat, any argument to be updated—whether it be by assignment to a THE_ pseudovariable as in this example or in any other way—must be a variable specifically.)

Pseudovariable references can be nested. Recall this type definition from the very end of the section "Types vs. Representations":

```
TYPE LINESEG POSSREP ( BEGIN POINT , END POINT ) ;
```

Let variable LS be declared to be of type LINESEG. Here then is a possible assignment involving that variable:

```
THE_X ( THE_BEGIN ( LS ) ) := 6.5 ;
```

Meaning: Assign the value 6.5 to the X component of the cartesian possrep of the BEGIN component of the LINESEG possrep of the argument variable corresponding to the parameter LS. (My apologies if you find you have to read that sentence more than once.)

Now, THE_ pseudovariables are extremely convenient from a usability point of view, as I think the foregoing examples demonstrate. However, they're logically unnecessary. For example, consider the following assignment from the REFLECT operator definition:

```
THE_X ( PT ) := - THE_X ( PT ) ;
```

This assignment, which uses a THE_ pseudovariable, is logically equivalent to the following one, which doesn't:

```
P := POINT ( - THE_X ( PT ) , THE_Y ( PT ) ) ;
```

Similarly, the assignment shown above involving nested THE_ pseudovariable references—

```
THE_X ( THE_BEGIN ( LS ) ) := 6.5 ;
```

—is logically equivalent to the following one, which involves no such references:

```
LS := LINESEG ( POINT ( 6.5 ,
                        THE_Y ( THE_BEGIN ( LS ) ) ) ,
                THE_END ( LS ) ) ;
```

So THE_ pseudovariables as such aren't strictly necessary in order to support the kind of component level updating I've been discussing. However, using them does seem intuitively more attractive than the alternative (for which it can be regarded as a shorthand); moreover, it also provides a higher degree of imperviousness to changes in the syntax of the corresponding selector.

One last point: It's convenient from a definitional point of view, at least, to treat references to THE_ pseudovariables as if they were regular variable references, and **Tutorial D** does. In other words (but now speaking *very* loosely, please note!), pseudovariables are variables.

Polymorphic Operators

The remarks earlier in this section concerning operators and their parameters—more specifically, the remarks concerning the types of those parameters—need some refinement if the operator in question is polymorphic. Speaking a trifle loosely, an operator is said to be *polymorphic* if it can take arguments of different types on different invocations. The equality operator "=" is an obvious case in point: We can perform equality comparisons between values of any type whatsoever (just so long as the values in question are of the *same* type, of course), and so "=" is polymorphic—it's defined for integers, and character strings, and supplier numbers, and line segments, and in fact for values of every possible type.

Analogous remarks apply to the assignment operator ":=", which is also defined for every type: We can assign any value to any variable, just so long as the value and variable in question are of the same type. Of course, the assignment will fail if it violates some integrity constraint, but it can't fail on a type error as such. (Not at run time, at any rate, because type errors are—or should be—caught at compile time, always.)

However, let me now qualify what I've just said, or at least elaborate on it slightly. What's really going on here, at least in the examples quoted (viz., ":=" and "="), isn't so much that there's a single operator that's associated with many different types; rather, it's that there are many different operators (one for each of many different types), but those different operators all have the same name. In a sense, then, it's the operator *names* that are polymorphic, not the operators as such. But that's because the examples quoted are all examples of what's sometimes called, more specifically, *overloading* polymorphism (also known as *ad hoc* polymorphism)—and in overloading polymorphism, it really is the operator names that are overloaded and not the operators as such. (Note, however, that the literature almost never admits to this fact but does indeed talk, confusingly, as if the overloading applied to the operators themselves.) Later in this chapter, by contrast, we'll meet another kind of polymorphism called *generic* polymorphism—and in the context of type inheritance there's still another kind, called *inclusion* polymorphism—and in these latter cases it really is the operators as such, not just the names, that are polymorphic.

Multiple Assignment

In Chapter 1 I said the following, more or less:

> The only update operator in the relational model is *assignment*, because (logically speaking) assignment is the only update operator we need.

Well, this observation is perfectly true. Note, however, that the latter part ("it's the only update operator we need") is true for all kinds of variables, not just for the relation variables I was talking about, at least implicitly, in Chapter 1. To spell it out:

If *T* is a type, the only update operator we need for variables of type *T* is indeed assignment (again, logically speaking).

However, what I didn't say previously was that the kind of assignment we need—in general, at any rate—is what's called *multiple* assignment. Multiple assignment is an operator that allows us to perform any number of individual assignments in parallel ("simultaneously"). For example, the following double DELETE is, logically, a multiple assignment operation:

```
DELETE S  WHERE SNO = SNO('S1') ,
DELETE SP WHERE SNO = SNO('S1') ;
```

Note the comma separator after the first DELETE, which indicates syntactically that the end of the statement overall hasn't yet been reached. That overall statement is logically equivalent to the following "explicit assignment" version:

```
S  := S  MINUS ( S  WHERE SNO = SNO('S1') ) ,
SP := SP MINUS ( SP WHERE SNO = SNO('S1') ) ;
```

Simplifying slightly, the semantics of multiple assignment in general are as follows:

■ First, all of the source expressions specified on the right sides of the individual assignments are evaluated.

■ Second, all of the individual assignments to the target variables specified on the left sides of those individual assignments are executed in parallel.

Note, however, that the foregoing explanation does require some slight refinement if two or more of the individual assignments specify the same target variable (see below). Ignoring that refinement for the moment, however, we can say that since the source expressions are all evaluated before any of the individual assignments are done, none of those individual assignments can depend on the result of any other (and so "executing them in parallel" is really only a manner of speaking). In othe words, the effect on the database in the foregoing example would be exactly the same if the two individual DELETEs were specified in the reverse order:

```
DELETE SP WHERE SNO = SNO('S1') ,
DELETE S  WHERE SNO = SNO('S1') ;
```

Also (*important!*), since multiple assignment is considered to be an atomic operation, no integrity constraint checking is performed "in the middle of" such an assignment. Indeed, this state of affairs is the primary reason for supporting multiple assignment in the first place.

Now let me get back to the question of repeated targets. Suppose two or more of the individual assignments involved in a given multiple assignment do in fact specify the same target variable. Then those particular individual assignments are effectively executed *not* in parallel but in sequence as written, and are thereby effectively reduced to a certain single assignment, involving WITH, to the variable in question. For example, the double assignment

```
S := S MINUS ( S WHERE SNO = SNO('S1') ) ,
S := S MINUS ( S WHERE SNO = SNO('S2') ) ;
```

—or equivalently

```
DELETE S WHERE SNO = SNO('S1') ,
DELETE S WHERE SNO = SNO('S2') ;
```

—is logically equivalent to the following single assignment:

```
S := WITH ( S := S MINUS ( S WHERE SNO = SNO('S1') ) :
                 S MINUS ( S WHERE SNO = SNO('S2') ) ;
```

In this example, the references to "S" in the second line denote the result of executing the parenthesized assignment in the WITH clause in the first line; in other words, they can be thought of, loosely, as referring to relvar S as it has become after the tuple for supplier S1 has been deleted. See the answer to Exercise 10 at the end of the chapter for further discussion.

An important special case of repeated targets occurs in connection with assignment to the same variable via two or more THE_ pseudovariables. Consider the following example once again (it's the update operator REFLECT from earlier in this chapter, but now I omit the explicit RETURN statement for simplicity):

```
OPERATOR REFLECT ( PT POINT ) UPDATES { PT } ;
    THE_X ( PT ) := - THE_X ( PT ) ;
    THE_Y ( PT ) := - THE_Y ( PT ) ;
END OPERATOR ;
```

As you can see, this definition contains the following pair of single assignments:

```
THE_X ( PT ) := - THE_X ( PT ) ;
THE_Y ( PT ) := - THE_Y ( PT ) ;
```

However, we could if we liked replace these two single assignments by the following double (and thus multiple) assignment:

```
THE_X ( PT ) := - THE_X ( PT ) ,
THE_Y ( PT ) := - THE_Y ( PT ) ;
```

And now we have an example of exactly the situation I mentioned above: viz., assignment via two or more THE_ pseudovariables to the same target variable. Thus, the statement overall is logically equivalent to the following:

```
PT := WITH ( PT := POINT ( - THE_X ( PT ) ,
                                 THE_Y ( PT ) ) ) :
          POINT ( THE_X ( PT ) , - THE_Y ( PT ) ) ;
```

Again I refer you to the answer to Exercise 10 at the end of the chapter for further discussion.

Summary So Far

From everything I've said in this chapter so far—in this section and its immediate predecessor, "The TYPE Statement," in particular—it should be clear that defining a new scalar type *T* involves all of the following (this is a revised and tightened up version of a list I gave previously in Chapter 2):

1. Defining a name for type *T*.

2. Defining the values that constitute type *T* (that's the type constraint).

3. Defining at least one possible representation for values of type *T*. Each such possrep definition automatically causes definition of (a) a corresponding selector and (b) for each component of that possrep, a corresponding THE_ operator (which can also be used as a pseudovariable).

4. Defining and providing implementation code for other operators (including assignment and equality comparison operators in particular, though in these cases the definitions and code will surely be provided automatically[16]) that apply to values and variables of type *T*—including, for those operators that return a result, defining the type of that result.

Note: It also involves defining the hidden physical representation for values of that type, but of course that's an implementation issue.

Observe that the foregoing definitions, taken together, imply among other things that (a) the system knows precisely which expressions are legal, and (b) for those expressions that are legal it knows the type of the result—which implies in turn that the total collection of available types is a closed set, in the sense that the type of the result of every legal expression is a type that's known to the system. Note in particular that this closed set must include type BOOLEAN, if comparisons are to be legal expressions! Finally, note that the fact that the system knows the type of the result of every legal expression means that it knows in particular exactly which assignments are valid, and also which equality comparisons.

TYPE GENERATORS

I turn now to types that aren't defined by means of the TYPE statement but are instead obtained by invoking some type generator. To repeat from Chapter 2, a type generator is basically just a special kind of operator; it's special because (a) it's invoked at compile time instead of run time, and (b) it returns a type instead of a value. In a conventional programming language, for example, we might write something like this:

---

[16] Even if they aren't, they must abide by the semantics as defined by the model—for otherwise the implementation would be in violation.

```
VAR SALES ARRAY INTEGER [1:12] ;
```

This statement defines a variable called SALES, whose legal values are one-dimensional arrays of 12 integers. In particular, the specification

```
ARRAY INTEGER [1:12]
```

denotes an invocation of the ARRAY type generator; it returns a specific array type, and that specific array type is a generated type. Points arising:

■ As noted in the answer to Exercise 9 in Chapter 2, type generators are referred to by many different names in the literature, including *type constructors*, *parameterized types*, *polymorphic types*, *type templates*, and *generic types*. I'll stay with the term *type generator*.

■ Type generators are *not* types. But the result produced by invoking such a generator is a type, a generated type, and it can be used wherever an ordinary "nongenerated" type can be used. For example, we might define some relvar to have an attribute of type ARRAY INTEGER [1:12].

■ Generated types are typically nonscalar (array types are a case in point), though they don't have to be. Nongenerated types, by contrast, are always scalar.

Now, generated types do have possible representations ("possreps"), but the possreps in question are *derived*. To be specific, they're derived in a fairly obvious way from

a. A generic possrep that's associated with the type generator in question, and

b. The specific possrep(s) that apply to the user visible component(s) of the specific generated type in question.

In the case of the generated type ARRAY INTEGER [1:12], for example:

a. There'll be some generic possrep defined for one-dimensional arrays in general, probably as a contiguous sequence of array elements that can be identified by subscripts in the range from *lower* to *upper*, inclusive, where *lower* and *upper* are the applicable bounds (1 and 12, in the example).

b. Elements of arrays of the type in question are defined to be of type INTEGER, and thus have whatever possreps are defined for type INTEGER.

    Note: In the case of a simple system defined type like INTEGER, the only possrep available will very likely be an "identity" possrep, according to which values of the type simply represent themselves (at least, that's one way to think about the matter). Here's a lightly edited version of what *The Third Manifesto* has to say in this connection:

> [In the case of a system defined type *T*], zero or more possible representations for values of type *T* shall be declared and thus made visible to the user. A possible representation *PR* for values of type *T* that is user visible shall behave in all respects as if *T* were user defined and *PR* were a declared possible representation for values of type *T*. If no possible representation for values of type *T* is user visible, then at least one selector operator *S*, of declared type *T*, shall be provided. Each such selector operator *S* shall have all of the following properties:
>
> 1. Every argument expression in every invocation of *S* shall be a literal.
>
> 2. Every value of type *T* shall be produced by some invocation of *S*.
>
> 3. Every successful invocation of *S* shall produce some value of type *T*.

    To get back to type generators and generated types as such: Of course, there'll also be operators that provide the required selector and THE_ operator functionality. For example, the expression (actually an array literal)

```
ARRAY INTEGER [  2 ,  5 ,  9 ,  9 , 15 , 27 ,
                33 , 32 , 25 , 19 ,  5 ,  1 ]
```

might be used to "select," or specify, a particular value of type ARRAY INTEGER [12] ("selector functionality").

    As for "THE_ operator functionality," conventional subscripted references do the necessary. For example,

```
SALES [ 7 ]
```

denotes a certain component of the possrep for the variable SALES. For a more complicated example, suppose we're given a variable PTV whose permitted values are one-dimensional arrays of values of type POINT. Then the expression

```
THE_X ( PTV [ 3 ] )
```

denotes the *x* coordinate of the third element (a point) of the possrep for PTV.

Those subscripted references can be used as pseudovariables too, of course, as in this example:

```
SALES [ 7 ] := 31 ;
```

Here's another example:

```
SALES [ 7 ] := SALES [ 4 ] + 25 ;
```

Array assignment and comparison operators also apply. For example, here's a valid array assignment:

```
SALES := ARRAY INTEGER [  2 ,  5 ,  9 ,  9 , 15 , 27 ,
                         33 , 32 , 25 , 19 ,  5 ,  1 ] ;
```

And here's a valid array comparison:

```
SALES = ARRAY INTEGER [  2 ,  5 ,  9 ,  9 , 15 , 27 ,
                        33 , 32 , 25 , 19 ,  5 ,  1 ]
```

Next, any given type generator will also have a set of generic type constraints and operators associated with it—generic, in the sense that the constraints and operators in question apply to every type that can be produced by invocation of the type generator in question. For example, in the case of the ARRAY type generator:

■ There'll obviously be a generic constraint to the effect that the lower bound mustn't be greater than the upper bound.

■ There could be a generic "reverse" operator that takes an arbitrary array of one dimension as input and returns another such as output: namely, the array containing the elements of the given one in reverse order. In fact, what we have here is, as promised earlier in this chapter, an example of *generic polymorphism*—"the same" reverse operator is available for use with any one-dimensional array. More generally, generic polymorphism is the kind of polymorphism exhibited by a generic operator, where (loosely speaking) a generic operator is an operator that's available in connection with every type that can be produced by invocation of some given type generator. As a matter of fact, the array assignment and equality comparison operators discussed above are also generic operators.

Tuples and Relations

Two type generators that are particularly important in the database world are (unsurprisingly) TUPLE and RELATION. Before I discuss those generators in detail, however, I'd like you to be sure you understand exactly what tuples and relations are. If you need to refresh your memory, therefore, please review the section "Basic Definitions" in Chapter 1, which contains precise definitions of these concepts, as well as of various subordinate matters. I'll leave it as an exercise for you to convince yourself that those definitions do indeed pin down the various notions precisely and do correspond to the constructs in question as you already, perhaps only informally, understand them. Let me make a couple of points, though:

- Even though tuples and relations do have user visible components—namely, their attributes, and their tuples too in the case of a relation—there's no suggestion that those components have to be physically stored as such, in the form in which they're perceived by the user. In fact, the physical representation of tuples and relations should generally be hidden from the user, just as it is for scalars.

- The generic operators that are associated with the RELATION type generator in particular include, of course, the familiar operators of the relational algebra. For example, consider join. Obviously, we can write, e.g.,

      S JOIN SP

  to join suppliers and shipments. Moreover, we can also write, e.g.,

      P JOIN S

to join parts and suppliers. In other words, the join operator can be applied to relations of different types on different invocations—which is, of course, just another way of saying that join is a generic operator (to be specific, one that's associated with the RELATION type generator). And a similar observation applies to all of the usual relational operators—restrict, project, and so on—and indeed to tuple operators too.

Tuple Types

Now I turn to to tuple types as such. Here first, repeated from the section "Row and Table Types" in Chapter 3, is a **Tutorial D** definition for a tuple variable (or tuplevar) called STV:

```
VAR STV TUPLE
  { SNO SNO , SNAME NAME , STATUS INTEGER , CITY CHAR } ;
```

Explanation:

■ The keyword VAR, which we've already seen in numerous examples in this book, just means the statement constitutes a variable definition specifically.

■ STV ("supplier tuple variable") is the name of the variable being defined.

■ The remainder of the definition, from the keyword TUPLE to the closing brace inclusive, specifies the type of that variable. The keyword TUPLE shows it's a tuple type, and the commalist in braces specifies the set of attributes that make up the corresponding heading. No significance attaches to the order in which the attributes are specified within those braces.

Note: Recall from the definitions in Chapter 1 that, formally speaking, an attribute is an $<A_j,T_j>$ pair,[17] and no two distinct attributes in the same heading have the same attribute name. As we'll see, however, **Tutorial D** doesn't use those angle brackets. It also doesn't use a comma to separate the attribute name A_j from the type name T_j (it uses one or more spaces instead). Analogous remarks apply to all uses of the keyword

---

[17] Note that qualifier "formally speaking," though. In less formal contexts we often ignore the type name, or at least elide it.

TUPLE in **Tutorial D**, also to all uses of the keyword RELATION (see later); I won't keep on saying as much, therefore, but will instead let this one paragraph do duty for all.

Now let's focus on the portion of the example that denotes the tuple type as such. Here it is again:

```
TUPLE { SNO SNO , SNAME NAME , STATUS INTEGER , CITY CHAR }
```

The type thus defined is, of course, a tuple type, and it's nonscalar. It's also a generated type, since it's obtained by invoking a type generator (viz., TUPLE). More generally, the example illustrates the style used for tuple type names in **Tutorial D**; as you can see, such names take the form TUPLE *H*, where *H* is the pertinent heading (and the degree and attributes of *H* are, respectively, the degree and attributes of the tuple type so named).

Note: The reason the *Manifesto* insists on tuple type names being of this particular form, or something logically equivalent to this particular form, has to do with the issue of *tuple type inference*. Of course, an analogous remark applies to relation type names and relation type inference also, as you would surely expect (see the next subsection below). For further explanation, see the answer to Exercise 12 at the end of the chapter.

Getting back to the tuple variable STV, the value of that variable at any given time is a tuple with, again as you can see, the same heading as that of the suppliers relvar S. As noted in Chapter 2, therefore, we might imagine a code fragment that (a) extracts a one-tuple relation—say the relation containing just the tuple for supplier S1—from the current value of that relvar, then (b) extracts the single tuple from that one-tuple relation, and finally (c) assigns that tuple to the variable STV. In **Tutorial D**:

```
STV := TUPLE FROM ( S WHERE SNO = SNO('S1') ) ;
```

Note that TUPLE FROM will fail if the cardinality of its argument relation is anything other than one (i.e., either zero or two or more).

Next, tuples are, of course, values. Like all values, therefore, they must be returned by some selector invocation (a tuple selector invocation, naturally, if the value is a tuple). Here's an example:

```
TUPLE { SNO SNO('S1') , SNAME NAME('Smith') ,
                       STATUS 20 , CITY 'London' }
```

This expression returns the tuple for supplier S1 shown in the picture of the suppliers relation in Chapter 1. The order in which the tuple components are specified is arbitrary, of course. Note, however, that in **Tutorial D** each component is specified by means of the pertinent attribute name by itself—i.e., without the corresponding type name—separated by at least one space from an expression denoting the pertinent attribute value. (There's no need to specify the attribute type as such, because it's necessarily the same as that of the specified expression.)

Here's another example of a tuple selector invocation (unlike the previous one, this one isn't a literal, because not all of its arguments are specified as literals in turn):

```
TUPLE { SNO SV , SNAME NAME('Johns') ,
                 STATUS TV + 2 , CITY CV }
```

I'm assuming here that SV, TV, and CV are variables of types SNO, INTEGER, and CHAR, respectively.

As these examples indicate, a tuple selector invocation in **Tutorial D** consists in general of the keyword TUPLE, followed by—to spell it out again—a commalist of pairs of the form

```
Aj xj
```

(where x_j is an expression denoting the corresponding attribute value v_j), that whole commalist being enclosed in braces. Note, therefore, that the keyword TUPLE does double duty in **Tutorial D**—it's used in connection with tuple selector invocations as we've just seen, and also with tuple type names as we saw earlier.

So tuple types certainly have selectors. But they don't have (nor do they need) any THE_ operators—at least, not as such; instead, they have operators that provide access to the corresponding attributes of values and variables of the tuple type in question, and those operators provide functionality somewhat analogous to that provided by THE_ operators in connection with scalar types. For example, if *tx* is a tuple expression denoting a tuple of the same type as tuple variable STV, the **Tutorial D** expression

```
CITY FROM tx
```

extracts the CITY value from the tuple that's the current value of *tx*.

Finally, tuple assignment and equality comparison operators are also available, with the obvious syntax in each case. (In fact, of course, tuple assignment in particular was illustrated earlier in this subsection.)

Relation Types

I turn now to relation types (the following discussion parallels that of the previous subsection, for the most part). Here first, repeated from Chapter 1, is a **Tutorial D** definition for the suppliers relvar S from the suppliers and parts database:

```
VAR S BASE
    RELATION { SNO SNO , SNAME NAME ,
                              STATUS INTEGER , CITY CHAR }
    KEY { SNO } ;
```

Explanation:

- Again the keyword VAR means this definition is a variable definition specifically; S is the name of the variable being defined, and the keyword BASE means the variable is a base relvar specifically (not, e.g., a view).

- The second and third lines of the definition together specify the type of that variable. The keyword RELATION shows it's a relation type, and the commalist in braces specifies the set of attributes that make up the corresponding heading. Again, of course, no significance attaches to the order in which the attributes are specified.

- The last line defines {SNO} to be a key for this relvar.

Now let's focus on the portion of the example that denotes the relation type as such. Here it is again:

```
RELATION { SNO SNO , SNAME NAME ,
                          STATUS INTEGER , CITY CHAR }
```

The type thus defined is, of course, a relation type, and it's nonscalar. It's also a generated type, since it's obtained by invoking the RELATION type generator. More generally, the example illustrates the style used for relation type names in **Tutorial D**: Such names take the form RELATION *H*, where *H* is the pertinent heading (and the degree and attributes of *H* are, respectively, the degree and attributes of the relation type so named).

Next, relations are values and must therefore be returned by some selector invocation (a relation selector invocation, naturally, if the value is a relation). Here's an example:

```
RELATION { TUPLE { SNO    SNO('S1') ,
                   SNAME  NAME('Smith') ,
                   STATUS 20 ,
                   CITY   'London' } ,
          TUPLE { SNO    SNO('S2') ,
                   SNAME  NAME('Jones') ,
                   STATUS 10 ,
                   CITY   'Paris' } ,
          TUPLE { SNO    SNO('S3') ,
                   SNAME  NAME('Blake') ,
                   STATUS 30 ,
                   CITY   'Paris' } ,
          TUPLE { SNO    SNO('S4') ,
                   SNAME  NAME('Clark') ,
                   STATUS 20 ,
                   CITY   'London' } ,
          TUPLE { SNO    SNO('S5') ,
                   SNAME  NAME('Adams') ,
                   STATUS 30 ,
                   CITY   'Athens' } }
```

The order in which the tuples are specified is arbitrary, of course. Here's another example (unlike the previous one, this one isn't a literal):

```
RELATION { tx , ty , tz }
```

I'm assuming here that *tx*, *ty*, and *tz* here are tuple expressions, all of which are of the same tuple type.

As the foregoing examples suggest, a relation selector invocation in **Tutorial D** consists in general[18] of the keyword RELATION, followed by a commalist enclosed in braces of tuple expressions (and those tuple expressions must all be of the same tuple type). Note, therefore, that the keyword RELATION does double duty in **Tutorial D**—it's used in connection with relation selector invocations as we've just seen, and also with relation type names as we saw earlier.

---

[18] But see Exercise 13 at the end of the chapter.

Like tuple types, relation types don't have, or need, any THE_ operators as such. In their place:

■ Given a relation *r*, the restrict operator of the relational algebra allows access to any arbitrary one-tuple "subrelation" of *r*. For example, let *r* be the relation that's the current value of the suppliers relvar S. Then the restriction *r* WHERE SNO = *sno* evaluates to the relation that's the one-tuple restriction of *r* corresponding to supplier number *sno*.

■ Given a relation *r* containing exactly one tuple, the operator TUPLE FROM *r* allows access to the single tuple in *r*.

Taken together, these operators provide functionality analogous to that provided by THE_ operators in connection with scalar types.

Finally, relational assignment and equality comparison operators are also available, with the obvious syntax in each case. (In fact, of course, relational assignment in particular was illustrated in an earlier section of this chapter, also at several points in Chapter 1.)

INITIAL VALUES

It's well understood in programming circles that referencing a variable before it has been assigned a value can lead to either run time errors or (worse) wrong answers. For such reasons, the *Manifesto* requires all variables, scalar or otherwise, to be initialized—i.e., assigned some initial value—at the time they're declared. Let's take a closer look. I'll consider the scalar case first.

The scalar case divides into two subcases, depending on whether the type in question is user defined or system defined. If it's user defined, the applicable initial value can be specified as part of the pertinent type definition, as in this example:

```
TYPE NAME ... INIT NAME ( '' ) ;
```

(Actually, *The Third Manifesto* requires that scalar type definitions—TYPE statements, in **Tutorial D**—always specify an explicit INIT clause, or something equivalent to such a clause. I've omitted such specifications from previous examples purely to avoid unnecessary distractions.)

Initial values can optionally be specified on scalar variable definitions too, as in this example:

```
VAR XNAME NAME INIT NAME ( 'zzz' ) ;
```

For a given scalar variable, then, the corresponding initial value—the value to be assigned to that variable at the time it's declared— is either

a. The INIT value, if there is one, specified in the pertinent variable definition, or

b. The INIT value—the required *default* initial value—specified in the pertinent type definition otherwise.

So much for user defined types. In the case of system defined types, of course, there *is* no corresponding explicit TYPE statement; thus, if *V* is a scalar variable of some system defined type, an INIT clause *must* be specified as part in the statement defining *V*.

I turn now to tuple and relation variables. Unlike scalar variables, these variables have no corresponding TYPE statement from which they might derive their initial value. However, we can (and do) still define a default initial value for such a variable by appealing to the default initial values for the types in terms of which the pertinent tuple or relation type is defined. I omit the details for simplicity. Of course, we can always specify an explicit initial value anyway, as part of the definition of the variable in question. Here's a tuplevar example:

```
VAR STV TUPLE
  { SNO SNO , SNAME NAME , STATUS INTEGER , CITY CHAR }
    INIT TUPLE
  { SNO SNO('S0') , SNAME NAME('') , STATUS 0, CITY '' } ;
```

Now, you might be thinking this example looks rather cumbersome, not to say repetitious—and you'd be right. The fact is, the specified initial value must of course be a value of the appropriate type, and the INIT clause thus effectively implies a corresponding type specification. So the foregoing example could be simplified to just:

```
VAR STV
  INIT TUPLE
  { SNO SNO('S0') , SNAME NAME('') , STATUS 0, CITY '' } ;
```

But it's not wrong to include both a type specification and an INIT clause, and doing so could at least permit the compiler to check that the specified initial value is indeed a value of the specified type.

Note: The foregoing remarks apply to scalar type definitions also, mutatis mutandis, though in that case the arguments for omitting the type specification if an INIT clause is included might not be quite so persuasive.

Finally, concerning relation variables: The only difference here is that if no INIT clause is specified, the implementation defined value that the variable is initialized to by default is, specifically, the empty relation of the pertinent type.

Now let me get back to the TYPE statement as such. Actually, the INIT clause on the TYPE statement serves another purpose as well (a more fundamental purpose, in some respects). Here's another lightly edited quote from the *Manifesto*:

> The definition of any given scalar type[19] shall be accompanied by a specification of an example value of that type.

The reason for providing such an example value is to guarantee that the type in question isn't empty (i.e., does contain at least one value—see Exercise 15 at the end of the chapter). In **Tutorial D**, the INIT clause serves to provide that example value.

Note: Although the INIT clause on the TYPE statement is indeed required, I'll continue to omit it from most of my examples from this point forward (for the same reason as before—i.e., simply to avoid unnecessary distractions).

ORDERED AND ORDINAL TYPES

A given scalar type *T* can be ordered, ordinal, or neither. To elaborate:

- *T* is an *ordered* type if and only if it has a total ordering, meaning that (a) the comparisons $v_1 < v_2$, $v_1 = v_2$, and $v_1 > v_2$ are all defined for arbitrary pairs of values v_1 and v_2 of type *T*, and (b) for any such pair of values v_1 and v_2, one of those comparisons returns TRUE and the other two return FALSE.

---

[19] With the sole exception of the system defined type *omega* (but type *omega* is defined only if type inheritance is supported, anyway). See the answer to Exercise 15 at the end of the chapter for further discussion.

■ *T* is an *ordinal* type if and only if (a) it's an ordered type and (b) the following operators are also defined for it:

    a. Niladic "first" and "last" operators, which return the first and last value, respectively, of type *T* with respect to the applicable total ordering, and

    b. Monadic "next" and "prior" operators, which, given a value *v* of type *T*, return the value of type *T* immediately succeeding *v* and the value of type *T* immediately preceding *v*, respectively, again with respect to the applicable total ordering.

    Note: The "next" operator will fail, of course, if the given value *v* is last according to the pertinent ordering. Likewise, the "prior" operator will fail if the given value *v* is first according to that ordering.

INTEGER is an obvious example of an ordinal type (in fact, any ordinal type must be isomorphic to type INTEGER, in the sense that it displays ordering behavior that directly parallels that of the integers). RATIONAL is an example of a type that's ordered but not ordinal, because if *p/q* is a rational number, then—in mathematics at least, if not in computer arithmetic—no rational number can be said to be the "next" one, immediately following *p/q*. And type POINT is an example of a type that's not ordered at all,[20] and hence certainly not ordinal either, a fortiori.

In support of the foregoing ideas, **Tutorial D** allows at most one of ORDINAL and ORDERED to be specified as part of the TYPE statement that defines a given type *T*. For example:

```
TYPE QTY ORDINAL POSSREP ( Q INTEGER ) INIT QTY ( 0 ) ;
```

If ORDERED is specified, associated "<" (etc.) operators must be defined for the type in question. If ORDINAL is specified, the same is true, but corresponding "first," "last," "next," and "prior" operators must be defined as well.

---

[20] At least as defined earlier in this chapter, also in Chapter 2—but that's not to say we couldn't define an ordering for it if we wanted to. See the answer to Exercise 18 at the end of the chapter.

A FINAL REMARK

Let me close by pointing out explicitly something that I rather hope has been obvious all through the foregoing: viz., that the operation of defining a type doesn't actually create the corresponding set of values. Rather, those values simply exist, at least conceptually, and always will exist; they're part of the fabric of our universe, as it were, and they can be neither created nor destroyed. Thus, all the "define type" operation—i.e., the TYPE statement, in the case of scalar types—really does is introduce a name by which the corresponding set of values can be referenced. Likewise, the DROP TYPE statement doesn't drop the set of values as such, it merely drops the name that was introduced by the corresponding TYPE statement.

EXERCISES

1. This chapter has touched on still more logical differences, including:

literal	vs.	constant
occurrence	vs.	encoding
ordered	vs.	ordinal
possible representation	vs.	physical representation
read-only operator	vs.	update operator
value	vs.	expression
value	vs.	occurrence
value	vs.	variable

What exactly is the logical difference in each case?

2. Every value is a value of exactly one type: true or false?

3. Does a value have a declared type?

4. The operation of defining a type doesn't actually create the corresponding set of values: true or false? Explain your answer.

5. Explain the following concepts: possrep; selector; THE_ operator.

6. What's a pseudovariable?

7. What's a polymorphic operator?

8. What do you understand by the term *type constraint*? When are type constraints checked? What happens if such a check fails?

9. Explain the term *multiple assignment*. Can you think of any examples of multiple assignment in practice, over and above the ones given in the body of the chapter?

10. Recall the following text from the body of the chapter (slightly abbreviated here):

> Suppose two or more of the individual assignments in a given multiple assignment specify the same target variable. Then those particular individual assignments are effectively executed in sequence as written, and are thereby effectively reduced to a certain single assignment to the variable in question.

What do you think is the reason for this rule?

11. What's a dbvar?

12. Here's a sample view definition expressed in **Tutorial D**:

```
VAR VX VIRTUAL ( S JOIN SP ) ;
```

VX here is a relvar, of course (a virtual relvar, to be precise). What's the type of that relvar?

13. Recall the following text from the body of the chapter:

> [A] relation selector invocation in **Tutorial D** consists in general of the keyword RELATION, followed by a commalist enclosed in braces of tuple expressions (and those tuple expressions must all be of the same tuple type).

What happens if that commalist of tuple expressions is empty?

14. A heading is a set of attributes and the empty set is a legitimate set; thus, we might define an empty heading to be a heading where the set in question is empty. Can you think of any uses for such a heading?

15. Can a type be empty?

16. Give an examples of a type for which it might be useful to define two or more distinct possible representations. Can you think of an example where distinct possible representations for the same type have different numbers of components?

17. Give an example of a scalar type with a nonscalar possrep component.

18. Consider a database concerning geometric figures. In connection with that database, suppose there's a user defined type called PARALLELOGRAM, with the intuitively obvious semantics. Here's an example of a value of that type (i.e., a specific parallelogram), with vertices A, B, C, D (in clockwise sequence, starting from A), and with center E:

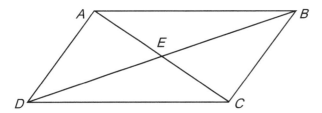

How many distinct possreps can you think of for this type? What associated operators do you think might be useful? *Note:* The purpose of this exercise is to get you thinking a little more deeply about the whole idea of user defined types—more deeply, that is, than would have been appropriate in the body of the chapter.

ANSWERS

1. Out of this list of logical differences, the only ones I want to elaborate on here are the ones between (a) literals and constants and (b) values and expressions. For the rest I refer you to the body of the chapter.

   First, literals vs. constants: Well, "constant" is basically just another word for "value"—every constant is a value, every value is a constant. However, the term is often used more specifically to designate something that's rather like a variable, except that it doesn't vary (apologies for the apparent contradiction in terms here). What I mean is, a constant in this latter sense is something that, like a variable, has been given a name, a name that isn't just a simple, explicit, literal representation of the value in question—but unlike a variable, of course, it can't ever be updated.

As an aside, I note that it might be better to refer to a constant in this latter sense more explicitly as a *named* constant. Here to invent some syntax on the fly is an example:

```
CONST PI RATIONAL INIT ( 3.14159 ) ;
```

As you can see, therefore, a named constant does resemble a variable in that it can be thought of as an abstraction of a storage location that contains a value (or, more precisely, contains a representation of an occurrence of a value); however, it differs from a variable in two obvious ways: First, it can never serve as the target for an assignment operation; second, every reference to the pertinent name always denotes the same value.

Turning now to literals: In contrast to all of the above, a literal is "self defining." It resembles a named constant in that it too designates a value, but it does so by means of a name that *is* "just a simple, explicit, literal representation of the value in question." Thus, its value is determined by the name in question, and that value is known at compile time (and, accordingly, the type of that value is also determined by the name in question and known at compile time). Every value of every type, tuple and relation types included, is—in fact, must be, by definition—denotable by means of some literal.

Note: A literal is actually a special case of a selector invocation. To be precise, a selector invocation is a literal if and only if all of the argument expressions in that selector invocation are literals in turn.

It follows from everything I've said so far that there is indeed a logical difference between a literal as such and the value it stands for. Be aware, however, that some systems, including certain object systems in particular, actually use the term *literal* to mean a value! For example, here's a quote (boldface added) from page 112 of *Object Data Management*, by R. G. G. Cattell (Addison-Wesley, 1991):

[There's a] distinction between *literal* and *entity* data types ...**Literal data consists of a simple value** such as an integer, date, or string; entity values are a group of values, which we call an object, referenced by an OID.

Caveat lector.

    Second, values vs. expressions: Values are an abstraction; they exist conceptually, but no one has ever actually seen or touched or tasted a value as such. What we typically tend to think of as a value, in (e.g.) some program or some database, is really just *a symbol that denotes* the abstraction in question. (I called such symbols "occurrences" in the body of the chapter.) And the only way we can access such symbols is by means of some expression (possibly just a simple literal, of course). To sum up:

> A value is an abstraction; an expression is a mechanism for accessing a symbolic representation of such an abstraction.

Thus, there is indeed a logical difference between (a) a value as such, on the one hand, and the (b) expression that's used to denote that value in some particular context, on the other.

2. True, absent type inheritance. With type inheritance, by contrast, a value might be of several types at once—for example, a given geometric figure might simultaneously be both a rectangle and a rhombus. Or, to repeat an example from Chapter 2, a given animal might simultaneously be both four legged and warm blooded. Even so, however, every value will still have exactly one *most specific* type. For example, if value *v* is indeed both a rectangle and a rhombus, then *v* must be a square, and the most specific type of *v* will thus be SQUARE[21]—a type that, in our inheritance model at least, *must* be explicitly defined if types RECTANGLE and RHOMBUS are. See my book *Type Inheritance and Relational Theory* (O'Reilly, 2016), if you want to know more.

3. Not really, because values as such aren't declared at all, they just exist. As noted in the answer to Exercise 1 above, however, the only way a value can be accessed within a program is by means of some expression—possibly just a

---

[21] Or possibly some proper subtype of SQUARE, if any such subtype exists.

literal—and such expressions do have declared types. But the declared type of an expression is exactly that, the declared type of the expression as such, *not* of the value the expression denotes.

4. True. As I put it in the previous answer, the values in question "just exist"—at least conceptually—and they always have existed, and always will exist. They're built into the very fabric of the universe, one might say, and they can therefore be neither created nor destroyed.

It follows that all the "define type" operation—the TYPE statement, in **Tutorial D**—really does is introduce a name by which the pertinent set of values can be referenced. Likewise, the DROP TYPE statement doesn't drop the values as such, it merely drops the name that was introduced by the corresponding TYPE statement.

5. *Possrep:* "Possrep" is short for possible representation. Let *T* be a scalar type, and let *v* be an occurrence in some context of some value of type *T*. By definition, *v* has exactly one physical representation and one or more possible representations (at least one, because there's obviously always one that's the same as the physical representation). Then:

- If *T* is user defined, then one or more possreps for values of type *T* must be explicitly defined.

- If *T* is system defined, zero or more possreps for values of type *T* can be explicitly defined, but at least one will be implicitly defined.

Each possrep consists of zero or more components, where each such component consists in turn of a name and a corresponding type. Possreps are explicitly exposed to the user via an associated selector and associated set of THE_ operators. Also, possreps are always named; by default, however, the possrep name is the same as that of the corresponding scalar type. Note that there's no requirement that any possrep be the same as any underlying physical representation; however, there's certainly a requirement that if *PR* is a possrep for type *T*, then (a) every value of type *T* must be representable via *PR*, and (b) every value representable via *PR* that satisfies the pertinent type constraint must be a value of type *T*.

Selector: A selector is an operator—read-only by definition—for selecting, or specifying, an arbitrary value of a given type. Every type, tuple and relation types included, has at least one associated selector.[22] Let *S* be a selector for type *T*. Then (a) every value of type *T* is producible by means of some invocation of *S* in which the argument expressions are all literals, and (b) every successful invocation of *S* produces a value of type *T*. To elaborate:

■ If *T* is a scalar type and user defined, definition of a possrep *PR* for *T* causes automatic definition of a corresponding selector operator (with the same name as *PR*, in **Tutorial D**), which allows a value of type *T* to be selected by supplying a value for each component of *PR*.

■ If *T* is a a scalar type and system defined, one or more possreps might or might not be defined for it. If one is defined (*PR*, say), then it behaves exactly as if *T* were user defined and *PR* were a corresponding possrep. If no possrep is defined, then at least one selector operator for type *T* must be provided by the system. In the latter case, however, invocations of such a selector will probably be limited to being simple literals.

■ If *T* is a tuple type, the (unique) corresponding selector allows a tuple of type *T* to be selected by supplying a value for each attribute of *T*.

■ If *T* is a relation type, the (unique) corresponding selector allows a relation of type *T* to be selected by supplying a value for each tuple of *T*. (In other words, a relation selector invocation effectively just enumerates the relevant tuples.)

Note that, ultimately, the only way any expression can ever yield a value of type *T* is via invocation of some selector for that type *T*. In fact, the selector notion is essentially a generalization of the familiar concept of a literal (all literals are selector invocations, but some selector invocations aren't literals; to be specific, a selector invocation is a literal if and only if all of its argument expressions are literals in turn).

---

[22] So long as the type in question is nonempty, that is—but empty type are relevant only in the context of inheritance, and further details are thus (for the most part) beyond the scope of this book. See the answer to Exercise 15.

THE_ operator: Let *T* be a scalar type. Then definition of a possrep *PR* for *T* causes automatic definition of a set of operators of the form THE_*A*, THE_*B*, ..., THE_*C* (**Tutorial D** syntax), where *A*, *B* ..., *C* are the names of the components of *PR*. Let *v* be a value of type *T*, and let *PR*(*v*) denote the possible representation corresponding to *PR* for that value *v*. Then invoking THE_*X* on *v* (*X* = *A*, *B*, ..., *C*) returns the value of the *X* component of *PR*(*v*).

THE_ operator invocations can also be used as pseudovariable references (loosely, "THE_ pseudovariables"). THE_ operator invocations and THE_ pseudovariable references can both be nested.

Note: I'd like to elaborate briefly on certain aspects of the foregoing definitions.

- To repeat, if *T* is a scalar type, it must have at least one corresponding possrep, *PR* say. But the components of *PR* don't necessarily have to be scalar in turn! Here's a simple example of a scalar type with a possrep in which one of the components is tuple valued:

  ```
  TYPE NADDR /* name and address */
       POSSREP { NAME NAME ,
                 ADDR TUPLE { STREET  CHAR ,
                              CITY    CHAR ,
                              STATE   CHAR ,
                              ZIP     CHAR } } ;
  ```

  And here's an example of a scalar type with a possrep in which one of the components is relation valued:

  ```
  TYPE POLYGON /* geometric figure */
       POSSREP { ID ... ,
                 VERTICES RELATION { VNO    INTEGER ,
                                     VERTEX POINT } } ;
  ```

- Similarly, if *T* is a tuple or relation type, *T* might have an attribute that's tuple or relation valued—recall the example in Chapter 2 of a relation with attributes SNO and PNO_REL, where PNO_REL was relation valued.

- I gave a BNF grammar for scalar type definitions in the body of the chapter, and one of the things I said in explaining that grammar was this: "The *<possrep component def commalist>* will usually not be empty." But it *might* be empty!—though I admit that such a situation would constitute something of a pathological case. If it were empty, however, it would mean that the type being defined has at most one value—in fact, exactly one value, since user defined empty scalar types are explicitly prohibited, and in fact can't even be defined (see the answer to Exercise 15 below). That value would be denoted by the only legal invocation of the corresponding selector, viz., *PR* ( ), where *PR* is the name of the possrep in question—which would in fact be a literal, and indeed the only legitimate literal, corresponding to possrep *PR*.

6. The term *pseudovariable*—more precisely, pseudovariable *reference*—refers to the use of an operational expression instead of a simple variable reference to denote the target for some assignment or other update operation. Note, however, that It's convenient for definitional purposes to regard pseudovariable references as if they were regular variable references; in other words, pseudovariables are variables, loosely speaking. Here's an example. Let CS be a variable of type CHAR, with current value the string 'Middle', and consider the following assignment:

```
SUBSTRING ( CS , 2 , 1 ) := 'u' ;
```

The effect of this assignment is to "zap" the second character position within CS, replacing the 'i' by a 'u' (after the update, therefore, the current value of CS will be the string 'Muddle').[23] The expression on the left side of the assignment symbol ":=" here is a pseudovariable reference.

For a second example, let LS ("London suppliers") be a view of relvar S ("suppliers"), defined as the restriction of S to just the suppliers in London, and consider the following DELETE statement:

```
DELETE LS WHERE STATUS > 15 ;
```

Logically speaking, this DELETE is equivalent to the following:

```
DELETE ( S WHERE CITY = 'London' ) WHERE STATUS > 15 ;
```

---

[23] More precisely, the argument 2 specifies the second character position within CS counting from the left, and the argument 1 specifies the length of the substring of interest. By way of another example, therefore, SUBTRING ('Muddle',3,2) denotes the string 'dd'.

In this expanded form—which isn't, nor is it meant to be, valid **Tutorial D** syntax—the target of the DELETE is specified by means of an operational expression, or in other words by means of a pseudovariable reference. As the example suggests, therefore, updating a view is logically equivalent to updating a certain pseudovariable (thus, views are pseudovariables, loosely speaking). Here's the expanded form (again not valid **Tutorial D** syntax):

```
( S WHERE CITY = 'London' ) :=
    ( S WHERE CITY = 'London' ) WHERE NOT ( STATUS > 15 ) ;
```

And this latter simplifies in turn to the following (which *is* valid **Tutorial D** syntax):

```
S := S WHERE NOT ( CITY = 'London' AND STATUS > 15 ) ;
```

For a third example, showing that even updating a base relvar is in fact logically equivalent to updating a certain pseudovariable (and hence that base relvars too are really pseudovariables, logically speaking), see the answer to Exercise 11 below.

7. The exercise asks for a definition of the term "polymorphic operator," but I think it's better to start with the term "polymorphism" as such. That term refers, in general, to the idea that a given operator might take arguments of different types on different invocations. Note, however, that there are at least three different kinds of polymorphism. To elaborate:

First, *overloading polymorphism* (also known as *operator overloading*, or just as *overloading*, or sometimes as *ad hoc polymorphism*): This not terribly accurate term means the same name is being used for two or more different operators (equality is a case in point). The reason the term is inaccurate is because it's really the name as such, not some operator, that's overloaded. For example, UNION is overloaded in **Tutorial D**, because it—i.e., the operator name—is used to denote both relational union and tuple union. Another, more obvious, example is "=", which as mentioned above is certainly overloaded; in fact, there's an "=" operator for *every* type—one for integers, one for supplier numbers, one for relations of type RELATION {SNO SNO, PNO PNO, QTY QTY}, and so on). Similar remarks apply to ":=" also.

Note: The foregoing definition and examples do at least tend to suggest that the operators in question should have similar semantics. An example of where this suggestion, or recommendation, is flouted is provided by those languages—C++ is a case in point—that use the symbol "+" to denote string concatenation as well as numeric addition. Precisely because we're all used to the fact that numeric addition is commutative, users of such a language might be tempted to fall into the trap of thinking string concatenation is commutative too, which of course it isn't.

Generic polymorphism: This term refers to the kind of polymorphism exhibited by a generic operator. A generic operator in turn is one that's available in connection with every type that can be produced by invocation of some particular type generator. For example, the operators of the relational algebra (join, project, restrict, and so on) are all generic: They're available for use with relations of every type that can be produced by invocation of the RELATION type generator—which is to say, they're available for relations of all possible types, and hence for all possible relations.[24]

Inclusion polymorphism: This term refers to the kind of polymorphism exhibited in connection with type inheritance. The details are beyond the scope of this book, but let me at least explain the basic idea, which is simply this: Any read-only operator that applies to values of a given type *T* necessarily applies to values of every proper subtype *T'* of *T*, because values of type *T'* *are* values of type *T*.[25] For example, if there's an AREA operator for rectangles, that operator must work for squares too, because squares *are* rectangles. Such operators are thus polymorphic, and the kind of polymorphism they exhibit is called inclusion polymorphism, on the grounds that the relationship between *T'* and *T* is that of set inclusion (the set of values constituting type *T'* is included in, or is a subset of, the set of values constituting type *T*). Note that this kind of polymorphism is a logical consequence of the very notion of type inheritance.[26]

---

[24] Of course, there are exceptions to this observation (or what might be thought of as exceptions, at any rate). For example, the operation of projecting a specified relation on a specified attribute is available only for relations that actually have such an attribute.

[25] A proper subtype of type *T*, in a system that supports type inheritance, is a subtype of *T* that's distinct from *T*. (Every type is always a subtype of itself, but not a proper one.)

[26] Let me add for the record that certain "overloading" examples might be considered examples of inclusion polymorphism instead if inheritance is supported. Further details are beyond the scope of this book.

8. The type constraint for a given type is a definition of the set of values constituting that type. It's checked whenever a selector for that type is invoked. If the check fails, the selector invocation fails.

9. Multiple assignment is an operator that allows several individual assignments to be performed in parallel (in effect, simultaneously). In the important special case in which the targets for some or all of the individual assignments are database relvars, no database constraint checking is done until all of those individual assignments have been executed in their entirety. *Note:* A *database constraint* is any constraint, other than a type constraint, that affects updates on the database.

Note that multiple assignment is involved implicitly in a variety of other operations—for example, updating several components of the same tuplevar in a single UPDATE, or updating several elements of the same array variable in a single assignment, or updating some join or union view, or updating some relvar in such a way as to cause a cascade delete. Note therefore, incidentally, that the individual "single" assignments involved in a given multiple assignment don't have to be relational assignments specifically. As a matter of fact, multiple assignment isn't even a new idea. Here for example is a multiple assignment expressed in Algol 60:

```
A := B := C := 7.5 ;
```

This assignment assigns the value 7.5 to all three of the variables A, B, and C "simultaneously."

For a detailed discussion of multiple assignment in general, with several further nonrelational examples, please see Chapter 11 ("Multiple Assignment") of my book *Date on Database: Writings 2000-2006* (Apress, 2006).

10. Let X be a variable of type INTEGER with current value 0, and consider the following multiple assignment:

```
X : = X + 1 , X := X + 3 ;
```

Intuitively speaking, we should surely expect X to wind up with a final value of 4. However, recall the following loose definition of multiple assignment from the body of the chapter (lightly reworded here):

a. First, all of the source expressions on the right sides of the individual assignments are evaluated.

b. Then all of the individual assignments to the target variables on the left sides of those individual assignments are executed in parallel.

Because those source expressions are all evaluated before any of the individual assignments are done, however, none of those individual assignments can depend on the result of any other, and so "executing them in parallel" is really just a manner of speaking. In the example, therefore, the effect of the foregoing procedure would be to set X to either 1 or 3, unpredictably. Precisely for such reasons, the definition of multiple assignment in general requires (to repeat) that if two or more of the individual assignments specify the same target variable, then those assignments are effectively executed in sequence as written. In the case of the foregoing double assignment to X, then, the precise semantics are defined in such a way as to make that assignment logically equivalent to the following *single* assignment—

```
X : = WITH ( X := X + 1 ) : X := X + 3 ;
```

—and the overall effect is thus indeed to set X to 4.

11. "Dbvar" is short for *database variable* (the term isn't in general use, though perhaps it should be). A database variable in turn is, loosely, just a container for relvars; more precisely, it's a variable whose value at any given time is a database value. Strictly speaking, there's a logical difference, analogous to that between relation values and relation variables, between database values and database variables; in other words, what we usually call a database is really a variable (typically a rather large one), and updating it has the effect of replacing one value of that variable by another such value, where the values in question are database values.

More precisely still, a database is actually a *tuple* variable—see the examples below—with one attribute (relation valued) for each relvar in the database in question. Note, therefore, that a database isn't really a set of relation variables, despite the fact that that's how we usually think of it; rather, the relvars within any given database are really *pseudovariables* (see the answer to Exercise 6 above for more on pseudovariables in general).

All of that being said, however, I bow to traditional usage in this book—most of the time, at any rate—and use the term *database* to refer to both database values and database variables, relying on context to make it clear which is intended.

Examples: For an example of a database value, see the suppliers and parts database value in Chapter 1. As for the matter of a database really being a tuple variable, the suppliers and parts database in particular can be thought of as a tuple variable (SPDB, say) of the following tuple type:

```
TUPLE { S   RELATION { SNO SNO , SNAME NAME ,
                       STATUS INTEGER , CITY CHAR } ,
        P   RELATION { PNO PNO , PNAME NAME , COLOR COLOR ,
                       WEIGHT WEIGHT , CITY CHAR } ,
        SP RELATION { SNO SNO , PNO PNO , QTY QTY } }
```

It follows that, e.g., the following conventional relational update—

```
DELETE SP WHERE STATUS < 22 ;
```

—is really shorthand for the following *tuple* update on tuplevar SPDB:

```
UPDATE SPDB : { SP := SP WHERE NOT ( STATUS < 22 ) } ;
```

And this statement in turn is shorthand for the following tuple assignment:

```
SPDB := TUPLE { S    ( S  FROM SPDB ) ,
                P    ( P  FROM SPDB ) ,
                SP ( ( SP FROM SPDB )
                     WHERE NOT ( STATUS < 22 ) ) } ;
```

The names S, P, and SP thus really do denote pseudovariables. Note, however, that if we're to be able to write explicit database assignments like the one in the foregoing example, then databases—or database variables, rather—like SPDB will obviously have to have user visible names, which in **Tutorial D** they don't. Thus, database assignments in **Tutorial D** have to be expressed in the form of relational assignments (multiple assignments, in general) to the relvars within the database in question.

Incidentally, if the name SPDB were user visible after all, then **Tutorial D** would certainly allow the foregoing tuple assignment to be written in the form of an explicit tuple UPDATE statement as shown above, thus—

```
UPDATE SPDB : { SP := SP WHERE NOT ( STATUS < 22 ) } ;
```

—or even as follows:

```
UPDATE SPDB : { DELETE SP WHERE STATUS < 22 } ;
```

Finally, note that a database isn't *just* a set of relvars—rather, it's a set of relvars that are subject to a certain constraint (what's referred to as *the total database constraint* for the database in question). And it seems reasonable to require that the database be *fully connected*, meaning that every relvar in the database is logically connected to every other, via that constraint. The definitions that follow are intended to help in formalizing this requirement.

■ Let *DB* be a set of relvars, and let *TC* ("total constraint") be the logical AND of all constraints that mention any relvar in *DB*.
   Note: "All constraints" here actually means all *database* constraints, of course, since type constraints don't mention relvars at all.

■ Assume without loss of generality that *TC* is in conjunctive normal form.
   Note: A truth valued expression is in conjunctive normal form, CNF, if and only if it's of the form (c_1) AND (c_2) AND ... AND (c_n), where the conjuncts (c_1), (c_2), ..., (c_n) involve no ANDs. The parentheses enclosing the individual conjuncts c_1, c_2, ..., c_n might not be needed in practice.

■ Let *A* and *B* be distinct relvars in *DB*.

■ Then *A* and *B* are *logically connected* if and only if there exist relvars R_1, R_2, ..., R_n in *DB* (*A* and R_1 not necessarily distinct, R_n and *B* not necessarily distinct, $n > 0$) such that there's at least one conjunct in *TC* that mentions both *A* and R_1, at least one that mentions both R_1 and R_2, ..., and at least one that mentions both R_n and *B*.

It should be clear that if a given database isn't fully connected in the foregoing sense, then the relvars it contains can be partitioned into two or more disjoint sets, each of which *is* fully connected.

12. The type of VX is, of course, the type of the expression S JOIN SP; in other words, it's RELATION H where H is the heading of the result of that expression. In fact, the type of *any* relational expression is RELATION H, where H is the pertinent heading, and that heading in turn is fully determined by the operators involved in the expression in question. Here for example is the definition of the operator JOIN:

> **Definition (join):** Let relations r_1 and r_2 be joinable—i.e., let them be such that attributes with the same name are of the same type (equivalently, let them be such that the set theory union of their headings is a legal heading). Then, and only then, the expression r_1 JOIN r_2 denotes the join of r_1 and r_2, and it returns the relation with heading the set theory union of the headings of r_1 and r_2 and body the set of all tuples t such that t is the set theory union of a tuple from r_1 and a tuple from r_2.

More generally, this exercise has to do with the question of *type inference* in all of its manifestations (including tuple and relation type inference as special cases). Type inference can be defined as the process of determining the type of the value denoted by a given expression, where the given expression is arbitrarily complex. That process in turn is completely defined by the rules governing the types of the results of the various operations involved in the expression in question. (In fact, of course, as noted both in this chapter and in Chapter 2, the type of the value denoted by expression *exp* is, precisely, the type of the result of the outermost operation involved in *exp*.)

13. Since "empty relations"—i.e., relations whose body contains no tuples—are perfectly legitimate, it follows that we must be able to invoke a selector that selects, or returns, just such a relation. I'll focus on shipments, just to be definite. Here first is a shipment selector invocation that returns a shipment relation containing just one tuple:

```
RELATION { TUPLE { SNO SNO('S1') ,
                   PNO PNO('P1') ,
                   QTY QTY(300) } }
```

The heading of this relation doesn't need to be stated explicitly, because it's the same—it must be the same—as that of the single tuple in its body; and this latter heading in turn is implied by the specified tuple value.

But what if we want to select the *empty* shipment relation? We can't write just

```
RELATION { }
```

(where the subexpression "{ }" is supposed to denote an empty set of shipment tuples), because such an expression—if it were permitted, which it isn't— provides no way of determining the pertinent heading. Instead, we need to specify that heading explicitly by writing something like this:

```
RELATION { SNO SNO , PNO PNO , QTY QTY } { }
```

Here then is a BNF grammar for *<relation selector inv>* (*inv* standing for "invocation"):

```
<relation selector inv>
    ::=   RELATION [ <heading> ] { <body> }

<heading>
    ::=   <attribute commalist>

<attribute>
    ::=   <attribute name> <type name>

<body>
    ::=   <tuple exp commalist>
```

Every tuple denoted by a *<tuple exp>* in a *<body>* must be of the same type, which must be the unique type corresponding to the implicit or explicit *<heading>*. That *<heading>* must be stated explicitly if the *<body>* is empty but can be, and usually is, implicit otherwise.

Subsidiary exercise: Why doesn't a similar problem arise in connection with tuple types?

14. Yes! There's exactly one tuple with an empty heading, and we call it the empty tuple or 0-tuple. In **Tutorial D**, we write it thus (I mean, this is the corresponding tuple selector invocation):

```
TUPLE {}
```

The type of this tuple looks the same, syntactically speaking:

```
TUPLE {}
```

But the braces "{ }" denote different things in the two cases. In the first case, they represent an empty set of tuple components; in the second, they represent an empty heading.

As for relations, there are exactly two relations with an empty heading—one has an empty body as well, and we call it TABLE_DUM (DUM for short); the other has a body containing exactly one tuple (viz., the empty tuple), and we call it TABLE_DEE (DEE for short).[27] These names can be thought of as shorthand for the relation selector invocations

```
RELATION { } { }
```

and

```
RELATION { } { TUPLE { } }
```

respectively. They can also be thought of as the names of two important relation constants.

As for uses for these relations: I can't get into too much detail here; I'll just say that they play roles in the relational algebra that's akin, somewhat, to the role played by the values 0 and 1 in ordinary arithmetic. For example, joining any relation *r* and TABLE_DEE just returns *r*—much like multiplying any number *n* by 1 in ordinary arithmetic just returns *n*. For further discussion, I refer you to Chapter 11 ("Why Is It Called Relational Algebra?") of my book *Logic and Relational Theory* (Technics, 2020).

---

[27] All empty tuples are duplicates of one another, of course! *Note:* Perhaps I should add that the names TABLE_DUM and TABLE_DEE are basically just wordplay on Tweedledum and Tweedledee, who were originally characters in a children's nursery rhyme and were subsequently incorporated into Lewis Carroll's *Through the Looking-Glass and What Alice Found There* (1871).

Note: If a relvar (as opposed to a relation) has an empty heading, then it must have just one key, and that key must be empty too. However, a relvar doesn't have to have an empty heading in order to have an empty key; in fact, a relvar will have an empty key if and only if it's constrained never to contain more than just one tuple (though it's true that the empty key will certainly be the *only* key for such a relvar). For further discussion of such matters, I refer you to my book *SQL and Relational Theory*, 3rd ed. (O'Reilly, 2015).

15. A relation type can never be empty, because if *T* is such a type, there's always at least one value of that type, viz., the empty relation of type *T*. By contrast, scalar and tuple types can be empty. To be specific:

■   The empty scalar type is certainly a valid type; in fact, there's exactly one such, and we call it *omega*. However, it wouldn't make much sense to define a variable to be of that type, because no value could ever be assigned to that variable! Despite this fact, type *omega* turns out to be critically important in connection with type inheritance. Further details are beyond the scope of this book.

■   A tuple type *T* is empty if and only if *T* has at least one attribute that is of some empty type. Of course, this is a recursive definition, so in fact there can be any number of empty tuple types. As with type *omega*, however, it turns out that the notion of an empty tuple type is important in connection with type inheritance, but not otherwise. Again further details are beyond the scope of this book.

Let me now focus on scalar types, for simplicity. Perhaps it has already occurred to you that a scalar type might be defined in such a way that it must be empty, meaning there can't possibly be any values of the type. For example, consider the following would-be scalar type definition:

```
TYPE MT POSSREP { X INTEGER }
       CONSTRAINT X < 0 AND X > 0 ;
```

In order to prevent such mistakes, **Tutorial D** requires TYPE statements to include an INIT clause, which (as explained in the body of the chapter) serves among other things to provide a sample value of the type in question. But in the case at hand no such value exists! Thus, e.g., the would-be definition

```
TYPE MT POSSREP { X INTEGER }
       CONSTRAINT X < 0 AND X > 0
       INIT ( 0 ) ;
```

will fail at compile time, because the specified sample value fails to satisfy the specified type constraint.

16. A triangle can possibly be represented by (a) its three vertices or (b) the midpoints of its three sides or (c) the three line segments constituting its sides or (d) the line segments constituting two of its sides together with the corresponding included angle (etc., etc.).

Note: Each of the foregoing triangle possreps involves the same number of components (i.e., three in every case). By contrast, a regular pentagon can possibly be represented by either (a) its center and one vertex (two components) or (b) three consecutive vertices (three components). *Subsidiary exercise:* Why wouldn't two consecutive vertices suffice?

17. As noted in the answer to Exercise 5, a polygon can possibly be represented by a relation containing one tuple for each of its vertices, each such tuple containing among other things the pertinent vertex number and the corresponding point in two-dimensional space:

```
TYPE POLYGON /* geometric figure */
     POSSREP { ID ... ,
               VERTICES RELATION { VNO     INTEGER ,
                                   VERTEX POINT } }
     CONSTRAINT ... ; ;
```

The CONSTRAINT specification might look like this:

```
CONSTRAINT
   WITH ( N := COUNT ( VERTICES ) ) :
   COUNT ( VERTICES { VNO } ) = N
   AND
   COUNT ( VERTICES { VERTEX } ) = N
   AND
   IS_EMPTY ( VERTICES WHERE VNO < 1 OR VNO > N )
```

Explanation: This CONSTRAINT specification involves three separate conditions all ANDed together. Let *p* be an arbitrary value of type POLYGON. Then the first condition ensures that no two tuples in the VERTICES relation for *p* have the same vertex number; the second ensures that no two tuples in the VERTICES relation for *p* have the same vertex; and the first and third together ensure that if *p* has *n* vertices, then the *n* tuples in the VERTICES relation for *p* contain exactly the VNO values 1, 2, ..., *n*.

Note: Actually the foregoing possrep is incomplete in several respects. One is as follows. Suppose for simplicity that the polygon is in fact a triangle. Clearly, then, the very same triangle can be specified by giving its three vertices in any of six different orders. Now, you might be thinking such a state of affairs surely doesn't matter, but in fact it does; in a right triangle, for example, we might want to be sure it's the "middle" vertex that corresponds to the right angle. In general, then, we'd need a way of pinning down the precise order in which the vertices are to be specified. E.g., in terms of polar coordinates, we might say they're specified in terms of increasing values of θ (but even then we'd need a way of breaking ties). See the answer to Exercise 18 below for further discussion of such matters.

18. *Note: This exercise raises a huge number of issues (as of course it was intended to), and I can't do much more than just scratch the surface of those issues here. For further discussion, I refer you to my book Type Inheritance and Relational Theory (O'Reilly, 2016).*

Let parallelogram *p* be as illustrated in the figure in the statement of the exercise; i.e., let it have vertices *A, B, C, D* (in clockwise sequence, starting from *A*), and center *E*. Then there are many different ways of possibly representing *p*. The first and most obvious one is just to use the four vertices *A, B, C,* and *D*. Of course, it's not the case that every set of four points defines a parallelogram, so we'll need to impose some appropriate constraints on points *A, B, C,* and *D*. But there are several different ways we might state those constraints. For example, we might say that sides *AB* and *DC* must be of equal length and sides *BC* and *AD* must be of equal length also; alternatively, we might say that sides *AB* and *DC* must be parallel and sides *BC* and *AD* must be parallel also; and there are clearly other possibilities as well. Note too that *A, B, C,* and *D* must all be distinct—in fact, no three of them can be collinear, which implies that they must all be distinct a fortiori. So here's a first attempt at a type definition:

```
TYPE PARALLELOGRAM    /* first attempt */
    POSSREP ( A POINT , B POINT , C POINT , D POINT )
    CONSTRAINT NOT COLLINEAR ( A , B , C )
           AND NOT COLLINEAR ( B , C , D )
           AND NOT COLLINEAR ( C , D , A )
           AND NOT COLLINEAR ( D , A , B )
           AND DIST ( A , B ) = DIST ( D , C )
           AND DIST ( B , C ) = DIST ( A , D ) ;
```

I'm assuming here that:

■ COLLINEAR returns TRUE if and only if its three POINT arguments lie on a straight line.

■ DIST returns the distance between its two POINT arguments as a value of type LENGTH.

However, there's at least one problem with the $A - B - C - D$ possrep, as you might have already realized: namely, that the vertices *A, B, C,* and *D* aren't all independent of one another—as soon as any three of them are pinned down, the fourth is fully determined.

Or is it? *Answer:* No! If we're given (say) *A, B,* and *C, and we also know that AC is a diagonal*, then *D* is indeed fully determined, because it must be on the opposite of the diagonal from B. But if *AC* is not a diagonal but a side, then either *AB* or *BC* could be a diagonal, and each of these possibilities corresponds to a different *D* (so given only *A, B,* and *C,* there are three different possible *D*'s altogether).

Well, I'll come back to the foregoing issue later; for now, please take it on trust that we can indeed use just three vertices (say *A, B,* and *C*) as the basis for a possrep if we want to. If we do that, it would have the effect of simplifying the type constraint considerably:

```
TYPE PARALLELOGRAM    /* second attempt */
    POSSREP ( A POINT , B POINT , C POINT )
    CONSTRAINT NOT COLLINEAR ( A , B , C ) ;
```

Note in particular that now we don't need to say that *AB* and *DC* must be of equal length, nor that *BC* and *AD* must be of equal length as well.

Of course, if we do go with a three-vertex possrep as just suggested, there's the problem that there are four different vertex triples we could use, without there being any obvious reason to choose any particular triple over the other three. There's also the problem that whichever triple we do choose, the vertex left out will necessarily "look and feel" different from the other three; for example, if we choose the *A* – *B* – *C* triple, then THE_A, THE_B, and THE_C operators will "automatically" be defined, but a THE_D operator won't be. Partly for such reasons, let's assume until further notice that we do go with the *A* – *B* – *C* – *D* possrep despite the redundancy,[28] and let's see what some of the implications of that decision might be.

"Updating a Parallelogram"

To repeat, choosing the *A* – *B* – *C* – *D* possrep has the obvious advantage that all four operators THE_A, THE_B, THE_C, and THE_D are available. But what about the corresponding pseudovariables? Well, it should be obvious that any attempt to "update a parallelogram" via just one of the four pseudovariables will necessarily fail. Why? Because if it didn't, the result wouldn't be a parallelogram any longer (unless the update was a "no op," I suppose). On the face of it, then, any such updating would seem to require some kind of multiple assignment. For example, let P be a variable of declared type PARALLELOGRAM, and let *p* be the current value of P. Now suppose we want to update P in such a way that, after the update, P contains a parallelogram obtained from *p* by extending side *AB* by one unit of length at the "*B*" end and simultaneously extending side *DC* by one unit of length at the "*C*" end (thereby ensuring that the result is still a parallelogram as such). So we might try a multiple assignment looking something like this:

```
THE_B ( P ) := SHIFT ( THE_B ( P ) ) ,  /* warning -   */
THE_C ( P ) := SHIFT ( THE_C ( P ) ) ;  /* invalid !!! */
```

I'm assuming for the sake of the example that SHIFT is a read-only operator that does whatever's necessary to "shift" its point argument as

---

[28] Actually *The Third Manifesto* would prohibit such a choice. See Appendix A, RM Prescription 5, part b.

required (more precisely, to return the point that marks the position that would be reached if its point argument had been so shifted; note that, to repeat, SHIFT is a read-only operator, not an update operator).

However, observe that the individual assignments in the foregoing multiple assignment both have the same target variable. According to the discussion of such matters in the answer to Exercise 10, therefore, the assignment overall is shorthand for the following:

```
P :=
WITH ( P := PARALLELOGRAM ( THE_A ( P ) ,
                            SHIFT ( THE_B ( P ) ) ,
                            THE_C ( P ) ,
                            THE_D ( P ) ) ) :
            PARALLELOGRAM ( THE_A ( P ) ,
                            THE_B ( P ) ) ,
                            SHIFT ( THE_C ( P ) ) ,
                            THE_D ( P ) ) ;
```

But now there's another problem! Here again is the first of the two foregoing PARALLELOGRAM selector invocations (i.e., the one inside the WITH specification):

```
PARALLELOGRAM ( THE_A ( P ) ,
                SHIFT ( THE_B ( P ) ) ,
                THE_C ( P ) ,
                THE_D ( P ) )
```

And this invocation will clearly fail (more precisely, the pertinent type constraint check will fail)—because if it didn't, whatever it returned certainly wouldn't be a parallelogram, because it would violate the constraint on parallelograms that sides *AB* and *DC* are supposed to be of equal length. *Note:* Perhaps I shoud remind you that (for good reason!) type constraints are checked on selector invocations, not "at semicolons."

In order to get around this problem, what we need to do is perform the entire update en bloc, using a single assignment and an explicit selector invocation instead of a multiple assignment and pseudovariables:

```
P := PARALLELOGRAM ( THE_A ( P ) ,
                     SHIFT ( THE_B ( P ) ) ,
                     SHIFT ( THE_C ( P ) ) ,
                     THE_D ( P ) ) ;
```

What this example shows is that if we do go for the $A - B - C - D$ possrep, then we probably won't be able to make much use of THE_A (etc.) as pseudovariables at all!—a state of affairs that tends to suggest that choosing such a possrep wasn't a very good idea in the first place. In other words, it's probably a good idea (in general, I mean, not just in this example) to choose a possrep in which the components are all independent of one another. For example, if we choose the $A - B - C$ possrep, we can at least still use THE_A, THE_B, and THE_C as pseudovariables, even if we can't use THE_D any longer. To be definite, therefore, let's assume the $A - B - C$ possrep specifically.

For the record, the foregoing update now simplifies to:

```
P := PARALLELOGRAM ( THE_A ( P ) ,
                     SHIFT ( THE_B ( P ) ) ,
                     SHIFT ( THE_C ( P ) ) ) ;
```

Resolving Ambiguities

Even with the $A - B - C$ possrep, though, there's still a problem: viz., which vertex is which? Let me elaborate. Let X, Y, and Z be any three noncollinear points. At first sight, then, it might seem that any permutation of X, Y, and Z could be used as the arguments corresponding to A, B, and C, respectively, in an invocation of the PARALLELOGRAM selector, and the result produced would be the same parallelogram—call it p—in every case. But then what would the value of, say, THE_A(p) be? What this thought experiment shows is that choosing $A - B - C$ as a possrep isn't sufficient in itself; we also need a way of saying which of A, B, and C is which.

Well, actually the foregoing paragraph doesn't quite state the problem accurately (nor is the problem quite as bad as that paragraph might suggest). Whichever three vertices we choose, it must be the case that two of them are opposite one another, in the sense that they're the terminal points of a diagonal. To be definite, let's agree that A and C are the opposite ones—so AC is a diagonal and not a side—and hence that B is the odd one out, as it were; in other words, let's require that the argument corresponding to parameter B always be that "odd one out." So now we need to find a way of distinguishing between the A and C vertices. The following will do the trick. Let V_1 and V_2 be the A and C vertices (not necessarily in that order), and let their cartesian coordinates be (x_1,y_1) and (x_2,y_2), respectively. Then:

■ If $x_1 = x_2$, then let A be that one of V_1 and V_2 with the smaller y coordinate.

■ Otherwise, let A be that one of V_1 and V_2 with the smaller x coordinate.

Of course, all I've done here is define a simple ordering according to which, given any two distinct points, one of those points is first with respect to that ordering and the other is second.

But we're still not done!—we've pinned down A and C precisely, but there are still two choices for B, one on either side of the AC diagonal. So here I'll appeal to the mathematical result that says that the point with cartesian coordinates (x,y) is on one side of diagonal AC if it makes the expression

$$(x_2 - x_1) (y - y_1) - (y_2 - y_1) (x - x_1)$$

positive, and on the other side if it makes that same expression negative.[29] Let's take B to be the vertex that makes it positive. Then the final version of the PARALLELOGRAM type definition looks like this:

```
TYPE PARALLELOGRAM    /* third and final attempt */
    POSSREP ( A POINT , B POINT , C POINT )
    CONSTRAINT NOT COLLINEAR ( A , B , C ) AND WITH
      ( X1 := THE_X ( A ) , Y1 := THE_Y ( A ) ,
        X  := THE_X ( B ) , Y  := THE_Y ( B ) ,
        X2 := THE_X ( C ) , Y2 := THE_Y ( C ) ) :
    IF X1 = X2 THEN Y1 < Y2 ELSE X1 < X2 END IF AND
      ( X2 - X1 ) × ( Y - Y1 ) > ( Y2 - Y1 ) × ( X - X1 ) ;
```

More Possreps

I said earlier that there were many different ways of possibly representing the parallelogram p. I've considered a few such possreps (or would-be possreps, I should say, because only the final one really does the job) in some detail, but here in outline are several more:

■ We could use any two adjacent vertices (A and B, say) and the center E. There are four possible choices for the pair of adjacent vertices.

---

[29] Drawing a diagram might help you understand why this is so.

- We could use any two adjacent sides (*AB* and *BC*, say). There are four possible choices for the pair of adjacent sides.

- We could use a pair of opposite sides (*AB* and *DC*, say). There are two choices here.

- We could use the diagonals *AC* and *BD*.

- We could use a pair of adjacent half-diagonals (*EA* and *EB*, say). Four choices here.

- We could use one vertex, the interior angle at that vertex, and the lengths of the sides that meet at that vertex (for example, the point *A*, the angle *DAB*, and the lengths of sides *AB* and *AD*). Four choices. (Or is it eight?)

And so on, probably. *Subsidiary exercise:* What type constraints would be required in each of the foregoing cases?

Operators

Here now are definitions (some just in outline) for a set of operators—all of them read-only—that would surely prove useful in practice in connection with parallelograms. Note that several of these definitions make use of type LINESEG ("line segment"), which was defined in the body of the chapter thus:

```
TYPE LINESEG POSSREP ( BEGIN POINT , END POINT ) ;
```

Now to the operators as such. The first few just return the sides of a parallelogram as line segments (note that, e.g., *AB* and *BA* are the same side but distinct line segments—why, exactly?):

```
OPERATOR AB ( P PARALLELOGRAM ) RETURNS LINESEG ;
   RETURN ( LINESEG ( THE_A ( P ) , THE_B ( P ) ) ) ;
END OPERATOR ;

OPERATOR BA ( P PARALLELOGRAM ) RETURNS LINESEG ;
   RETURN ( LINESEG ( THE_B ( P ) , THE_A ( P ) ) ) ;
END OPERATOR ;
```

Similarly for operators BC and CB, of course (I'll skip the details). But CD and DC, and AD and DA, all involve vertex *D*, and of course we don't have a corresponding THE_D operator. Now, we can define an operator that provides the functionality—at least the read-only functionality—of such a hypothetical "THE_D" operator, but I don't think it would be a good idea to call it THE_D as such. Let's call it DVX instead ("*D* vertex"):

```
OPERATOR DVX ( P PARALLELOGRAM ) RETURNS POINT ;
   RETURN ( expression denoting vertex D ) ;
END OPERATOR ;
```

Now I can define CD and DC:

```
OPERATOR CD ( P PARALLELOGRAM ) RETURNS LINESEG ;
   RETURN ( LINESEG ( THE_C ( P ) , DVX ( P ) ) ) ;
END OPERATOR ;

OPERATOR DC ( P PARALLELOGRAM ) RETURNS LINESEG ;
   RETURN ( LINESEG ( DVX ( P ) , THE_C ( P ) ) ) ;
END OPERATOR ;
```

And similarly for AD and DA, of course (again I'll skip the details).

Now let's do for the diagonals the same kind of thing we've just done for the sides—i.e., define operators that return the corresponding line segments:

```
OPERATOR AC ( P PARALLELOGRAM ) RETURNS LINESEG ;
   RETURN ( LINESEG ( THE_A ( P ) , THE_C ( P ) ) ) ;
END OPERATOR ;

OPERATOR CA ( P PARALLELOGRAM ) RETURNS LINESEG ;
   RETURN ( LINESEG ( THE_C ( P ) , THE_A ( P ) ) ) ;
END OPERATOR ;

OPERATOR BD ( P PARALLELOGRAM ) RETURNS LINESEG ;
   RETURN ( LINESEG ( THE_B ( P ) , DVX ( P ) ) ) ;
END OPERATOR ;

OPERATOR DB ( P PARALLELOGRAM ) RETURNS LINESEG ;
   RETURN ( LINESEG ( DVX ( P ) , THE_B ( P ) ) ) ;
END OPERATOR ;
```

Now, we're probably going to need to work with the actual lengths of these various sides and diagonals from time to time. To that end, let me define an auxiliary operator (LEN) that returns the length of an arbitrary line segment:

```
OPERATOR LEN ( LSG LINESEG ) RETURNS LENGTH ;
   RETURN ( DIST ( THE_BEGIN ( LSG ) ,
                   THE_END ( LSG ) ) ) ;
END OPERATOR ;
```

Hence:

```
OPERATOR LS ( P PARALLELOGRAM ) RETURNS LENGTH ;
   /* "length of long side of" */
   RETURN ( MAX { LEN ( AB ( P ) ) , LEN ( BC ( P ) ) } ) ;
END OPERATOR ;

OPERATOR SS ( P PARALLELOGRAM ) RETURNS LENGTH ;
   /* "length of short side of" */
   RETURN ( MIN { LEN ( AB ( P ) ) , LEN ( BC ( P ) ) } ) ;
END OPERATOR ;

OPERATOR LD ( P PARALLELOGRAM ) RETURNS LENGTH ;
   /* "length of long diagonal of" */
   RETURN ( MAX { LEN ( AC ( P ) ) , LEN ( BD ( P ) ) } ) ;
END OPERATOR ;

OPERATOR SD ( P PARALLELOGRAM ) RETURNS LENGTH ;
   /* "length of short diagonal of" */
   RETURN ( MIN { LEN ( AC ( P ) ) , LEN ( BD ( P ) ) } ) ;
END OPERATOR ;
```

Next I'll define some operators to return the interior angles at the vertices of a given parallelogram:

```
OPERATOR DAB ( P PARALLELOGRAM )
                         SYNONYMS { BAD , BCD , DCB }
   RETURNS ANGLE ;
   RETURN ( WITH LAB := LEN ( AB ( P ) ) ,
                 LAD := LEN ( AD ( P ) ) ,
                 LDB := LEN ( DB ( P ) ) ) :
      ARCCOS ( ( LAB ^ 2 + LAD ^ 2 - LDB ^ 2 )
                         / ( 2 × LAB × LAD ) ) ;
END OPERATOR ;
```

Operator DAB returns the interior angle at vertex *A*. Note the SYNONYMS specification, which defines some alternative names for that same operator.

(More precisely, BAD really is that same operator; BCD and DCB ought by rights to return the interior angle at vertex *C*, not *A*, but of course the interior angles at *C* and *A* are equal.) ABC is similar:

```
OPERATOR ABC ( P PARALLELOGRAM )
                        SYNONYMS { CBA , ADC , CDA }
    RETURNS ANGLE ;
    RETURN ( WITH LBA := LEN ( BA ( P ) ) ,
                  LBC := LEN ( BC ( P ) ) ,
                  LAC := LEN ( AC ( P ) ) ) :
       ARCCOS ( ( LBA ^ 2 + LBC ^ 2 - LAC ^ 2 )
                            / ( 2 × LBA × LBC ) ) ;
END OPERATOR ;
```

A couple of obvious further operators:

```
OPERATOR AREA_OF ( P PARALLELOGRAM ) RETURNS AREA ;
    /* "area of" */
    RETURN ( expression denoting area of P ) ;
END OPERATOR ;

OPERATOR CTR_OF ( P PARALLELOGRAM ) SYNONYMS { CTR }
                                    RETURNS POINT ;
    /* "center of" */
    RETURN ( expression denoting center E of P ) ;
END OPERATOR ;
```

Well, there's obviously a great deal more that could be said in connection with this example, but I think I've given you quite enough to chew on, so I'll stop.

Chapter 5

Types in SQL:

A Closer Look

This chapter consists primarily of a detailed treatment of SQL's support for user defined types. As usual, however, I have nothing to say regarding aspects of that support that have to do with type inheritance (apart from a few unavoidable brief mentions here and there). Here repeated from Chapter 3 is the—or at least a—pertinent formal reference ("SQL:2011")

> International Organization for Standardization (ISO): *Database Language SQL*, Document ISO/IEC 9075:2008 (2011)

User defined types were introduced in the 1999 version of the standard ("SQL:1999").[1] The following books taken in combination provide an extensive description of that version:

> Jim Melton and Alan R. Simon: *SQL:1999—Understanding Relational Components* (Morgan Kaufmann, 2002)

> Jim Melton: *Advanced SQL:1999—Understanding Object-Relational and Other Advanced Features* (Morgan Kaufmann, 2003)

As a matter of fact, these two books are the only publications I know of, apart from the standard itself (which, I feel bound to observe, isn't exactly a model of clarity), that deal with SQL:1999—or indeed with any other version of

---

[1] SQL:1999 was actually the fourth version of the standard; earlier versions appeared in 1987, 1989, and 1992, and also (but only in the U.S.) 1986—but SQL/86, as it was known at the time, subsequently became the first or 1987 version of the international standard as such. *Note:* Since my concern in this book is primarily with concepts, I'll limit my attention in this chapter—most of the time, at any rate—to the pertinent SQL features as described in the original 1999 version of the standard. Be aware, though, that numerous further versions have appeared since 1999: viz., SQL:2003; SQL:2006; SQL:2008; SQL:2011; SQL:2016; and SQL:2023 (the most recent version at the time of writing).

the standard more recent than SQL:1992, come to that. In fact, the second of those books is the only one I know of that deals with SQL's "object oriented" aspects at all, and for that reason I'll be appealing to it from time to time in what follows. I'll refer to it as just "Melton" for short. *Note:* I should add that Jim Melton has strong credentials in this area, since he has been, for many years now, the editor of all parts of the official SQL standard.

I turn now to technical matters. Well, the first thing I need to do is warn you of something: namely, that *user defined type support in SQL doesn't correspond in any neat and tidy way to user defined type support in general as described in the previous chapter*. Instead, it involves a large number of new and rather different concepts—concepts that seem, in some cases at least, not to have been as carefully thought out as they might have been, or in my opinion should have been. As a result, I suspect you might find this chapter rather tough going in places. If so, then I apologize. However, I don't accept full responsibility for such a state of affairs; the fact is, certain aspects of the material to be discussed just seem to be innately quite complex. What's more, it's hard to see just why those complexities are there, at least in some cases.

With that warning out of the way, I can now tell you that SQL supports two kinds of user defined types, *DISTINCT* types and *structured* types, both of which are defined by means of a new statement, CREATE TYPE. (I depart from the style of the standard here in setting the word "DISTINCT," in the phrase "DISTINCT type(s)," in all caps, in order to stress the fact that it's being used in a very specialized sense.) To elaborate briefly:

■ DISTINCT types are scalar types, and I'll discuss them first.

■ As for structured types, they can be regarded as either scalar or nonscalar, depending on context. At least, that's the official story—but I don't really believe it; as far as I can see, there's essentially no context in which a structured type behaves as if it were truly scalar. In fact, structured types in general seem to me much more to resemble *tuple* types (as described in the previous chapter), but with this one big difference:

    a. In **Tutorial D**, if *T* is a tuple type, then *T* has a name of the form TUPLE *H*, where *H* is the pertinent heading.

    b. But in SQL, if *T* is a structured type, then *T* has a separate name of its own, quite separate and distinct from the corresponding heading *H*—

or, rather, separate and distinct from what might be regarded as SQL's counterpart to that heading *H*.

In what follows I'll limit my attention to DISTINCT types specifically until further notice.

DEFINING A DISTINCT TYPE

I'll begin with an example, an SQL definition for weights as a DISTINCT type:

```
CREATE TYPE WEIGHT AS DECIMAL(4,1) FINAL ;
```

(You'll recall that, prior to this point, weights in the SQL version of our running example have been just simple numeric values—actually values of type DECIMAL (4,1). In the relational version, by contrast, they've always been of a user defined type.)

The first thing to note about the example, then, is that even though it's indeed a DISTINCT type definition, "DISTINCT" (perhaps a little confusingly) does *not* appear as a keyword anywhere in that definition. Ths state of affairs notwithstanding, the example does at least illustrate the syntax for defining a DISTINCT type, which—in its simplest form, at any rate (i.e., ignoring various optional features)—looks like this:

```
CREATE TYPE <type name> AS <underlying type name> FINAL ;
```

To elaborate: First, the *<underlying type name>* is the name of a system defined scalar type, and it defines the representation of values of the DISTINCT type in question. But note the qualifiers *system defined* and *scalar* in that sentence!—DISTINCT types can't be defined in terms of either user defined types or nonscalar types.[2] Note carefully too that the representation in question is the *actual* (i.e., *physical*) representation, not just some possible representation. In fact, SQL doesn't really support any kind of "possrep" notion at all.

Second, FINAL means that this type can't have any proper subtypes. DISTINCT types are required to be "final" in this sense (and so FINAL is

---

[2] Of course, the qualifier *system defined* raises an obvious question in itself—namely, what exactly *is* a system defined type anyway, in SQL? See the section "Scalar Types" (especially the subsection "A Remark on Numeric Types") in Chapter 3 for further discussion.

assumed anyway if it isn't stated explicitly). They can't have any proper supertypes, either. *Note:* I mention these points for completeness. In general, of course, I'm trying to say as little as possible regarding type inheritance in this book anyway.

Third (*important!*), note that CREATE TYPE includes nothing analogous to **Tutorial D**'s CONSTRAINT specification. Which is to say, *SQL doesn't support type constraints*[3]—apart from the obvious but implicit constraint that values of the type in question must be representable in terms of the underlying type in question. In the case of type WEIGHT, for example, there's no way to specify in the pertinent CREATE TYPE statement that, for any given WEIGHT value, the corresponding DECIMAL (4,1) value must be greater than zero and less than 500, say. Rather, *every* value of type DECIMAL (4,1)—even if it's less than or equal to zero, or greater than or equal to 500—corresponds to some unique WEIGHT value, and *every* WEIGHT value corresponds to some unique DECIMAL (4,1) value. There's a one to one correspondence between them. Note in particular, therefore, that even negative weights are apparently legitimate, in SQL (!).

> *Aside:* Given the foregoing consequences—to my mind, the truly bizarre consequences—of not supporting type constraints, I'm sure you're wondering *why* they're not supported . It seems like such an obvious omission, doesn't it! Unfortunately, the reason for the omission is rather complicated; at the same time, it doesn't have much to do with the major topic of the present book, so I don't to want to get too sidetracked. Suffice it to say, then, that:
>
> a. The reason for the omission is a direct consequence of SQL's approach to type inheritance.
>
> b. That approach differs from the inheritance model defined in *The Third Manifesto* in certain crucial respects. (Just to remind you from Chapter 4, *The Third Manifesto* most certainly does support type constraints, whether or not inheritance is in effect.)

---

[3] I'm talking here about DISTINCT types specifically, of course—but in fact a precisely analogous criticism applies to structured types also (see later in this chapter).

c. On the other hand, SQL's approach does conform, more or less, to the approach typically found in object oriented languages. In other words, OO languages suffer from the same kinds of problems in this connection—negative weights, etc.—as SQL does, and they do so for essentially the same reason.

d. The reason why the SQL and OO approaches are the way they are has to do with what I regard as a very fundamental flaw: namely, the heavy reliance in both cases on *pointers*. Of course, pointers are prohibited in the relational world—but they're supported by SQL (also by OO in general), as we'll see later in this chapter—and that, to repeat, is the root of the problem. nonsquare

The foregoing state of affairs is discussed at length, and carefully analyzed, in Chapter 13 ("The S by C Controversy") of my book *Type Inheritance and Relational Theory* (O'Reilly, 2016), and I refer you to that book for a more detailed explanation. Here I'll just note that, although SQL doesn't support type constraints as such, it does at least support database constraints; so we can avoid problems like negative weights by specifying an explicit database constraint, repeatedly, for each and every variable, each and every column, and each and every field[4] that's defined to be of the pertinent type (type WEIGHT, in the example). In other words, SQL does at least provide a workaround, albeit one that's likely to require a great deal of extra definitional work on the part of the user. *End of aside.*

DISTINCT TYPES: SELECTORS AND THE_ OPERATORS

As I said in Chapter 2, types without operators are useless; so what operators apply to values and variables of a DISTINCT type? Well, first of all, selectors and THE_ operators are supported (not by those names, however). For example, let type WEIGHT be as defined in the previous section—

---

[4] Recall from Chapter 3 that *fields* in SQL are either (a) components of a row type *R* that's defined by means of SQL's ROW type generator or (b) components of a row *r* that's a value of such a row type *R*.

```
CREATE TYPE WEIGHT AS DECIMAL(4,1) FINAL ;
```

—and let DW ("decimal weight") be a local SQL variable, with definition as follows:

```
DECLARE DW DECIMAL(4,1) ;
```

Then:

- The expression

```
WEIGHT ( DW )
```

returns the corresponding weight value ("selector functionality").

- And if WT is an SQL variable of declared type WEIGHT—

```
DECLARE WT WEIGHT ;
```

—then the expression

```
DECIMAL ( WT )
```

returns the corresponding DECIMAL (4,1) value ("THE_ operator functionality"). *Note:* A similar remark applies not just to SQL variables as such but also to columns of SQL tables and fields of SQL rows.

So if we were to define column WEIGHT in table P in the suppliers and parts database (SQL version) to be of type WEIGHT instead of DECIMAL (4,1), then the following would be a valid SQL SELECT expression:

```
SELECT PNO ,
       DECIMAL ( WEIGHT ) AS DECWT
       /* "THE_ operator functionality" */
FROM   P
WHERE  WEIGHT >
       WEIGHT ( DW )
       /* "selector functionality" */
```

And the following would be a valid SQL DELETE statement:

```
DELETE
FROM    P
WHERE   WEIGHT = WEIGHT ( 14.7 ) ;
                 /* "selector functionality" */
```

(The expression WEIGHT (14.7) in this latter example is effectively a WEIGHT literal, though SQL doesn't use such terminology.)

I'll continue to assume throughout the rest of this chapter that column WEIGHT in table P in the suppliers and parts database (SQL version) has been defined to be of type WEIGHT instead of (as originally) type DECIMAL (4,1), barring explicit statements to the contrary.

Now, since the representation (the "underlying type," that is) for any given DISTINCT type always has, and indeed has to have, exactly one component, the corresponding "selectors" and "THE_ operators" are really nothing more than simple type conversion operators, or CASTs—and as a matter of fact explicit CASTs can be used in their place. The CAST operators in question are system defined (that is, creating DISTINCT type *DT* with underlying type *UT* automatically causes the system to create operators for casting from *DT* to *UT* and vice versa). Thus, for example,

```
CAST ( DW AS WEIGHT )
```

could be used instead of, and is logically equivalent to,

```
WEIGHT ( DW )
```

Similarly,

```
CAST ( WT AS DECIMAL(4,1) )   or just   CAST ( WT AS DECIMAL )
```

could be used instead of, and is logically equivalent to,

```
DECIMAL ( WT )
```

Also, if DT_1 and DT_2 are distinct DISTINCT types (if you see what I mean), then explicit CASTs can be defined if desired—and so long as such operations make sense, of course—for mapping between values of type DT_1 and values of type DT_2.

DISTINCT TYPES: STRONG TYPING

With one important exception (see below), strong typing does apply to DISTINCT types. One immediate consequence of this state of affairs is that comparisons between values of a DISTINCT type and values of the underlying representation type are illegal. For example, the following are *not* valid, even if (as before) the SQL variable DW in the first example is of type DECIMAL (4,1):

```
SELECT PNO , DECIMAL ( WEIGHT ) AS DECWT
FROM    P
WHERE   WEIGHT > DW                /* warning: illegal! */

DELETE
FROM    P
WHERE   WEIGHT = 14.7 ;            /* warning: illegal! */
```

For similar reasons, comparisons between values of distinct DISTINCT types are also not legal, even if the types in question have the same underlying representation type. For example, let DISTINCT types DT1 and DT2 be defined as follows—

```
CREATE TYPE DT1 AS DECIMAL(4,1) FINAL ;
CREATE TYPE DT2 AS DECIMAL(4,1) FINAL ;
```

—and let variables V1 and V2 be defined as follows:

```
DECLARE V1 DT1 ;
DECLARE V2 DT2 ;
```

Then the comparison

```
V1 = V2
```

will fail on a type error.

The one exception to the foregoing has to do with assignment operations. For example, suppose we want to retrieve some WEIGHT value into the variable DW. If that variable is declared as before to be of type DECIMAL (4,1), then some type conversion clearly has to occur. Now, we can certainly perform that conversion explicitly, as here:

```
SELECT  DECIMAL ( WEIGHT )
INTO    DW
FROM    P
WHERE   PNO = 'P1' ;
```

(Note the semicolon—the INTO makes this a statement, not just an expression.) However, the following is also legal, and an appropriate coercion will occur:

```
SELECT  WEIGHT /* instead of DECIMAL(WEIGHT) */
INTO    DW
FROM    P
WHERE   PNO = 'P1' ;
```

Coercions in the opposite direction are legal as well. For example:

```
UPDATE  P
SET     WEIGHT = 19.0 /* instead of WEIGHT = WEIGHT(19.0) */
WHERE   PNO = 'P4' ;
```

Please note, however, that (to say it again) assignment as such is the *only* exception to the strong typing rule. In particular, if operator *Op* has a parameter *P* of declared type WEIGHT, then (at least according to my reading of the standard) invoking *Op* with an argument *A* corresponding to *P* of declared type DECIMAL (4,1) won't work—despite the fact that such an invocation might be thought of, informally, as causing *A* to be assigned to *P*, and therefore legitimate according to the foregoing discussion.

DISTINCT TYPES: METHODS

So far we've covered the following operators in connection with DISTINCT types: selectors, THE_ operators, comparisons, and assignments. But further operators can be defined as required, of course. However, SQL doesn't call them operators, it calls them *routines*, and there are three kinds: *functions*, *procedures*, and *methods*.[5] Now, functions and procedures correspond very roughly to what in previous chapters I've been calling read-only and update operators, respectively. As for methods, they can be regarded as functions too,[6] but

---

[5] I note for the record that functions and procedures were first introduced as an extension to SQL:1992, as part of the "Persistent Stored Modules" feature (PSM).

[6] Well, that's the official story—but methods, like procedures but unlike true functions, are allowed to update their arguments.

functions that are tightly associated (as regular functions aren't) with some specific type—necessarily a user defined type[7]—and they're invoked using a different syntactic style, as we'll see..

Most of the present section has to do with methods specifically. But before I get to methods as such, let me give an example of a function as such (i.e., one that's not a method). The function is called ADDWT ("add weights"), and it allows two WEIGHT values to be added together and returns another WEIGHT value as a result. Here's the definition (a CREATE FUNCTION statement):

```
CREATE FUNCTION ADDWT ( W1 WEIGHT , W2 WEIGHT )
                                    RETURNS WEIGHT
   RETURN ( WEIGHT ( DECIMAL ( W1 ) + DECIMAL ( W2 ) ) ) ;
```

Again let WT be an SQL variable of type WEIGHT. Given the foregoing definition, then, all of the following are legal expressions, and they're all of type WEIGHT:

```
ADDWT ( WT , WT )
ADDWT ( WT , WEIGHT ( 14.7 ) )
ADDWT ( WEIGHT ( 14.7 ) , WT )
ADDWT ( WEIGHT ( 14.7 ) , WEIGHT ( 3.0 ) )
```

Note, however, that the following

```
ADDWT ( WT , 14.7 )
```

and

```
ADDWT ( 14.7 , WT )
```

are *not* legal expressions (why not, exactly?). However, we could make them legal by defining two further ADDWT functions (thereby overloading the name ADDWT, observe), one taking a WEIGHT parameter and a DECIMAL (4,1) parameter in that order, and the other taking a DECIMAL (4,1) parameter and a WEIGHT parameter in *that* order. I'll leave the details as an exercise.

---

[7] Note this point carefully! One implication is that what SQL calls the *subject parameter* (and any corresponding subject argument)—see further discussion below—must necessarily be of some user defined type. But the user defined type in question can be either a DISTINCT type or a structured type.

The remainder of this section is concerned with methods specifically. I'll begin with a definition, based on one in my book *The New Relational Database Dictionary*, O'Reilly, 2016):

> **Definition (method):** A term, much used in OO contexts in particular, to mean either (a) an operator as such or (b) an implementation version of such an operator. Note that the first of these meanings has to do with the model, while (obviously rnough) the second has to do with implementation.

Note: The term *method* is sanctioned by usage—at least in the OO world—but really doesn't seem very appropriate. *Chambers Dictionary* defines the word thus: *the mode or rule used in carrying out a task or accomplishing an aim.* I don't see how an operator can be a "mode or rule." Nor are matters improved by the fact that the two technical meanings are often confused anyway; that is, confusion between the two realms (model vs. implementation) is, I'm sorry to say, not uncommon in the OO world. In fact, it's quite usual to find the term used with both meanings in the same text, or even in the same sentence. Here's an example:

> The attributes[8] associated with an object are private, and only an object's methods may examine or update these data; the methods are public.

This quote is from *Object Data Management*, by R. G. G. Cattell (Addison-Wesley, 1991), page 105. To elaborate briefly: In the phrase "only an object's methods may examine or update these data," the term *methods* refers to the implementation; in the phrase "methods are public" it refers to the model.

However, if we overlook the foregoing terminological inexactitudes (as Winston Churchill might have described them), we see that *method* is basically, as I've claimed, nothing but an OO term for operator. Indeed, methods were added to SQL in 1999, along with user defined types, as part of an explicit attempt to make SQL more "object like." Here's a quote from Melton (page 113):

> SQL's object facilities were quite consciously designed to be similar to Java's.

---

[8] The term *attributes* here is to be understood generically, not in the specialized sense in which it's used in a relational context.

Though I think it's telling that in his very next paragraph Melton goes on to say this (page 113, italics in the original):

> It's somewhat unclear in the SQL standard exactly what an object *is*.

Anyway, let's get back to the operator ADDWT as discussed above. Suppose now that we want to use a method instead of a conventional function to provide ADDWT functionality. Now, just why we might want to do such a thing is far from clear—I mean, the advantages of methods over conventional functions aren't exactly obvious—but let's assume we do have a good reason. In order to avoid confusion with ADDWT as defined above, then (i.e., via CREATE FUNCTION), let's agree to call that method MADDWT ("method [to] add weights"). So what we have to do is this. First, we extend the definition of type WEIGHT to add an appropriate method *signature*, thus:

```
CREATE TYPE WEIGHT AS DECIMAL(4,1) FINAL
          METHOD MADDWT ( W2 WEIGHT ) RETURNS WEIGHT ;
```

In general, a signature in SQL looks like this:

```
METHOD <method name>
          ( <parameter def commalist> )
                    RETURNS <result type name>
```

Here for the record is the standard's own definition of the term:

> [A signature consists of the] name of an SQL-invoked routine,[9] the position and declared type of each of its SQL parameters, and an indication of whether it is an SQL-invoked function or an SQL-invoked procedure.

Note: The foregoing is indeed the standard's own definition, but subsequent uses of the term (in the standard as such, I mean) and SQL's own syntax rules both seem to suggest that the type of the result is part of the signature too. What definitely, and perhaps a little surprisingly, appears *not* to be part of the signature is any indication as to which parameters if any are subject to update.

In the example, then, the signature is the text between the keyword FINAL and the semicolon—

---

[9] Functions, procedures, and methods are referred to generically in the standard as "SQL-invoked routines."

```
METHOD MADDWT ( W2 WEIGHT ) RETURNS WEIGHT
```

—and so W2 in particular is a parameter to the MADDWT method. In fact, it corresponds directly to the second parameter, also called W2, in the function version of ADDWT as previously discussed. So what happened to the first parameter, W1? Well, I'll get to that.

So now we've defined the signature, but of course we must also define the method as such (the implementation code, that is; note the specification FOR WEIGHT in particular):

```
CREATE METHOD MADDWT ( W2 WEIGHT ) RETURNS WEIGHT
      FOR WEIGHT
      RETURN ( WEIGHT ( DECIMAL ( SELF ) +
                         DECIMAL ( W2 ) ) ) ;
```

Methods in SQL always have this kind of two-part, lockstep definition—signature in CREATE TYPE, implementation code in CREATE METHOD. Functions and procedures, by contrast, are defined more conventionally, via CREATE FUNCTION and CREATE PROCEDURE respectively—where by "more conventionally" I mean the signature and the implementation code are defined together, instead of being split across two separate statements.

Note: CREATE FUNCTION and CREATE PROCEDURE are analogous, somewhat, to CREATE METHOD. CREATE FUNCTION in particular was illustrated earlier in this section, of course. However, functions and procedures aren't tightly tied to one particular type as methods are—only methods have "FOR *<type name>*" specified as part of their definition, and only methods have their signature included in the type definition for the type identified by that specified *<type name>*.

Aside: A few comments here:

■ First of all, separating the definition of the signature from the definition of the implementation code does make some sense (and I do have some sympathy for it), inasmuch as the first is a model issue and the second is an implementation issue. On the other hand, exactly the same is true of functions and procedures—so why aren't they treated in similar fashion? (Well, I suppose the answer here is purely historical, so let's leave it at that.)

■ Second, note that the fact that the signature for a given method has to be specified as part of the pertinent type definition means that creating a new method for an existing type is slightly nontrivial, involving as it does an alteration to the definition of the type in question.

■ Third, the signature and the implementation code are both provided automatically in the important special case in which (a) the type defined in the CREATE TYPE statement in question is a structured type, not a DISTINCT type (see later in this chapter), and (b) the method in question is a constructor, an observer, or a mutator function for the type in question (again see later). *Note:* The methods referred to in part (b) of the foregoing sentence are indeed methods, despite the fact that SQL confusingly calls them functions.

■ Last (you've probably realized this already, but I want to spell it explicitly): The relationship between a given CREATE TYPE statement and the corresponding CREATE METHOD statements is one to many—a given CREATE TYPE statement corresponds to many CREATE METHOD statements, in general, whereas a given CREATE METHOD statement corresponds to exactly one CREATE TYPE statement. (CREATE TYPE identifies the corresponding methods by means of one or more METHOD clauses; CREATE METHOD identifies the corresponding type by means of the FOR clause.)

End of aside.

An important difference between methods, on the one hand, and functions and procedures on the other, is that methods are "selfish." What this means is that one parameter—SQL calls it the *subject* parameter—is singled out for special semantic treatment (see below), and hence, necessarily, special syntactic treatment also (again see below). The term *selfish method* derives in general from the fact that the subject parameter is typically unnamed and so has to be referenced within the method's implementation code in some ad hoc way, typically by means of the keyword SELF. Both of these points apply to SQL in particular (note the appearance of the keyword SELF in the MADDWT code above). Note too that MADDWT has two parameters, but only one, the second, is explicitly named and mentioned. To be specific, it's explicitly named and mentioned in both:

a. The CREATE TYPE statement (i.e., in the signature in the pertinent METHOD clause), and

b. The CREATE METHOD statement, inside the parentheses following the operator name.

By contrast, the first parameter—the one that corresponds to the parameter W1 in the functional version, ADDWT—is the SELF parameter, and it has no name.

Note: The parentheses following the operator name, in both CREATE TYPE and CREATE METHOD, are required even if there's nothing for them to enclose (i.e., even if the method has no parameters other than the implicit subject one).

Here then is an example of a MADDWT invocation:

```
WT . MADDWT ( WEIGHT ( 14.7 ) )
```

The symbol WT here denotes the "subject argument"—the "W1 argument," that is, meaning the argument corresponding to the subject parameter. (I'm assuming here once again that WT has been declared to be an SQL variable of type WEIGHT.) MADDWT is the name of the method being invoked, of course, and WEIGHT (14.7) is the "W2 argument," meaning the argument corresponding to the explicitly defined W2 parameter. The invocation overall constitutes an expression, and it returns the result of evaluating the argument expression WT + WEIGHT (14.7).

In general, then, a MADDWT invocation takes the form

```
<first argument> . MADDWT ( <second argument> )
```

Here are some more examples (note the last one in particular, which includes a second, nested, MADDWT invocation):

```
WT . MADDWT ( WT )
WEIGHT ( 14.7 ) . MADDWT ( WT )
WEIGHT ( 14.7 ) . MADDWT ( WEIGHT ( 3.0 ) )
WZ . MADDWT ( WX . MADDWT ( WY ) )
```

So much for what I referred to above as the "special syntactic treatment" (i.e., of the subject parameter, also of the corresponding subject argument in an invocation). As for the special semantic treatment, it consists in using the type of the subject argument,[10] and that type alone, to control the binding process—that is, the process of determining, preferably at compile time, which particular piece of implementation code needs to be invoked in response to some particular method invocation. Such considerations are significant, or at least potentially significant, if the method name in question is overloaded.

Note: The idea of singling out one particular argument for special treatment as just described is fairly typical of OO languages in general. It does have the advantage of making life easier for the implementation, in that it simplifies the binding process just referred to. At the same time, however, it has several disadvantages; in particular, it can make life more difficult for the user. For a detailed discussion of such matters, I refer you to Chapter 11 ("Substitutability") of my book *Type Inheritance and Relational Theory* (O'Reilly, 2016).

Finally, a brief note on terminology: To generalize slightly from the MADDWT example, the syntax for a method invocation in SQL is basically an expression of the form

```
<subject argument exp> .
                <method name> ( <argument exp commalist> )
```

Such an expression is sometimes characterized, not as invoking a method as such, but rather as "sending a message" to the argument denoted by the *<subject argument exp>*—a message that says, in effect, "apply the method called *<method name>* to yourself, using further arguments as specified in the *<argument exp commalist>*." Some people find this alternative characterization helpful.

ENTR'ACTE

The primary aim of this chapter is, of course, to describe SQL's user defined types (i.e., its DISTINCT and structured types). Now, I've already said more or

---

[10] Actually the *most specific* type (see the answer to Exercise 2 in Chapter 4)—but that notion is really significant only for structured types, and then only in the context of type inheritance, which as I've already explained we're not much concerned with in this book.

less everything I want to say regarding DISTINCT types; however, there are a few further topics having to do with SQL's type support in general that I need to elaborate on somewhat before I can move on to structured types as such, and that's the purpose of the present section (note the title!). The topics in question are *type generators*, *row types*, and *table types*. Of course, I did touch on all of these topics in Chapter 3, but now I need to say a little more about them.

Type Generators

Tutorial D supports two type generators, TUPLE and RELATION. Well, I suppose **Tutorial D**'s TYPE statement might be regarded as a type generator as well, but (speaking a trifle loosely) types generated by an invocation of that statement are always scalar, whereas the types generated by means of TUPLE or RELATION are nonscalar. For several reasons, however, matters aren't quite so clearcut in SQL:

- First of all, there's the fact, discussed at length in Chapter 3, that several scalar built-in types in SQL (e.g., CHARACTER, FLOAT, DECIMAL) aren't really types at all but type generators. *Note:* The SQL term is *type constructors*, but I'll stay with *type generators* for consistency with earlier chapters.

- Second, SQL explicitly supports several nonscalar type generators: ROW, ARRAY, and MULTISET. Of course, there's an obvious omission here!— namely, TABLE. Now, you might be thinking we don't actually need a TABLE type generator anyway, because MULTISET and ROW in combination will take care of the requirement.[11] However, although a table might indeed be regarded as a multiset of rows—more specifically, a multiset of rows in which the rows in question are all of the same type— there are in fact some serious logical differences between the two concepts, differences that I did touch on briefly in Chapter 2. In particular, multisets of rows in SQL can't be operated upon by means of SQL's regular table operators, and so they simply aren't regular SQL tables, by definition.

- Third, SQL's CREATE TYPE statement is used to define both (a) user defined scalar types (meaning DISTINCT types specifically, as described in

---

[11] There's evidence to suggest that that was exactly what the SQL language designers thought as well.

previous sections in this chapter), and also (b) structured types, which—in my opinion, that is, though not in that of the standard—are always nonscalar (I mean, they're not "encapsulated").

■   Last, SQL also supports another scalar type generator, called REF.

Now, I've already said as much as I intend to say in this book regarding SQL's system defined scalar types, its array and multiset types, and its DISTINCT types. So that leaves (a) row and table types, (b) structured types, and (c) REF types. I'll discuss row and table types in the rest of the present section, and structured types and REF types in the rest of the chapter.

Row Types

Note: This subsection and the next are revised and considerably expanded versions of the corresponding material from Chapter 3.

Row types are SQL's analog of **Tutorial D**'s tuple types, of course. In particular, they're like **Tutorial D**'s tuple types in that they're simply available for use whenever they're needed (typically as the declared type of some row variable); they don't need to be independently defined, and in fact they can't be. For example, here's the definition of an SQL row variable called PRV ("part row variable"):

```
DECLARE PRV
       ROW ( PNO     CHAR(6)      ,
             PNAME   VARCHAR(12) ,
             COLOR   VARCHAR(10) ,
             WEIGHT  WEIGHT       ,
             CITY    VARCHAR(25) ;
```

As you can see, the type of variable PRV is indeed a row type, and the row type in question is specified by means of an invocation of the ROW type generator. What's more, that invocation is not "free standing," as it were, but instead forms part of the row variable definition in question. Let me remind you, though, that SQL refers to the components of a row type that's produced by invocation of the ROW type generator—also to the components of values and variables of such a row type—not as columns but as *fields*. In the example, therefore, the SQL row variable PRV has five fields, called PNO, PNAME, COLOR, WEIGHT, and CITY, respectively. *Note:* I'm assuming for the sake of the example, just to be definite, that (a) fields PNO, NAME, COLOR, and CITY are each of a system defined type, and (b) field WEIGHT is of a user defined type (probably a DISTINCT type), also called WEIGHT.

Next (*important!*), note that the fields that go to make up a given row type are ordered, left to right. In the case of variable PRV, for example, PNO is the first field of that variable, PNAME is the second, and so on—but in general there are $5! = 5 \times 4 \times 3 \times 2 \times 1 = 120$ different row types (!) all consisting of the same five fields. (Contrast the situation in the relational world, where, given any particular set of attributes, there's just one corresponding tuple type.)

SQL also supports row assignment. For example:

```
SET PRV = ROW ( 'P1' , 'Nut' , 'Red' ,
                         WEIGHT(12.0) , 'London' ) ;
```

The expression on the right side here is a row selector invocation (SQL would call it a *row value constructor* invocation);[12] in fact, it's a row literal, though SQL doesn't use that term. *Note:* Actually, the keyword ROW in an SQL row value constructor invocation is optional (probably because earlier versions of SQL didn't support it), and in practice is almost always omitted. Thus, the foregoing example could be simplified slightly to just:

```
SET PRV = ( 'P1' , 'Nut' , 'Red' ,
                     WEIGHT(12.0) , 'London' ) ;
```

The parentheses are required, though.

By the way, the foregoing example also illustrates the somewhat peculiar fact that, while fields within a given row type *RT* have names—and those field names are explicitly considered to be part of the type—fields within rows of type *RT don't* have such names. As a consequence, literals of that type also don't have such names; instead, they consist simply of a sequence of unnamed literals of the applicable field types. It follows that, in SQL, the very same row literal might denote a value of any number of different row types, and the intended type of such a literal can't be determined, in general, just by looking at it. (Contrast the situation with tuple types and literals in **Tutorial D**.) The full consequences of this state of affairs are unclear.

---

[12] As you'll have noticed by now, SQL uses the term *constructor* in numerous contexts. However, I have to say that, in the case at hand at any rate, the term does seem rather inappropriate, because it suggests that values don't simply exist as I claimed in Chapters 2 and 4, but rather have to be "constructed." That's one reason why, in contexts like the one under discussion at any rate, I greatly prefer the term *selector*.

Here now is a slightly more complicated example:

```
SET PRV = ( P WHERE PNO = 'P1' ) ;
```

In this case the expression on the right side isn't a row selector invocation, it's a *row subquery*—i.e., it's an SQL table expression in parentheses that's acting as a row expression. Simplifying slightly, the table *t* returned by that table expression is required to contain exactly one row *r*; so long as it does so, *t* is coerced to *r*, and *r* is then assigned to the row variable referenced on the left side.[13] A **Tutorial D** analog of the foregoing assignment would look like this (note the explicit extraction here of the pertinent tuple from the single-tuple relation containing it):

```
PRV := TUPLE FROM ( P WHERE PNO = 'P1' ) ;
```

But SQL has no explicit "ROW FROM" counterpart, as such, to **Tutorial D**'s TUPLE FROM operator.

Row assignments are also involved, implicitly, in SQL UPDATE statements.

I turn now to row equality comparisons.[14] Here's a simple example:

```
PRV = ( 'P1' , 'Nut' , 'Red' ,   WEIGHT(12.0) , 'London' )
```

By way of another example, consider the following SELECT expression, which contains an explicit row equality comparison in the WHERE clause:

```
SELECT PNO
FROM   P
WHERE  ( COLOR , CITY ) = ( 'Red' , 'London' )
```

This SELECT expression is logically equivalent to the following:

```
SELECT PNO
FROM   P
WHERE  COLOR = 'Red' AND CITY = 'London'
```

---

[13] As explained in Chapter 3, it's an error if *t* contains more than one row—but it's not an error if *t* contains no rows at all! In that case, *t* is treated as if it contained exactly one row, viz., a row of all nulls.

[14] I remind you that row comparisons in SQL actually permit, not just equality sd duvh, but all six of the usual comparison operators. See the answer to Exercise 8 in Chapter 3 for a detailed discussion of such matters.

I'll give one more example, in order to illustrate another point. Consider the following CREATE TABLE statement:

```
CREATE TABLE NADDR
     ( NAME VARCHAR(25) NOT NULL ,
       ADDR ROW ( STREET CHAR(50) ,
                  CITY   VARCHAR(25) ,
                  STATE  CHAR(2) ,
                  ZIP    CHAR(5) ) NOT NULL ,
       UNIQUE ( NAME ) ) ;
```

Observe that column ADDR of this table (i.e., table NADDR) is defined to be of a certain row type, with fields STREET, CITY, STATE, and ZIP. (In general, of course, fields of a given row type can be of any type whatsoever, including other row types in particular.) References to such fields make use of dot qualification as illustrated in the following retrieval example (the syntax is *<exp>.<field name>*, where *<exp>* is a row expression and *<field name>* is the name of a field of the row type of that expression):

```
SELECT NT.NAME
FROM   NADDR AS NT
WHERE  NT.ADDR.STATE = 'CA'
```

NT here is an example of what SQL calls a *correlation name*. For technical reasons, having to do with avoiding a certain syntactic ambiguity that might otherwise occur, SQL requires explicit correlation name qualifiers to be used in field references like the one in the example (NT.ADDR.STATE).[15]

Here by contrast is an update example:

```
UPDATE NADDR
SET    ADDR.STATE = 'VT'
WHERE  NAME = 'Joe' ;
```

Observe that this latter example doesn't use correlation names at all. (Actually the example seems to be illegal anyway, because according to the standard ADDR.STATE doesn't seem to be legal as a SET clause target. However, I presume this state of affairs is just an oversight on the part of the standard, and I choose to ignore it here.)

---

[15] In some contexts, that is, but not in others! The very next example (an UPDATE example) illustrates this point. Further details are beyond the scope of this book.

Aside: Two further points:

■ First, since a field within a row type can itself be of some row type, field references can involve lots of dots (as in, e.g., R1.F2.F3.F4.F5).

■ Second, observe that I've defined a column constraint (NOT NULL) on column ADDR in the CREATE TABLE statement for table NADDR, in order to prevent nulls from appearing as entries in the column in question. In general, however, such a constraint won't prevent nulls from appearing in *fields within* entries in the column in question. (Note that a row with nulls in some of its fields—even in all of its fields!—is correctly considered to be logically distinct from a null row, in SQL.[16]) If we want to prohibit nulls entirely, therefore, we'll have to specify a whole series of additional constraints—probably as part of the pertinent CREATE TABLE statement—along the lines of the one shown here:

```
CHECK ( ADDR.STREET IS NOT NULL )
```

What we can't do is attach NOT NULL specifications to the definitions of fields STREET, CITY, etc. as such (i.e., as part of the definition of column ADDR of table NADDR).

End of aside.

Table Types

This subsection will be quite short, because table types in SQL are like snakes in Ireland—there aren't any. That is, SQL doesn't really support the concept of a table type at all; more specifically, it doesn't support a TABLE type generator (or table type constructor, as SQL would presumably call it). In other words, it has

---

[16] This statement is an oversimplification A more accurate statement is as follows: A NOT NULL constraint on column ADDR of table NADDR will correctly ensure that no entry in that column is null. However, it will also ensure that no entry in the column has a null in every field, which is incorrect. At the same time, it *won't* prevent such an entry from having nulls in some of its fields and not in others—which is correct, but confusing, and not very useful.

nothing directly analogous to **Tutorial D**'s RELATION type generator. Of course, it does have a mechanism, CREATE TABLE, for defining what by rights should be called table variables. Here's an example (it's a CREATE TABLE analog of the DECLARE ROW example from the previous subsection):

```
CREATE TABLE P
     ( PNO    CHAR(6)     NOT NULL ,
       PNAME  VARCHAR(12) NOT NULL ,
       COLOR  VARCHAR(10) NOT NULL ,
       WEIGHT WEIGHT      NOT NULL ,
       CITY   VARCHAR(25) NOT NULL ,
       UNIQUE ( PNO ) ) ;
```

Note carefully, however, that (as I pointed out in connection with a similar example in Chapter 3), there's nothing here—no sequence of linguistic tokens—that can logically be called "an invocation of the TABLE type generator." (The truth of this statement might become more apparent when you realize that the specification UNIQUE (PNO), which defines a certain integrity constraint, doesn't have to come after the column definitions as I've shown it but can appear almost anywhere—e.g., between the definitions of columns COLOR and WEIGHT. Not to mention the NOT NULL specifications on the individual column definitions, which also define certain integrity constraints.) In fact, to the extent that the variable P can be regarded (in SQL) as having any type at all, that type is nothing more than *bag of rows*, where the rows in question have fields named, in left to right order, PNO, NAME, COLOR, WEIGHT, and CITY, of types CHAR (6), VARCHAR (12), VARCHAR (10), WEIGHT, and VARCHAR (25), respectively.

As a matter of fact, SQL's treatment of tables is really quite strange when you come to think about it. Melton (page 15) describes them, quite correctly, as "SQL's most fundamental data structure"; yet, to repeat, there's no table type generator! One consequence of this state of affairs is that no column of any table in SQL can be of a "table type"—in other words, SQL doesn't support table valued columns. (As noted in Chapters 2 and 3, it does support columns that contain values that are multisets, or *bags*, of rows, but such values aren't tables in the SQL sense—and such columns aren't table valued columns, therefore—because SQL's table operators don't apply to them.)

Further evidence that SQL doesn't really regard tables as "first class objects" is provided by the fact that it fails to provide direct support for either table assignment or table comparisons. Of course, it's true that workarounds are available for such operations[17]—but workarounds shouldn't be necessary in the first place.

Note: Despite everything I've said in this subsection so far, let me remind you that SQL does support something it calls "typed tables." I'll be discussing these in great detail in the section "Typed Tables Revisited," later in this chapter. For now, let me just note that, to repeat from Chapter 3, the term is hardly very appropriate, because if *TT* is a "typed table" that has been defined to be "of type *T*," then *TT* is in fact *not* of type *T*, and neither are its rows.

DEFINING A STRUCTURED TYPE

I turn now to structured types.[18] I'll begin by reminding you of the following definition of WEIGHT as a DISTINCT type:

```
CREATE TYPE WEIGHT AS DECIMAL(4,1) FINAL ;
```

Here for purposes of contrast and comparison is a (possible, if unlikely) definition of WEIGHT as a structured type instead:

```
CREATE TYPE WEIGHT AS ( W DECIMAL(4,1) ) FINAL ;
```

Points arising:

■ The two definitions don't exactly look very different, do they! In fact, the only thing that tells us, syntactically speaking, that we're dealing with a structured type definition and not a DISTINCT one is basically just that the specification "DECIMAL (4,1)" in the first definition has been replaced by the specification "W DECIMAL (4,1)" in parentheses in the second. Note in particular that, just as there's no "DISTINCT" keyword in a DISTINCT type definition, so there's no "STRUCTURED" keyword in a structured type definition.

---

[17] Regarding workarounds for table comparisons in particular, see the answer to Exercise 8 in Chapter 3.

[18] Which according to Melton (page 24) were originally called *abstract* types. But abstract types in general are supposed to behave as far as the user is concerned just like scalar types (i.e., they're supposed to be "encapsulated"), and as I've already indicated SQL's structured types don't do that—they behave much more like tuple types instead.

■ What comes between those parentheses in a structured type definition is, syntactically speaking, a commalist of definitions of the components, called *attributes*, that make up the "structure" of the structured type in question. (In the example, of course, there's just one such attribute.) Each attribute is named and has a declared type of its own. Note the terminology, by the way: In SQL, tables have columns (as of course we know very well), and rows have fields (as we know from various earlier discussions); well, now we know that, by contrast, structured types have attributes.

Here now are a couple of slightly more realistic examples of structured type definitions:

```
CREATE TYPE POINT
  AS ( X FLOAT , Y FLOAT ) FINAL ;

CREATE TYPE LINESEG
  AS ( BEGIN POINT , END POINT ) NOT FINAL ;
```

(Actually the second example fails because BEGIN and END are reserved words in SQL, but I choose to ignore that detail here.)

In its simplest form, then—i.e., ignoring a variety of optional features[19]— the syntax for creating a structured type is:

```
CREATE TYPE <type name>
  AS ( <attribute commalist> ) [ NOT ] FINAL ;
```

Points arising:

1. I said above that it's the parenthesized commalist of attributes following the keyword AS that tells us we're dealing with a structured type definition and not a DISTINCT one, and in the example that's perfectly true. In more complicated cases certain additional distinguishing features come into play (or might come into play, at any rate), but such features are beyond the scope of the present discussion.

2. FINAL means this type can't have any proper subtypes; NOT FINAL means it can. Purely for the sake of the example—not for any really good

---

[19] I remind you, though, that one "optional feature" I'm *not* ignoring here is the specification of any kind of type constraint—because in fact, as noted in the section "Defining a DISTINCT Type" earlier, no such feature exists.

reason—I've specified FINAL for type POINT and NOT FINAL for type LINESEG.[20] Of course, proper subtypes as such are, again, beyond the scope of this book.

3. To repeat, each *<attribute>* in the *<attribute commalist>*—which mustn't be empty, by the way—consists of an *<attribute name>* followed by a *<type name>*. That *<type name>* in turn identifies the type of the physical representation of values of the attribute in question.

    Note: SQL apologists might dispute my use of the qualifier *physical* in the foregoing sentence. However, I stand by it—despite the fact that the standard says, paraphrasing slightly, that "physical representations of values of user defined types are undefined." Moreover, Melton appears to agree with me on this issue. On page 56 of his book, he gives an example of changing the representation (i.e., the attributes) of a certain type, and then goes on to say, paraphrasing slightly:

    > Perhaps obviously, [the] data in the database would have to be converted to [the new representation], but that's not relevant to the example.

    Such conversion would clearly not be necessary if representations weren't physical. Likewise, on page 31 he says this:

    > [The] fact that [SQL's] object model doesn't allow for private attributes, but only public attributes, makes it impossible to completely hide the implementation details of types.

    This statement clearly implies, again, that the attributes in question constitute the physical implementation of the type in question.

STRUCTURED TYPES: OBSERVERS AND MUTATORS

When I was describing DISTINCT types earlier, I followed up the section on defining such a type with one on THE_ operators and selectors (or SQL's analogs of those operators, rather) for such types. Now I turn to SQL's analog of those same operators in the case of structured types—THE_ operator

---

[20] Structured types had to be NOT FINAL in SQL:1999, but this limitation has since been dropped.

functionality (including THE_ peudovariable functionality) in the present section, and selector functionality in the next.

Let *T* be a structured type with an attribute *A* (possibly others as well). Then the act of defining *T* automatically causes definition of two operators for *A*, one *observer function* and one *mutator function* (actually they're methods, but SQL calls them functions). These two operators provide functionality analogous to that of a THE_ operator and a corresponding THE_ pseudovariable, respectively. For example, let LS, PT, and ZX be SQL variables of types LINESEG, POINT, and FLOAT, respectively:

```
DECLARE LS LINESEG ;
DECLARE PT POINT ;
DECLARE ZX FLOAT ;
```

Then all of the following are valid assignments:

```
SET ZX = PT.X ;            /* "observes" X attribute of PT */

SET PT.X = ZX ;            /* "mutates" X attribute of PT  */

SET ZX = LS.BEGIN.X ;      /* "observes" X attribute of   */
                           /* BEGIN attribute of LS       */

SET LS.BEGIN.X = ZX ;      /* "mutates" X attribute of    */
                           /* BEGIN attribute of LS       */
```

That said, I must make it clear that SQL's mutators actually *aren't* mutators!—not in the conventional OO sense of that term, at any rate. In other words, they aren't update operators. (In fact, I've already said they're functions, and functions of course are read-only by definition.) However, they can be used in such a way as to achieve, in effect, conventional mutator functionality. For example, the statement

```
SET PT.X = ZX ;
```

(which, believe it or not, doesn't explicitly contain a mutator invocation) is defined to be shorthand for the statement

```
SET PT = PT.X ( ZX )
```

(which does). To elaborate:

■ The expression

```
PT . X ( ZX )
```

denotes an invocation of the mutator called X (see the discussion of method invocation syntax some ten pages back or so).

■ PT and ZX denote the subject argument and an additional argument, respectively, to that invocation.

■ That invocation returns a point with x coordinate equal to the value currently contained in ZX and y coordinate equal to the y coordinate of the point currently contained in PT.

■ Finally, the SET statement causes that point to be assigned to PT.

However, I'll continue to talk about SQL's "mutators" as if they really were update operators, for simplicity.

STRUCTURED TYPES: CONSTRUCTORS

Let T be a structured type. Then defining T *doesn't* cause automatic definition of a corresponding selector operator (contrast the situation with DISTINCT types). However, something resembling selector functionality can be achieved as follows:

■ First of all, defining structured type T does cause automatic definition of a *constructor function* for T,[21] having that same name T.

■ Note carefully, however, that the constructor function for type T returns *the same value on every invocation*: namely, that value of type T whose attributes all have the applicable default value (see the bullet item immediately following). Thus, for example, the constructor function invocation

---

[21] So long as T is *instantiable*, that is—but instantiability (or lack thereof, rather) is another of those topics that have significance only in the context of type inheritance, and I'm going to ignore it here. Suffice it to say that (at least as far as this book is concerned) all SQL types are instantiable.

```
POINT ( )
```

returns the point with default values for attributes X and Y.

■ Let *A* be an attribute of structured type *T*. In general, then, the default value for *A* can optionally be specified along with the definition of *A* within the definition of *T*. If no default value is specified explicitly, the default value—the "default default"—will be null. *Note:* For reasons beyond the scope of the present discussion, however, the default for *A* must be null if *A* is of either a row type or some user defined type.

■ In the case of type POINT, no default value has been defined explicitly for that type's component attributes X and Y, and so the constructor function invocation shown above—viz., POINT ( )—returns a kind of "pseudopoint" whose X and Y components are both null.

■ Assume we now assign that "pseudopoint" to the variable PT:

```
SET PT = POINT ( ) ;
```

Now we can invoke the X and Y mutators on PT to get the point we really want, perhaps as follows:

```
PT . X ( 5.0 ) . Y ( 2.5 )
```

This expression overall returns the point with cartesian coordinates (5.0,2.5).[22] See the next bullet item for further explanation.

■ In practice, we'd probably bundle up the initial point construction and those subsequent point mutations into a single expression, like this:

```
POINT ( ) . X ( 5.0 ) . Y ( 2.5 )
```

Explanation: First, POINT ( ) is, as we've just seen, a POINT constructor function invocation, and by default it returns a "pseudopoint,"

---

[22] Note that the literals 5.0 and 2.5 are of type DECIMAL (2,1)—or should that be NUMERIC (2,1)?—whereas attributes X and Y are of type FLOAT. Thus, I'm relying here on SQL's support for coercion. I would *not* rely on such coercions if I were doing all this "for real."

with *x* and *y* coordinates both null.[23]   Second, the result of that invocation—
i.e., that pseudopoint— becomes the subject argument to the X mutator
invocation, which effectively replaces that pseudopoint by another such,
this one having *x* coordinate 5.0 and *y* coordinate null. Third, the result of
that invocation then becomes the subject argument to the Y mutator
invocation, which effectively replaces that second pseudopoint by a real
point with *x* coordinate 5.0 and *y* coordinate 2.5.

■   Finally, note that (despite the nomenclature, but like observers and mutators
before them) constructor functions are actually methods. Unlike other
methods, however, they—constructor functions, that is—have no subject
parameter. (So when that method is invoked, where do you think the
corresponding message gets sent to?)

Here now is a more complex example (and I'll leave it to you to explain the
details of this one to yourself to your own satisfaction):

```
LINESEG ( ) . BEGIN ( POINT ( ) . X ( 5.0 ) . Y ( 2.5 ) )
            . END   ( POINT ( ) . X ( 7.3 ) . Y ( 0.8 ) )
```

Actually there's another way of obtaining selector functionality with SQL's
structured types, one you might find a little more user friendly. Let me elaborate.
First of all, in the definition of the pertinent type, we can give the signature for a
constructor method (not to be confused with a constructor function, naturally,
despite the fact that as previously noted a constructor function is in fact a
method). The constructor method for a given structured type *T* has—rather, is
required to have—the same name as type *T* itself. Here's an example:

```
CREATE TYPE POINT
   AS ( X FLOAT , Y FLOAT ) FINAL
         CONSTRUCTOR METHOD
                     POINT ( X FLOAT , Y FLOAT ) RETURNS POINT
                     SELF AS RESULT ;
```

(The specification SELF AS RESULT is required.) Next we define the
constructor method implementation code:

---

[23] I note in passing that a "pseudopoint" with both coordinates null is not itself considered to be null (i.e., it's
not "a null point"). Compare the remarks earlier in this chapter on the logical difference between a null row
and a row all of whose fields are null.

```
CREATE CONSTRUCTOR METHOD
                POINT ( X FLOAT , Y FLOAT ) RETURNS POINT
       FOR POINT
          BEGIN
             SET SELF.X = X ;
             SET SELF.Y = Y ;
             RETURN SELF ;
          END ;
```

And now the expression

```
NEW POINT ( X , Y )
```

will return the point whose *x* and *y* coordinates are equal to the values of variables X and Y (whatever those values might be), respectively. *Explanation:* That keyword NEW causes the following to happen:

a. First, the POINT constructor *function* is invoked. That function invocation returns a pseudopoint with X and Y attributes both null.

b. That pseudopoint is then passed as the subject argument to an invocation of the POINT constructor *method*.

c. That method invocation will then assign the specified X and Y values to the attributes of the new point.

   By the way, I hope I haven't confused you with all the different X's and Y's in the foregoing example. Just to spell out the differences, though: The X and Y in the construction method signature (in CREATE TYPE) and in the constructor method definition (in CREATE CONSTRUCTOR METHOD)—also the X and Y on the right side of the two assignments in this latter—are parameters; the X and Y in the expressions SELF.X and SELF.Y are attributes of the POINT type; and the X and Y in the NEW expression are SQL variables of some numeric type.

STRUCTURED TYPES: COMPARISONS

By now I've said as much as I want to say regarding assignments involving values and variables of some structured type, except to state for the record that strong typing does apply to such operations (in fact, strong typing applies to all operations involving operands of some structured type). In the case of comparisons in particular, however, there's a little more to be said.

Let T be a structured type. Then the comparison operators that apply to values of type T aren't specified as part of the definition of type T as such; instead, they're specified by means of a separate statement that's associated with type T. Now, that separation in itself isn't necessarily a bad thing,[24] but it does give rise to certain anomalies, for want of a better word. Consider the following example:

```
CREATE ORDERING FOR POINT EQUALS ONLY BY STATE ;
```

Points arising:

- As you can see, the "separate statement" in question is called CREATE ORDERING. That in itself is a little odd, inasmuch as if (as is the case in the example) EQUALS ONLY is specified—which is likely to be a common situation in practice—then that specification explicitly means that the type in question doesn't *have* an ordering! That is, if values v_1 and v_2 of the type in question, the comparisons $v_1 < v_2$ and $v_1 > v_2$ are explicitly undefined; in fact, they'll fail on a syntax error.

- To spell it out, EQUALS ONLY means that "=" and "<>" (not equals) are the only valid comparison operators for values of the type in question.[25] The alternative to EQUALS ONLY is FULL, meaning that "<", "<=", etc., are all allowed in addition to "=" and "<>".

- BY STATE means that two values v_1 and v_2 of the type in question—the *structured* type, that is— are equal if and only if every attribute of v_1 has the same value as the corresponding attribute of v_2. *Note:* Alternatives to BY STATE are possible but are beyond the scope of this book.

---

[24] I can't be persuaded it's a good thing, though. It's not like that business of separating signatures and implementation code, which (as I pointed out earlier) can be seen as separating model and implementation issues. By contrast, which comparison operators apply is purely a model issue.

[25] Though I suppose you could define your own methods or functions or procedures to perform, e.g., "<" comparisons, if you wanted to. But if you did, the system presumably wouldn't understand the semantics of what you've done.

■ To repeat, CREATE TYPE and CREATE ORDERING are separate statements, but it's not possible to have more than one CREATE ORDERING for a given CREATE TYPE. It is, however, possible for a given CREATE TYPE to have no associated CREATE ORDERING at all!—in which case no comparisons at all, *not even equality comparisons*, can be done on values of the structured type in question[26] (a state of affairs with far reaching consequences, as you might imagine).

    Note: Perhaps I should remind you at this point that *The Third Manifesto* actually *requires* equality to be supported for every type (and defines its semantics, too). In fact, as pointed out near the end of the section "Equality Comparisons" in Chapter 2, we couldn't even say whether or not a given value is of a given type, absent such support.

STRUCTURED TYPES: AN EXAMPLE

Let's look at an example of how structured types might actually be used. Here again, repeated from near the beginning of the section "Defining a Structured Type," is structured type POINT as originally defined:

```
CREATE TYPE POINT
  AS ( X FLOAT , Y FLOAT ) FINAL ;
```

This type can now be used in SQL variable and column definitions. For example, let's extend our previous definition of table NADDR from the "Entr'acte" section to include an additional column called LOCATION, whose value within any given NADDR row is the geographic point on the map corresponding to the ADDR value in that row:

```
CREATE TABLE NADDR
    ( NAME VARCHAR(25) NOT NULL ,
      ADDR ROW ( ... ) NOT NULL ,
              /* fields omitted for simplicity */
      LOCATION POINT   NOT NULL ,
      UNIQUE ( NAME ) ) ;
```

---

[26] Except possibly by user defined operators, as mentioned in the previous footnote. But regarding those "far reaching consequences" in general, see the answer to Exercise 2 in Chapter 3.

Column LOCATION is of type POINT,[27] and we can access the components of a given LOCATION value—i.e., values of the X and Y attributes of the structured type POINT—using dot qualification syntax, more or less as if that LOCATION value were just a simple row value. Here are a couple of examples:

```
SELECT  NT.LOCATION.X , NT.LOCATION.Y
FROM    NADDR AS NT
WHERE   NT.NAME = 'Joe'

UPDATE  NADDR
SET     LOCATION.X = 7.3 ,
        LOCATION.Y = 0.8
WHERE   NAME = 'Joe' ;
```

Note that the SELECT example not only uses dot qualifications, it uses explicit correlation names as qualifiers—such explicit names being required in this context (at least in the SELECT clause, though not in the WHERE clause). By contrast, the UPDATE example doesn't use correlation names at all.[28]

When used as in these examples, therefore, SQL structured types effectively behave rather like a row type, as you can see. Note in particular that, at least in the case at hand, structured types certainly do seem to be nonscalar,[29] inasmuch as they certainly do have user visible components—again, just like a row type. The only differences are that:

- The components are called attributes instead of fields.

- The structured type, unlike the analogous row type, has a separately and explicitly declared name (POINT, in the example). I'll have more to say regarding the implications of this state of affairs at the very end of the section "Typed Tables: Some Questions," later.

---

[27] I'm pretending for the sake of the example, not very realistically, that values of column LOCATION ("geographic points on the map") are geometric points, with a cartesian possrep. In practice, of course, we'd surely want to use conventional map coordinates instead—probably with a latitude and longitude possrep.

[28] Full details of these matters—i.e., exactly when correlation names can and can't be used, and when they must or mustn't be—are beyond the scope of this book. Compare footnote 15, earlier.

[29] I.e., they're not "encapsulated," to use the jargon. Perhaps we could say they've been "decapsulated" (assuming they're encapsulated in the first place, which I really don't think they are).

TYPED TABLES REVISITED

So far, then, SQL's structured types look as if they might not be too hard to understand. But there's more to come, much more. The crucial point to understand is this:

SQL allows a base table[30] to be defined to be "OF" some structured type.

And if it is, then all kinds of further considerations come into play.

In order to illustrate some of those further considerations, let me first extend the foregoing definition of type POINT slightly, as follows (note the last line in particular):

```
CREATE TYPE POINT
   AS ( X FLOAT , Y FLOAT ) FINAL
      REF IS SYSTEM GENERATED ;
```

To elaborate:

■ Type POINT is defined once again to be a structured type with two attributes, X and Y, each of which is of type FLOAT.

■ REF is a type generator, and the corresponding generated types are known as *reference types* (REF types for short).

■ If REF IS SYSTEM GENERATED is specified in connection with structured type *T*, it causes a specific reference type called "REF (*T*)" to be generated.[31] (*T* is POINT, of course, in the example.)

■ Values of that reference type (REF values for short) then serve as unique identifiers (unique IDs for short) for rows within tables, if any, that are defined to be "OF" type *T* (see further discussion below).

---

[30] Or a view—but details of the view case are beyond the scope of this book. For simplicity, I'll take the unqualified term *table* to mean a base table specifically throughout the rest of this chapter, barring explicit statements to the contrary.

[31] Other specifications—e.g., REF IS USER GENERATED—are also supported, but the details are beyond the scope of this book. (Actually REF IS SYSTEM GENERATED is the default. In the example, therefore, I could have left the original POINT type definition unchanged.)

In the example, therefore, the system automatically generates a type called REF (POINT), the values of which are references to rows within tables, if any, that are defined to be "OF" type POINT. So let's define such a table:

```
CREATE TABLE POINTS OF POINT
      ( REF IS PID SYSTEM GENERATED ) ;
```

Table POINTS is an example of what SQL calls, not very aptly, both a *typed table* and a *referenceable table*—though in fact all typed tables are referenceable tables and all referenceable tables are typed tables, so there's really no need for both terms. To quote the standard:

> A referenceable table is necessarily also a *typed table* ... A typed table is called a referenceable table.

What makes matters worse (in my opinion, anyway) is the fact that a "referenceable table" is actually *not* "referenceable"!—rather, its rows are. Indeed, it's important to understand that rows in a "typed" or "referenceable" table are the *only* construct in SQL that can and do have a REF value to identify them. Thus, to say table *T* is "referenceable" is to say that

a. The rows within *T* at any given time have certain identifying REF values associated with them, and

b. Those REF values can be used elsewhere—in particular, in rows in tables elsewhere in the database—as references to the rows in question.

I'll explain in just a few moments (a) how the association between those REF values and the rows in question is established, and (b) how those REF values can then be used to reference those rows.

> *Aside:* I remind you from Chapter 3 that SQL uses the terminology of referencing in two quite different senses. One is as sketched above. The other, and older, sense has to do with foreign keys—a foreign key value in some given row in a referencing table is said to reference the row in the referenced or target table that contains that same value in the corresponding target key position. I'll have a little more to say about foreign keys vs. REF values later in the chapter. *End of aside.*

More terminology: Let "typed table" *TT* be defined to be "OF" structured type *T*. Then that keyword "OF" is really not appropriate, because—as noted a few pages back, also in Chapter 3—table *TT* is actually *not* "of" type *T*, and neither are its rows![32] To elaborate:

a. First of all—but please understand that this point is purely hypothetical (I mean, it's not the way SQL actually works)—if table *TT* had just one column and that column were of type *T*, then we might reasonably say something to the effect that table *TT* was of type TABLE (*T*) and its rows were of type ROW (*T*). (Not in SQL, though, because "TABLE (*T*)" and "ROW (*T*)" aren't legitimate SQL constructs.)

b. But in fact no typed table in SQL has just one column, ever! To be specific, typed table *TT* has one column for each attribute of the corresponding structured type *T*—and you'll recall that structured types do always have at least one attribute—*together with one additional column* (see point d. below). Thus, table POINTS in the example has columns called X and Y, both of type FLOAT and both of them explicitly visible to the user,[33] together with an additional column as discussed under point d. below. The one thing it most definitely *doesn't* have is a column of type POINT—even though having such a column is exactly what the OF POINT specification in the pertinent CREATE TABLE statement would surely seem to suggest.

c. By the way, if we want to impose a NOT NULL constraint on those columns X and Y in table POINTS (which of course I would strongly suggest we do want), we can do so by extending the CREATE TABLE statement for that table to include some appropriate "column options," like this:

---

[32] Which accounts for all of those quotation marks, of course, surrounding "OF" and "typed table" in particular, in the text of this section prior to this point. I'll drop them from now on because I know how annoying they can be—but I do wish language designers could be a little more careful in their choice of concepts and terminology and keywords. Quite apart from anything else, poor choices like the ones at hand make the language just that much harder to teach, learn, and understand.

[33] So in this context once again, the structured type definitely seems to be nonscalar (or "decapsulated")—again, just like a row type. (In the case at hand, to be specific, the user has to be explicitly aware that (a) type POINT has attributes called X and Y, and therefore that (b) table POINTS has columns with those same names and (c) those attributes, and therefore those columns, are all of type FLOAT.)

```
CREATE TABLE POINTS OF POINT
    ( REF IS PID SYSTEM GENERATED ,
      X WITH OPTIONS NOT NULL ,
      Y WITH OPTIONS NOT NULL ) ;
```

And if we additionally want to say that no two rows existing in table POINTS at the same time can have both the same X value and the same Y value, we can extend the CREATE STATEMENT still further, thus:

```
CREATE TABLE POINTS OF POINT
    ( REF IS PID SYSTEM GENERATED ,
      X WITH OPTIONS NOT NULL ,
      Y WITH OPTIONS NOT NULL ,
      UNIQUE ( X , Y ) ) ;
```

d. As noted under point b. above, table *TT* actually has another column as well: to be specific, a column of the applicable REF type, viz., REF (*T*). However, the syntax for defining that column is not the normal column definition syntax—instead, it's that REF specification once again, which takes the general form:

```
REF IS <column name> SYSTEM GENERATED
```

In the example, of course, that specification looks like this:

```
REF IS PID SYSTEM GENERATED
```

This specification implicitly defines the extra column and gives it the specified name (PID, in the example).[34] The column in question is said to be a *self-referencing* column, and it's used to contain those unique IDs or "references" for the rows of the table being defined; thus, each row of the table being defined actually contains its own ID. So we see in the example that table POINTS actually has *three* columns (PID, X, and Y, in that left to right order), not just two. It follows that what the standard calls the "row type" of that table is as follows:

```
ROW ( PID REF ( POINT ) , X FLOAT , Y FLOAT )
```

---

[34] Don't get confused here—the CREATE *TYPE* statement specifies REF IS SYSTEM GENERATED, the CREATE *TABLE* statement specifies REF <*column name*> IS SYSTEM GENERATED. Incidentally, it's not at all clear why it should be necessary to define the table to be OF some structured type in the first place, instead of just defining an appropriate column in the usual way, in order to obtain this "automated" unique ID functionality. But that's the way it is.

Note: Self-referencing columns like PID are implicitly defined to be both UNIQUE and NOT NULL.

e. But where do those IDs come from? *Answer:* The ID for a given row is automatically assigned, and placed in the row in question in the self-referencing column position, at the time the row is first inserted into the table. And it remains associated with that row, unchanged, until such time as the row in question is deleted. Moreover, no row in that table from that time forward will ever have that same ID.

Note: Of course, the INSERT operation that causes that row to be inserted provides the X and Y values, but not the PID value (at least, not explicitly). For example:

```
INSERT INTO POINTS ( X , Y )
       VALUES ( 35.8 , -9.4 ) ;
```

As you can see, the foregoing INSERT statement explicitly mentions X and Y as "insert targets" and explicitly specifies values to be inserted in those target positions. What it explicitly *doesn't* do is mention PID as a target, nor does it specify a value to be inserted in that position. But the user certainly has to know about the PID column, as well as (obviously) about columns X and Y as such.[35] So do you think points are encapsulated, at least as far as table POINTS is concerned? No, neither do I.

One final terminological point: The fact that a row contains its own ID—i.e., its own REF value—is regarded by some people as transforming the row in question into an *object* in the OO sense.[36] For example:

Once an instance [*sic*] of a structured type has a unique identity, then it really behaves exactly as an object is expected to behave in an object-oriented environment. For all practical purposes, it *is* an object.

---

[35] It also doesn't explictly mention either PID as a target column or the REF value to be inserted in that PID position.

[36] Or perhaps it's the rest of the row (i.e., the row with the REF value excluded) that's the object. At any rate, there's certainly nothing else in SQL that has any claim to being an object. And the text "its rows can be manipulated through method invocations"—part of the quote on the next page from Melton's page 109—suggests rather strongly that it is indeed the whole row that's the object, not the row excluding its ID.

This quote is from Melton, page 30—though I remind you that Melton also says (on page 113) that "it's somewhat unclear in the SQL standard exactly what an object *is*." (As for that term *instance*, I'll come back to that later.)

Here's another quote from Melton (page 109):

> [A] typed table is, in many ways, no different than an ordinary SQL table, but it has the important characteristic that its rows can be manipulated through method invocations in addition to ordinary SQL data manipulation statements.

However, these remarks shouldn't be construed as meaning that a row from a table *TT* that has been defined to be OF type *T* can be used as an argument to a method invocation (or indeed an invocation of any SQL routine) where the corresponding parameter is declared to be of type *T*, because it can't. Nor can table *TT* as such, of course.

TYPED TABLES: SOME QUESTIONS

Now, I have to say I think there's something very problematic going on with all of this. On the surface, of course, the idea seems straightforward—the idea, that is, that (a) any given row *r* has a unique ID, and (b) that ID is recorded in a field within row *r* itself, and (c) that ID never changes so long as row *r* exists, even if *r* is updated. But does this idea really stand up to careful analysis? More specifically, what exactly does the phrase "any given row *r*" mean? For one thing, is *r* a value, or is it a variable?

Well, it can't be a value, because then, contrary to what the foregoing paragraph suggests, it could never change; in fact, like all values, it would be self-identifying, and thus it wouldn't need any form of additional ID anyway. So it must be a variable. Indeed, it *is* a variable, because as just indicated SQL allows it to be updated.

Further evidence that it must be a variable is provided by the fact that those REF values we've been talking about are really *addresses*—slightly abstract addresses, perhaps, but addresses nonetheless—and values don't have addresses, variables do. (Or as I put it in Chapter 4: Values don't have location, variables do.) In other words, if a given REF value is used to access the unique corresponding row, then that REF value is being used as a *pointer* to that row. But rows in the database aren't just free floating, as it were, they're contained within tables—and those tables in turn are variables too! (They're SQL's analog of relvars. I suppose we might call them *tablevars*, or *tabvars*.) So now we're faced with the notion that one variable might contain another: specifically, the notion—I would say the logical absurdity—of a table variable containing row variables.

Now, I want to examine this idea (the idea, that is, that the rows we're talking about are variables, and the corresponding REF values are pointers to those variables) in a little more detail, because it's important.

First of all, some might dispute my claim that those REF values are acting as pointers; however, I think the discussions in the next section, regarding operations, support that claim rather strongly, and I stand by it. (I note in passing that certain remarks of Melton's indicate that he agrees with me on this issue.) Of course, if they *are* pointers, then the tables containing them can't possibly represent relations (or relvars) in the relational model sense, because the relational model doesn't allow pointers. Indeed, it's not clear why such tables are supported in SQL at all; certainly there seems to be no useful functionality that can be achieved with them that can't equally well—in fact, better—be achieved without them. And in connection with *that* issue, I'd like to mention something else, too. A tutorial article on SQL:1999 ("SQL:1999, Formerly Known as SQL3," by Andrew Eisenberg and Jim Melton) appeared in *ACM SIGMOD Record 28*, No. 1 (March 1999). Observing that, while it did indeed describe the object features of SQL, the article did nothing to justify them, Hugh Darwen and I wrote a letter to the editor of *SIGMOD Record* at the time, as follows:

> With reference to [the subject article]—in particular, with reference to the sections *Objects ... Finally* and *Using REF Types*—we have a question: What useful purpose is served by the features described in those sections? To be more specific, what useful functionality is provided that can't be obtained via features already found in SQL:1992?

Our letter was never published, however, and our questions remain unanswered to this day.

Second: In Chapter 11 ("Array Variables") of his book *A Discipline of Programming* (Prentice-Hall, 1976), Edsger W. Dijkstra makes the point (also rather strongly) that the elements of an array variable can't themselves be variables. His observation is specific to arrays as such, of course, but the point that no variable can be a "subvariable" of another is generally valid and applies to variables of all kinds. In particular, it applies to relvars; that is, a relvar is most certainly not, as has sometimes been suggested (and as SQL seems to think, given its support for tables that contain rows that contain pointers to rows in other tables), a collection of tuplevars.

Third: Regardless of whether or not they're considered to be contained in table variables, those row variables certainly constitute a violation of *The Information Principle* (see Chapter 2). I refer you to my book *SQL and Relational Theory*, 3rd ed. (O'Reilly, 2015) for a discussion of some of the (serious!) consequences of such violation.

Another good question to ponder in this connection is the following: Is this notion of table variables containing row variables consistent with the notion that table (or relation) assignment is fundamentally the only update operator we need?

I have another question too. When someone says a certain REF value is being used to identify a certain row, I want to ask: Which row is it, exactly, that's that "certain row"? Surely, the only possible answer to this question is: It's the row identified by that particular REF value. (Certainly SQL doesn't require any other kind of "row identifier.") So it seems to me that, as well as involving a logical absurdity as noted above, there's something horribly circular about the whole idea.

> *Aside:* I suppose it *might* be possible to rescue the idea, in part, by inventing a scheme along the following lines: 1. Assume the existence of operations that (a) insert a single row into a table and (b) update a specific row within a table. 2. When row *r* is inserted into table *T*, it's given a unique identifier (perhaps the timestamp of the insertion). 3. That identifier never changes, even when the row is updated.
>
> > Given such a scheme, however, it still wouldn't really be rows as such that had unique identifiers, it would be *row insertion events*. (Note that two rows r_1 and r_2 might be identical in all respects except for the time of their insertion.) And I'm not at all comfortable with the importance such a scheme would attach to the "update row" and (more particularly) "insert row" operations—especially since there aren't any such operations in the relational model, nor is there any logical need for them. What's more, of course, the whole scheme still seems to involve the notion of "variables containing variables," with all that that entails. *End of aside.*

Well, simply in order to be able to continue with the rest of the chapter, I'm just going to have to overlook all of the foregoing concerns. But I assure you I'm not at all happy about it.

One final point to close this section: Recall from Chapters 2 and 4 that—deliberately, of course—there's no "define tuple type" operator in **Tutorial D**; instead, there's a TUPLE type generator, which can be invoked in (e.g.) the definition of a tuple variable. As a direct consequence of this state of affairs, the only names tuple types have in **Tutorial D** are names of the form

```
TUPLE {  A₁ T₁ ,  A₂ T₂ ,  ..., Aₙ Tₙ }
```

while tuples as such take the form

```
TUPLE {  A₁ v₁ ,  A₂ v₂ ,  ..., Aₙ vₙ }
```

Some important consequences of this discipline are that it's immediately clear in **Tutorial D** when two tuple types are one and the same, and when two tuples are of the same type, and when two tuples are equal.

Now, as we saw in the "Entr'acte" section earlier in this chapter, SQL's row types are similar, somewhat, to **Tutorial D**'s tuple types in the foregoing respect. But structured types are different: There *is* an explicit "define structured type" operator (viz., CREATE TYPE), and structured types do have additional and explicit names. So consider the following SQL definitions:

```
CREATE TYPE POINT1 AS ( X FLOAT , Y FLOAT ) FINAL ;
CREATE TYPE POINT2 AS ( X FLOAT , Y FLOAT ) FINAL ;

DECLARE V1 POINT1 ;
DECLARE V2 POINT2 ;
```

POINT1 and POINT2 are distinct (not DISTINCT!) types; thus, variables V1 and V2 are of different types, and they can't be compared with one another, nor can either one be assigned to the other.

Note: Despite the foregoing state of affairs, you might be thinking that at least every value of either type is also a value of the other. However, such thinking is erroneous. It's true that every value of either type *has the same representation* as some value of the other—but there's a logical difference between values as such and their representation, and the values as such aren't the same. Rather, values of V1 are values of type POINT1, values of V2 are values of type POINT2, and never the twain shall meet. To say it again in different words: No value of type POINT1 is a value of type POINT2, and no value of type POINT2 is a value of type POINT1. (What's more, if we define tables T1 and T2 to be of types POINT1 and POINT2, respectively, then those two tables—even though they have "the same" columns X and Y—*clearly* have different row types, because of those additional self-referencing columns. Thanks to Hugh Darwen for this observation.)

TYPED TABLES: OPERATIONS

I turn now to the question of operations involving typed tables. Recall this definition for table NADDR from a few pages back:

```
CREATE TABLE NADDR
    ( NAME VARCHAR(25) NOT NULL ,
      ADDR ROW ( ... ) NOT NULL ,
                /* fields omitted for simplicity */
      LOCATION POINT   NOT NULL ,
      UNIQUE ( NAME ) ) ;
```

Now let's revise this definition so that column LOCATION contains, not values of the structured type POINT as such, but pointers to rows in table POINTS instead. Here first to remind you is the original (i.e., the simplest) definition of this latter table:

```
CREATE TABLE POINTS OF POINT
    ( REF IS PID SYSTEM GENERATED ) ;
```

And here's the revised definition of table NADDR (note the fourth line):

```
CREATE TABLE NADDR
    ( NAME VARCHAR(25)                         NOT NULL ,
      ADDR ROW ( ... )                         NOT NULL ,
      LOCATION REF ( POINT ) SCOPE POINTS NOT NULL ,
      UNIQUE ( NAME ) ) ;
```

Points arising (pardon the pun):

■ Note first that table NADDR is still a regular table, not a typed table—a table doesn't have to be a typed table in order to have a column of some REF type. (It has to be, and in fact is, a typed table if and only if the column in question is a self-referencing column—which is to say, if and only if that column is defined by means of a clause on the pertinent CREATE TABLE statement of the form REF IS *<column name>* SYSTEM GENERATED.)

■ To say it again in different words: Any column of any table can be of some REF type, in general. In the example, values of column LOCATION are defined to be values of type REF (POINT).

■ The specification SCOPE POINTS limits the REF values appearing in that column to ones also appearing in column PID of table POINTS, thereby guaranteeing that the REF values in question do indeed point to rows currently appearing in table POINTS as such (except as noted in the next bullet item but one).

■ The table named in a SCOPE clause must be a typed table specifically. No given REF value can ever appear in the self-referencing columns of two or more such tables.[37]

■ *Dangling references* can occur. A dangling reference is a REF value that points to a row that doesn't exist. Such a situation can arise if suitable precautions aren't taken when a row is deleted from a referenced table. The result of "dereferencing" a dangling reference—see further discussion in a few moments—is defined to be null.

■ Dangling references can be prevented by specifying REFERENCES ARE CHECKED immediately following the REF (...) specification in the pertinent column definition in the referencing table. However, REFERENCES ARE NOT CHECKED is the default.

■ If REFERENCES ARE CHECKED is specified, an accompanying ON DELETE *<option>* clause can be specified as well, just as with a conventional foreign key specification. The available *<option>*s are RESTRICT, CASCADE, SET NULL, SET DEFAULT, and NO ACTION. NO ACTION is the default. Further details of these *<option>*s are beyond the scope of this book.

---

[37] Unless one of the tables concerned is a "subtable" of the other. But subtables and supertables are yet another aspect—a very suspect one, too, I'd have to say—of SQL's support for inheritance in general, and are beyond the scope of this book for that reason. I note, however, that subtables and supertables are required to be typed tables specifically. For further discussion I refer you once again to my book *Type Inheritance and Relational Theory* (O'Reilly, 2016).

Aside: To repeat, values of column LOCATION in the example are defined to be values of type REF (POINT). But this raises an obvious question: What does the result from a query of the form SELECT LOCATION FROM NADDR look like? More specifically, if the result is displayed, what do the displayed LOCATION values look like? Are there any REF literals? (*Answer:* No, there aren't. The only thing the standard has to say about such matters is this: "In a host variable, a REF value is materialized as an *N*-octet value, where *N* is implementation defined.") *End of aside*.

Now suppose we want to retrieve the *x* and *y* coordinates of the location for the person named Joe. In essence, then, what we need to do is this:

a. Start with the row for Joe in table NADDR.

b. Next, follow the pointer that's the LOCATION value in that row over to the corresponding row in table POINTS.

c. Finally, extract the X and Y column values from that corresponding POINTS row.

So what we need is a *dereferencing* operator, or in other words an operator that follows a pointer as just described. (Actually I've already mentioned such an operator a couple of times in passing in previous chapters. See, eg., the answer to Exercise 5 in Chapter 2.) In SQL, that operator is written in concrete syntax as a hyphen followed by a ">" symbol. Thus, the following is an SQL formulation of the desired query:

```
SELECT  LOCATION -> X , LOCATION -> Y
FROM    NADDR
WHERE   NAME = 'Joe'
```

This expression yields a result of two columns, X and Y, both of type FLOAT. The two subexpressions in the SELECT clause might be read as "the X value in the row that the LOCATION value points to" and "the Y value in the row that the LOCATION value points to," respectively. (So note the small syntactic, or intuitive, oddity here, viz.: The items specified in the SELECT clause don't actually come from the table specified in the FROM clause.)

By the way, note carefully that what appears following the dereferencing operator in concrete syntax is, technically, an attribute name, not a column name.

Thus, the following, which might have been thought to have been an expansion or clarification of the expression shown above, is actually illegal and will fail on a syntax error:

```
SELECT  LOCATION -> POINTS.X , LOCATION -> POINTS.Y
FROM    NADDR
WHERE   NAME = 'Joe'
```

It fails—somewhat counterintuitively, I'd have to say—because "POINTS.X" and "POINTS.Y" aren't attribute names, and (to repeat) attribute names are what the dereferencing operator requires.

What makes the foregoing even more counterintuitive (at least to my mind) is that the following, by contrast, *is* legal and *doesn't* fail:

```
SELECT POINTS.X , POINTS.Y
FROM   POINTS
```

Exercise: Why exactly doesn't it fail?

> *Aside:* As a matter of fact SQL also supports another dereferencing operator, explicitly called DEREF. Here's an example:
>
> ```
> SELECT DEREF ( LOCATION ) AS JOE_POINT
> FROM   NADDR
> WHERE  NAME = 'Joe'
> ```
>
> Technically, this expression yields a result table of just one column, called JOE_POINT, of type POINT. However, the significance of this fact—the fact, that is, that the result table has just that one column, a state of affairs that appears to constitute the sole situation in SQL in which it might be argued that structured types are "encapsulated" or scalar—is unclear, to say the least. It's unclear because the observer and mutator functions associated with type POINT can be, and in fact must be, used to access the X and Y coordinates of the JOE_POINT value or values within rows in that result table. In other words, SQL might try to pretend that the result table has just one column, but users are aware, and indeed must be aware, that values of that column have X and Y components. *End of aside.*

What about updates on table NADDR? Well, DELETEs are straightforward, and there's nothing special to say about them. INSERTs are another matter, though. The question is: When we insert a row into that table, what do we do about the necessary LOCATION value? Well, languages that, like SQL, support pointers and a dereferencing operator usually support a corresponding *referencing* operator as well, which, given a variable V, returns the address of—i.e., a pointer to—V.[38] But SQL doesn't. As a consequence, what we *can't* do is write an expression of the form ADDR_OF (r), where r is a row in table POINTS, in order to obtain the address of that row r. Instead, we need to write an expression—typically a *scalar subquery* (see Chapter 3)—that will explicitly extract the PID value from the row in question, and then plug that value into the row we're inserting into table NADDR. For example:

```
INSERT INTO NADDR ( NAME , ADDR , LOCATION )
          VALUES ( 'Joe' , ... ,
                 ( SELECT PID
                   FROM   POINTS
                   WHERE  X = 5.0 AND Y = 2.5 ) ) ;
```

A similar approach can be used with UPDATE statements, if necessary.

Aside: Note that, while we can certainly retrieve POINTS data by following pointers from table NADDR, we can't update POINTS data in the same way (i.e., we can't do what might be called "update via dereferencing"). For example, the following is illegal:

```
UPDATE NADDR
SET    LOCATION -> X = 7.3 ,  /* warning: illegal! */
       LOCATION -> Y = 0.8    /* warning: illegal! */
WHERE  NAME = 'Joe' ;
```

By contrast, the following, which achieves the presumably intended effect, *is* legal:

```
UPDATE POINTS
SET    X = 7.3 ,
       Y = 0.8
WHERE  PID =
     ( SELECT LOCATION
       FROM   NADDR
       WHERE  NAME = 'Joe' ) ;
```

---

[38] We've met this operator before too (see the section "Row and Table Types" in Chapter 3). *Note:* As I pointed out at the time, the operator is actually rather unusual, inasmuch as it's certainly read-only, and yet (as with an update operator) its argument—its sole argument—must be a variable specifically (why?).

End of aside.

Now, so far I've considered only queries on, or via, a table that has pointers into another (necessarily typed) table. What about queries on a typed table as such? In fact such queries basically just follow SQL's normal rules. For example, the following expression will return the *y* coordinates of all points currently represented in table POINTS that have *x* coordinate 5.0:

```
SELECT Y
FROM   POINTS
WHERE  X = 5.0
```

Updates are reasonably straightforward too, except for a couple of issues. The first is that (of course) we can't insert into or update column PID, since values in that column are provided by the system and never change. The second is that (as noted a few pages back) care might be needed in connection with deletions in order to avoid producing "dangling references"—i.e., REF values that point to a row that no longer exists.

> *Aside:* Well, actually there's a third, rather complicated point that I think I should mention too, because if it's correct it's certainly very odd (maybe it's not correct, but I think it is). On page 76 of his book, Melton says this:
>
>> You can never change the most specific type of a structured type instance [*sic*] to any type other than the one it had when it was created, not even to a proper supertype or a proper subtype.
>
> (Regarding the "most specific type" notion in general, see the answer to Exercise 2 in Chapter 4.)
> Now, it's true that this remark of Melton's refers to instances, not values or variables; but if "instance" means *value*, the remark is trivially true and wouldn't be worth making, so I have to assume it means *variable*. So let structured type *T* have an attribute RECT, say, of declared type RECTANGLE, say; let typed table *TT* be declared to be of type *T*; finally, let a row *r* be inserted into *TT* in which the RECT value is of most specific type RECTANGLE. Thus, the most specific type of that row *r* as such has a RECT component of most specific type RECTANGLE. And if *r* is updated—I

assume for the sake of the argument that *r* counts as a variable!—in such a way that it now contains a value of most specific type SQUARE (where SQUARE is a proper subtype of type RECTANGLE) in the RECT position, the most specific type of *r* is apparently still considered to have a RECT component of most specific type RECTANGLE, not SQUARE. Square nonsquares! (Nonsquare squares are possible too, of course.)[39]

Now, perhaps the root of the problem here is that term *instance*. What SQL means by that term is certainly far from clear. The 2011 version of the standard uses the phrase "instance of a value," suggesting that *instance* perhaps means what I called in Chapter 4 an *appearance* (since "appearance of a value" does make sense, while "value of a value" doesn't). By contrast, the 1999 version of the standard defines an instance to be a *physical representation* of a value. And on page 74 Melton's book says this: "Making a type INSTANTIABLE [*a technical term I'm not going to explain further here*] imposes no requirement on your application to actually create any instances of the type," which suggests rather strongly (to me, at any rate) that an instance is a variable— especially since these "instances" do certainly seem to be updatable. Yet on page 79 that same book states explicitly (indeed, it stresses the point) that "instances are *values*, not objects." But then on the very next page it talks about "instances of values," and elsewhere it talks about "constructing a value." And here are a few more quotes, selected almost at random:

> [Your] applications can ... update the attributes of UDT instances (page 52).[40]

> [You] can ... modify the value of an attribute of some UDT instance (page 53).

> [Instances] of structured [UDTs] ... are values, rather than objects (page 53).

---

[39] Such nonsenses couldn't occur if type constraints were supported, of course—but they aren't.

[40] "UDT" here and elsewhere in these quotes is an abbreviation for *user defined type*.

> Updating structured type instances ... isn't much more complicated than creating them (page 85).

> [Instances] of [structured UDTs] are values (page 119).

Overall, I'd have to say there does seem to be a considerable degree of muddle surrounding this notion. *End of aside.*

I'll finish up this section with two further observations:

■ First, here's a quote from the *Manifesto* book (it's somewhat paraphrased here, however, in order to make it fit the present context better):

> In a relational database, no table or row has any "hidden" component that (a) can be accessed only by invocation of some special operator instead of by means of a simple column reference, or that (b) causes invocations of the usual operators on tables or rows to have irregular effects.

Do you think self-referencing columns abide by this principle? Well, only you can answer this question—but I know you know what my own answer would be.

■ Second, I really do think those REF values are pointers. The thing about pointers is: They *point*—I mean, they have a direction to them, and they have a single, specific target. Note the asymmetry inherent in this state of affairs. In the NADDR example from a couple of pages back, to get from a given row in table NADDR to the corresponding row in table POINTS (or to the X and Y values in that row, rather), we can write something like this:

```
SELECT  LOCATION -> X , LOCATION -> Y
FROM    NADDR
WHERE   NAME = ...
```

However, to go in the opposite direction—i.e., to get from a given row in table POINTS to the corresponding row(s) in table NADDR (or to the NAME and ADDR values in those corresponding rows, rather)—we have to write something like this:

```
SELECT NAME , ADDR
FROM   NADDR
WHERE  LOCATION =
     ( SELECT PID
       FROM   POINTS
       WHERE  X = ... AND Y = ... )
```

Asymmetric, as I said.

Now contrast the situation with keys and foreign keys in the relational world. Key and foreign key values are regular data values, and they're thus, like all data values in a relational database, what might be called "*n*-way associative." For example, the part number P1, in some tuple in relvar SP (or indeed in any tuple anywhere in the database), is simultaneously linked—speaking purely logically, of course—not just to the pertinent part tuple in relvar P but to all shipment tuples in relvar SP, and indeed to all tuples anywhere in the database, that happen to contain that same part number. As a consequence, queries like

```
SELECT *
FROM   P
WHERE  PNO IN
     ( SELECT PNO
       FROM   SP
       WHERE  ... )
```

and

```
SELECT *
FROM   SP
WHERE  PNO IN
     ( SELECT PNO
       FROM   P
       WHERE  ... )
```

in SQL are much more symmetric.

Note: The foregoing symmetry is even more obvious in **Tutorial D**. Here are **Tutorial D** analogs of those two SQL queries:

```
P  MATCHING ( SP WHERE ... )

SP MATCHING ( P  WHERE ... )
```

Given all of the above, which do you think REF values more closely resemble?—pointers, or foreign keys?[41]

"SCALARNESS" REVISITED

I've said I don't really think there's any context in which a structured type behaves as if it were truly scalar (or "encapsulated"). To be specific, it always seems to be the case that its attributes are, either implicitly or explicitly, visible to the user—and that's more or less the definition of what it means *not* to be scalar. But am I being entirely fair here? Let's take a closer look.

Consider the following definition for the structured type POINT once again:

```
CREATE TYPE POINT
  AS ( X FLOAT , Y FLOAT ) FINAL ;
```

Given this definition, the X and Y observer and mutator functions (which are provided automatically by the system, remember) allow us to refer to the cartesian coordinates of any given point PT via dot qualification, thus: PT.X, PT.Y.[42] If we wanted to, though, we could effectively define additional observer and mutator functions RHO and THETA for this type (where RHO and THETA correspond to polar instead of cartesian coordinates, of course). And if we did, then a user of the type could behave more or less as if it had been defined with attributes RHO and THETA instead of X and Y. In particular, such a user could refer to the polar coordinates for any given point PT via dot qualification, thus: PT.RHO, PT.THETA. The net effect would thus be to make type POINT look a little bit like, in our terms, a scalar type with two distinct possreps.[43]

Numerous points (sorry) arise in connection with the foregoing paragraph, though. First of all, I've said we could additionally define polar observer and mutator functions, or methods, and that's true—but I don't think we could define a polar constructor method, because, although a given structured type is allowed to have any number of constructor methods, they must of course all have different signatures. Now, you'll recall that a signature in SQL consists of (a) the

---

[41] For further (and extensive) discussion of the logical difference between pointers and foreign keys in general, I refer you to my book *Keys, Foreign Keys, and Relational Theory* (Technics, 2023).

[42] *Exercise:* What exactly is PT here, syntactically speaking?

[43] But only a liitle bit like! The fact is, the type is *not* scalar, and the "possrep" is *not* a possrep as such.

operator name, (b) a sequence of parameter declared types, and (c) an indication of whether the operator in question is a procedure or a function. In the case of type POINT, then, a cartesian constructor method and a polar constructor method (a) would both be functions, (b) would both have the same operator name POINT, and (c) would both have two parameters, each of declared type FLOAT. In other words, they'd both have the same signature—and "distinct operators with the same signature" is a contradiction in terms.

Next, suppose we did in fact define what I've called "two different possreps" for type POINT nevertheless. One problem that raises its head immediately, then, is that those two "possreps" wouldn't be named; in particular, therefore, there wouldn't be a POLAR "selector" as such.[44] Nevertheless, we'd presumably still be able to "select" a point by its polar coordinates as illustrated in this example:

```
POINT ( ) . RHO ( 2.7 ) . THETA ( 1.0 )
```

A more significant problem is that (as we saw earlier in the chapter), SQL doesn't support type constraints. As a consequence, the logical relationship between the two "possreps" wouldn't be explicitly visible to the user but would effectively be hidden inside the code implementing those observer and mutator methods. In fact, the RHO and THETA mutators would have to be responsible for maintaining that relationship. Assuming it's maintained at all, I suppose I should add.

Despite all of these difficulties, however, it does seem as if—with discipline—SQL's nonscalar structured types might be made to behave somewhat like **Tutorial D**'s scalar types with possreps. There's at least one difference, though (possibly only a minor one):

- In **Tutorial D**, specification of a given possrep implies that THE_ operators and pseudovariables *will* be defined, automatically, for each component of that possrep.

- In SQL, by contrast, the possrep notion as such doesn't exist; thus, it would be entirely possible to define, say, a RHO observer and/or mutator, but no THETA observer and/or mutator, for type POINT.

---

[44] Of course, there isn't a CARTESIAN (or POINT, rather) selector as such, either; but there is a corresponding constructor.

On balance, therefore, I think I'd still have to say that SQL's structured types are really much more nonscalar than they are scalar.

EXERCISES

The following are basically all just review questions, and most of the answers can be found in the body of the chapter. There's no corresponding answers section as such.

1. What's the difference between a DISTINCT type and a structured type? How does the syntax for defining a DISTINCT type differ from that for defining a structured type? What's the most obvious difference between a structured type in SQL and a tuple type in **Tutorial D**?

2. Why doesn't SQL support type constraints? What are the consequences of that lack of support?

3. Suppose we decide to make supplier status values be of some user defined type, STATUS say (a DISTINCT type, just to be definite). Show an appropriate type definition, and revise the CREATE TABLE statement for table S accordingly. Define a local variable of type STATUS. Give examples of (a) assigning some value to that variable; (b) assigning the value of that variable to the STATUS component of some row in table S; and (c) selecting rows from that table whose STATUS value is greater than some prescribed literal value.

4. With one important exception, strong typing applies to DISTINCT types. What do you understand by this statement? What's the exception?

5. Explain the logical differences, if any, among the following: (a) routine; (b) function; (c) procedure; (d) method; (e) operator.

6. What are the advantages of using a method over a more conventional function? What are the disadvantages?

7. What's a signature?

8. Let DISTANCE, SPEED, and TIME be three different object types (or *classes*, to use the more conventional OO term), with the intuitively obvious semantics. Suppose you're told to implement a method corresponding to the well known formula $s = u \times t$ (where s *is* distance, u is speed, and t is time). Which object type would you attach that method to? Why?

9. What's an instance (i.e., of a type)?

10. What's a dangling reference? Can the dangling reference problem occur with foreign keys in the relational model? Or with foreign keys in SQL?

11. Explain the following terms: (a) selfish method; (b) dereferencing; (c) binding.

12. Identify as many logical differences as you can between an SQL-style table and "a bag of rows."

13. "SQL doesn't support table types." Explain this statement. Do you think this position on SQL's part is reasonable? Justify your answer.

14. Explain the differences between attributes, columns, and fields.

15. In SQL, how can a table value be assigned to a table variable? How can two table values be compared for equality? How can we test to see whether one table value is a subset of another (loosely speaking)? What about a proper subset?

16. What do you understand by the terms *observer* and *mutator*?

17. What's the difference between a constructor function and a constructor method?

18. Equality comparisons can't be performed on values of a given structured type unless an appropriate CREATE ORDERING has been executed for that type. If they can't, what are some of the consequences?

19. What's a referenceable table? What columns does such a table have? Is such a table in fact referenceable? If it isn't, what does it mean to describe it as referenceable?

20. Does SQL support the possrep notion? Justify your answer.

21. Are SQL's user defined types encapsulated? What about row types? What about table types? Explain your answer.

22. What's a typed table? How do such tables differ from other tables? Do you think the terminology is reasonable?

23. Show the steps we'd have to go through to convert our usual suppliers, parts, and shipments tables into typed tables. Give some examples of retrievals and updates—in particular, ones that have no obvious relational counterpart—against those typed tables.

24. What's an object? In SQL? In OO generally?

Appendix A

The Third Manifesto

I referred to *The Third Manifesto*, or just the *Manifesto* for short, several times in the body of this book. Just to remind you, the *Manifesto* is an attempt by Hugh Darwen and myself to define precisely what we think a true relational DBMS should look like to the user. In particular, as I explained in Chapter 1, it proposes a detailed theory of types, a theory that we believe is in the spirit of the relational model and works well with that model. Thus, since the present book is all about types and type theory, it seemed appropriate to include the *Manifesto* itself as an appendix. It's quite short, but dense.

PREAMBLE

Note: This section isn't part of the Manifesto as such, and what it has to say is mostly not new. It's intended primarily just as a reminder regarding certain terms and concepts from earlier in the present book that the Manifesto relies on, or appeals to (many times, in most cases).

- **D**: The *Manifesto* makes repeated reference to a hypothetical language it calles **D** (note the boldface). However, that name **D** is merely a useful generic label; any language that conforms to the principles laid down in the *Manifesto* is a valid **D**. Conversely, any language that doesn't conform to those principles isn't a valid **D**. (For the record, SQL isn't a valid **D**.)

- **Tutorial D**: The book *Databases, Types, and the Relational Model: The Third Manifesto*, 3rd ed., by Hugh Darwen and myself (Addison-Wesley, 2007)—"the *Manifesto* book" for short—contains among other things a fairly formal definition of one particular **D** that it calls **Tutorial D** (again, note the boldface). **Tutorial D** is a computationally complete programming language with fully integrated database functionality. However, it's deliberately not meant to be industrial strength; rather, it's a "toy" language, whose principal purpose is to serve as a teaching vehicle, and many features that would be required in an industrial strength language are intentionally omitted. In particular, it includes no exception handling, no I/O facilities, and no authorization features of any kind.

- *"RM" and "OO"*: The *Manifesto* defines a number of prescriptions and proscriptions that the language **D** is required to abide by. Prescriptions that arise directly from the relational model are called *Relational Model Prescriptions* ("RM Prescriptions"). Prescriptions that don't arise from that model are called *Other Orthogonal Prescriptions* ("OO Prescriptions").[1] Proscriptions are similarly divided into RM and OO categories. The *Manifesto* also includes a number of *Very Strong Suggestions*, likewise divided into RM and OO categories.

- *Expression*: The term *expression* refers to the representation in concrete syntactic form of a read-only operator invocation. Observe in particular that variable references are regarded as expressions in exactly this sense, and so are constant references.

- *Literal*: A literal is an expression denoting a selector operator invocation in which every argument expression is a literal in turn. Observe that there's a logical difference between a literal as such and the value it denotes.

- *Argument and argument expression*: An argument is what's substituted for a parameter when an operator is invoked; it's denoted by an argument expression, which is part of the representation in concrete syntactic form of the operator invocation in question. An argument is either a value or a variable. If the parameter in question is subject to update, the argument must be a variable (and the corresponding argument expression must be a variable reference specifically, denoting the variable in question); otherwise the argument must be a value (though the corresponding argument expression might still be a simple variable reference, denoting in this case the current value of the variable in question).

- *Scalar*: Loosely, a type is *scalar* if and only if it has no user visible components, and *nonscalar* if and only if it's not scalar; and values, variables, attributes, operators, parameters, and expressions of some type *T*

---

[1] A would-be joke, originally. It probably doesn't wear very well.

are scalar or nonscalar according as type *T* itself is scalar or nonscalar. But these definitions are only informal, and the *Manifesto* nowhere relies on them in any formal sense. For the purposes of this appendix, in fact, the term *scalar type* can be taken to mean just a type that's neither a tuple type nor a relation type, and the term *nonscalar type* can be taken to mean a type that is either a tuple type or a relation type. The terms *scalar value*, *nonscalar value, scalar operator, nonscalar operator,* etc., can all be interpreted analogously.

Two last preliminary points:

- *Type theory*: As noted above, the relational model in fact requires a supporting theory of types, and part of the purpose of the *Manifesto* is precisely to provide such a theory. Several of the RM Prescriptions are aimed toward this goal.

- *Type inheritance*: The *Manifesto* book also includes a detailed proposal for a model of type inheritance, a model that's described in excruciating detail in my book *Type Inheritance and the Relational Model* (O'Reilly, 2016). However, everything to do with that model is ignored in the *Manifesto* as such, except for very brief mentions in RM Prescription 1, OO Prescription 2, and OO Very Strong Suggestion 1. The concepts of the inheritance model extend, but do not invalidate, the concepts of the *Manifesto* as such.

RM PRESCRIPTIONS

1. A **scalar data type** (**scalar type** for short) is a named set of scalar values (**scalars** for short). Given an arbitrary pair of distinct scalar types named *T1* and *T2*, respectively, with corresponding sets of scalar values *S1* and *S2*, respectively, the names *T1* and *T2* shall be distinct and the sets *S1* and *S2* shall be disjoint; in other words, two scalar types shall be equal—i.e., the same type—if and only if they have the same name (and therefore the same set of values). **D** shall provide facilities for users to define their own scalar types (*user defined* scalar types); other scalar types shall be provided by the system (*built in* or *system defined* scalar types). With the sole exception of the system defined empty type *omega* (which is defined only if type inheritance is supported—see OO Prescription 2),

the definition of any given scalar type *T* shall be accompanied by a specification of an **example value** of that type. **D** shall also provide facilities for users to destroy user defined scalar types. The system defined scalar types shall include type **boolean** (containing just two values, here denoted TRUE and FALSE), and **D** shall support all four monadic and 16 dyadic logical operators, directly or indirectly, for this type.

2. All scalar values shall be **typed**—i.e., such values shall always carry with them, at least conceptually, some identification of the type to which they belong.

3. A **scalar operator** is an operator that, when invoked, returns a scalar value (the **result** of that invocation). **D** shall provide facilities for users to define and destroy their own scalar operators (*user defined* scalar operators). Other scalar operators shall be provided by the system (*built in* or *system defined* scalar operators). Let *Op* be a scalar operator. Then:

   a.   *Op* shall be **read-only**, in the sense that invoking it shall cause no variables to be updated other than ones local to the code that implements *Op*.

   b.   Every invocation of *Op* shall denote a value ("produce a result") of the same type, the **result type**—also called the **declared type**—of *Op* (as well as of that invocation of *Op* in particular). The definition of *Op* shall include a specification of that declared type.

   c.   The definition of *Op* shall include a specification of the type of each parameter to *Op*, the **declared type** of that parameter. If parameter *P* is of declared type *T*, then, in every invocation of *Op*, the expression that denotes the argument corresponding to *P* in that invocation shall also be of type *T*, and the value denoted by that expression shall be **effectively assigned** to *P*. *Note:* The prescriptions of this paragraph c. shall also apply if *Op* is an update operator instead of a read-only operator (see below).

It is convenient to deal with update operators here as well, despite the fact that such operators are not scalar (nor are they nonscalar—in fact, they are not typed at all). An **update operator** is an operator that, when invoked, is allowed to update at least one variable that is not local to the code that implements that operator. Let *V* be such a variable. If the operator accesses *V* via some parameter *P*, then that parameter *P* is **subject to update**. **D** shall provide facilities for users to define and destroy their own update operators (*user defined update operators*). Other update operators shall be provided by the system (*built in* or *system defined* update operators). Let *Op* be an update operator. Then:

d. No invocation of *Op* shall denote a value ("produce a result").

e. The definition of *Op* shall include a specification of which parameters to *Op* are subject to update.

If parameter *P* is subject to update, then, in every invocation of *Op*, the expression that denotes the argument corresponding to *P* in that invocation shall be a variable reference specifically, and, on completion of the execution of *Op* caused by that invocation, the final value assigned to *P* during that execution shall be **effectively assigned** to that variable.

4. Let *T* be a scalar type, and let *v* be an appearance in some context of some value of type *T*. By definition, *v* has exactly one **physical representation** and one or more **possible representations** (at least one, because there is obviously always one that is the same as the physical representation). Physical representations for values of type *T* shall be specified by means of some kind of *storage structure definition language* and shall not be visible in **D**. As for possible representations:

a. If *T* is user defined, then at least one possible representation for values of type *T* shall be declared and thus made visible in **D**. For each possible representation *PR* for values of type *T* that is visible in **D**, exactly one **selector** operator *S*, of declared type *T*, shall be provided. That operator *S* shall have all of the following properties:

1. There shall be a one to one correspondence between the parameters of *S* and the components of *PR* (see RM Prescription 5). Each parameter of *S* shall have the same declared type as the corresponding component of *PR*.

2. Every value of type *T* shall be produced by some invocation of *S* in which every argument expression is a literal.

3. Every successful invocation of *S* shall produce some value of type *T*.

b. If T is system defined, then zero or more possible representations for values of type T shall be declared and thus made visible in **D**. A possible representation PR for values of type T that is visible in **D** shall behave in all respects as if T were user defined and PR were a declared possible representation for values of type T. If no possible representation for values of type T is visible in **D**, then at least one **selector** operator S, of declared type T, shall be provided. Each such selector operator shall have all of the following properties:

1. Every argument expression in every invocation of S shall be a literal.

2. Every value of type T shall be produced by some invocation of S.

3. Every successful invocation of S shall produce some value of type T.

5. Let some declared possible representation PR for values of scalar type T be defined in terms of components $C1$, $C2$, ..., Cn ($n \geq 0$), each of which has a name and a declared type. Let v be a value of type T, and let $PR(v)$ denote the possible representation corresponding to PR for that value v. Then $PR(v)$ shall be **exposed**—i.e., a set of read-only and update operators shall be provided such that:

a. For all such values v and for all i ($i = 1, 2, ..., n$), it shall be possible to "retrieve" (i.e., read the value of) the Ci component of $PR(v)$. The read-only operator that provides this functionality shall have declared type the same as that of Ci.

b. For all variables V of declared type T and for all i ($i = 1, 2, ..., n$), it shall be possible to update V in such a way that if the values of V before and after the update are v and v' respectively, then the possible representations corresponding to PR for v and v' (i.e., $PR(v)$ and $PR(v')$, respectively) differ only in their Ci components.

Such a set of operators shall be provided for each possible representation declared for values of type T.

6. **D** shall support the **TUPLE** type generator. That is, given some heading H (see RM Prescription 9), **D** shall support use of the **generated type** TUPLE H as a basis for defining (or, in the case of values, selecting):

a. Values of that type (see RM Prescription 9)

b. Variables of that type (see RM Prescription 12)

c. Attributes of that type (see RM Prescriptions 9 and 10)

d. Components of that type within declared possible representations (see RM Prescription 5)

e. Read-only operators of that type (see RM Prescription 20)

f. Parameters of that type to user defined operators (see RM Prescriptions 3 and 20)

The generated type TUPLE H shall be referred to as a **tuple type**, and the name of that type shall be, precisely, TUPLE H. The terminology of **degree**, **attributes**, and **heading** introduced in RM Prescription 9 shall apply, mutatis mutandis, to that type, as well as to values and variables of that type (see RM Prescription 12). Tuple types TUPLE $H1$ and TUPLE $H2$ shall be equal if and only if $H1 = H2$. The applicable operators shall include operators analogous to the RENAME, *project*, EXTEND, and JOIN operators of the relational algebra (see RM Prescription 18), together with tuple assignment (see RM Prescription 21) and tuple comparisons (see RM Prescription 22); they shall also include (a) a tuple selector operator (see RM Prescription 9), (b) an operator for extracting a specified attribute value from a specified tuple (the tuple in question might be required to be of degree one—see RM Prescription 9), and (c) operators for performing tuple "nesting" and "unnesting."

Note: When we say "the name of [a certain tuple type] shall be, precisely, TUPLE H," we do not mean to prescribe specific syntax. The *Manifesto* does not prescribe syntax. Rather, what we mean is that the type in question shall have a name that does both of the following, no more and no less: First, it shall specify that the type is indeed a tuple type; second, it shall specify the pertinent heading. Syntax of the form "TUPLE H" satisfies these requirements, and we therefore use it as a convenient shorthand; however, all appearances of that syntax throughout this *Manifesto* are to be interpreted in the light of these remarks.

7. **D** shall support the **RELATION** type generator. That is, given some heading *H* (see RM Prescription 9), **D** shall support use of the **generated type** RELATION *H* as the basis for defining (or, in the case of values, selecting):

   a. Values of that type (see RM Prescription 10)

   b. Variables of that type (see RM Prescription 13)

   c. Attributes of that type (see RM Prescriptions 9 and 10)

   d. Components of that type within declared possible representations (see RM Prescription 5)

   e. Read-only operators of that type (see RM Prescription 20)

   f. Parameters of that type to user defined operators (see RM Prescriptions 3 and 20)

The generated type RELATION *H* shall be referred to as a **relation type**, and the name of that type shall be, precisely, RELATION *H*. The terminology of **degree**, **attributes**, and **heading** introduced in RM Prescription 9 shall apply, mutatis mutandis, to that type, as well as to values and variables of that type (see RM Prescription 13). Relation types RELATION *H1* and RELATION *H2* shall be equal if and only if *H1* = *H2*. The applicable operators shall include the usual operators of the relational algebra (see RM Prescription 18), together with relational assignment (see RM Prescription 21) and relational comparisons (see RM Prescription 22); they shall also include (a) a relation selector operator (see RM Prescription 10), (b) an operator for extracting the sole tuple from a specified relation of cardinality one (see RM Prescription 10), and (c) operators for performing relational "nesting" and "unnesting."

Note: When we say "the name of [a certain relation type] shall be, precisely, RELATION *H*," we do not mean to prescribe specific syntax. The *Manifesto* does not prescribe syntax. Rather, what we mean is that the type in question shall have a name that does both of the following, no more and no less: First, it shall specify that the type is indeed a relation type; second, it shall specify the pertinent heading. Syntax of the form "RELATION *H*" satisfies these requirements, and we therefore use it as a convenient shorthand; however, all appearances of that syntax throughout this *Manifesto* are to be interpreted in the light of these remarks.

8. **D** shall support the **equality** comparison operator "=" for every type *T*. Let *v1* and *v2* be values, and consider the equality comparison *v1* = *v2*. The values *v1* and *v2* shall be of the same type *T*. The comparison shall return TRUE if and only if *v1* and *v2* are the very same value. *Note:* It follows from this prescription that if (a) there exists an operator *Op* (other than "=" itself) with a parameter *P* of declared type *T* such that (b) two successful invocations of *Op* that are identical in all respects except that the argument corresponding to *P* is *v1* in one invocation and *v2* in the other are distinguishable in their effect, then (c) *v1* = *v2* must evaluate to FALSE.

   Note: By "operator" here we mean one that is a function, i.e., determinate. That two evaluations of RANDOM (5), for example, might differ in their results is irrelevant. Also, an operator whose implementation references a variable that is not defined locally within that implementation is indeterminate.

9. A **heading** *H* is a set of ordered pairs or **attributes** of the form <*A,T*>, where:

   a. *A* is the name of an **attribute** of *H*. No two distinct pairs in *H* shall have the same attribute name.

   b. *T* is the name of the **declared type** of attribute *A* of *H*.

The number of pairs in *H*—equivalently, the number of attributes of *H*—is the **degree** of *H*.

   Now let *t* be a set of ordered triples <*A,T,v*>, obtained from *H* by extending each ordered pair <*A,T*> to include an arbitrary value *v* of type *T*, called the **attribute value** for attribute *A* of *t*. Then *t* is a **tuple value** (**tuple** for short) that **conforms** to heading *H*; equivalently, *t* is of the corresponding tuple type (see RM Prescription 6). The degree of that heading *H* shall be the **degree** of *t*, and the attributes and corresponding types of that heading *H* shall be the **attributes** and corresponding **declared attribute types** of *t*.

   Given a heading *H*, exactly one **selector** operator *S*, of declared type TUPLE *H*, shall be provided for selecting an arbitrary tuple conforming to *H*. That operator *S* shall have all of the following properties:

1. There shall be a one to one correspondence between the parameters of *S* and the attributes of *H*. Each parameter of *S* shall have the same declared type as the corresponding attribute of *H*.

2. Every tuple of type TUPLE *H* shall be produced by some invocation of *S* in which every argument expression is a literal.

3. Every successful invocation of *S* shall produce some tuple of type TUPLE *H*.

10. A **relation value** *r* (**relation** for short) consists of a *heading* and a *body,* where:

   a. The **heading** of *r* shall be a heading *H* as defined in RM Prescription 9; *r* **conforms** to that heading; equivalently, *r* is of the corresponding relation type (see RM Prescription 7). The degree of that heading *H* shall be the **degree** of *r*, and the attributes and corresponding types of that heading *H* shall be the **attributes** and corresponding **declared attribute types** of *r*.

   b. The **body** of *r* shall be a set *B* of tuples, all having that same heading *H*. The cardinality of that body shall be the **cardinality** of *r*. *Note:* Relation *r* is an *empty relation* if and only if the set *B* is empty.

   Given a heading *H*, exactly one **selector** operator *S*, of declared type RELATION *H*, shall be provided for selecting an arbitrary relation conforming to *H*. That operator *S* shall have all of the following properties:

   1. The sole argument to any given invocation of *S* shall be a set *B* of tuples, each of which shall be denoted by a tuple expression of declared type TUPLE *H*.

   2. Every relation of type RELATION *H* shall be produced by some invocation of *S* for which the tuple expressions that together denote the argument to that invocation are all literals.

3. Every successful invocation of *S* shall produce some relation of type RELATION *H*: to be specific, the relation of type RELATION *H* with body *B*.

11. **D** shall provide facilities for users to define **scalar variables**. Each scalar variable shall be named and shall have a specified (scalar) **declared type**. Let scalar variable *V* be of declared type *T*; for so long as variable *V* exists, it shall have a value that is of type *T*. Defining *V* shall have the effect of initializing *V* to some value—either a value specified explicitly as part of the operation that defines *V*, or some implementation defined value otherwise. *Note:* Omitting an explicit initialization value does not preclude the implementation from checking that no reference is made to scalar variable *V* until an explicit assignment to *V* has occurred. Analogous remarks apply to tuple variables (see RM Prescription 12), real relvars (see RM Prescription 14), and private relvars (again, see RM Prescription 14).

12. **D** shall provide facilities for users to define **tuple variables**. Each tuple variable shall be named and shall have a specified **declared type** of the form TUPLE *H* for some heading *H*. Let variable *V* be of declared type TUPLE *H*; then the degree of that heading *H* shall be the **degree** of *V*, and the attributes and corresponding types of that heading *H* shall be the **attributes** and corresponding **declared attribute types** of *V*. For so long as variable *V* exists, it shall have a value that is of type TUPLE *H*. Defining *V* shall have the effect of initializing *V* to some value—either a value specified explicitly as part of the operation that defines *V*, or some implementation defined value otherwise.

13. **D** shall provide facilities for users to define **relation variables** (**relvars** for short)—both database relvars (i.e., relvars that are part of some database) and application relvars (i.e., relvars that are local to some application). **D** shall also provide facilities for users to destroy database relvars. Each relvar shall be named and shall have a specified **declared type** of the form RELATION *H* for some heading *H*. Let variable *V* be of declared type RELATION *H*; then the degree of that heading *H* shall be the **degree** of *V*, and the attributes and corresponding types of that heading *H* shall be the **attributes** and corresponding **declared attribute types** of *V*. For so long as variable *V* exists, it shall have a value that is of type RELATION *H*.

14. Database relvars shall be either *real* or *virtual*. A **virtual relvar** *V* shall be a database relvar whose value at any given time is the result of evaluating a certain relational expression at that time; the relational expression in question shall be specified when *V* is defined and shall mention at least one database relvar other than *V*. A **real relvar** (also known as a **base relvar**) shall be a database relvar that is not virtual. Defining a real relvar *V* shall have the effect of initializing *V* to some value—either a value specified explicitly as part of the operation that defines *V*, or the empty relation of type RELATION *H* otherwise (where RELATION *H* is the type of relvar *V*).

Application relvars shall be either *public* or *private*. A **public relvar** shall be an application relvar that constitutes the perception on the part of the application in question of some portion of some database. A **private relvar** shall be an application relvar that is completely private to the application in question and is not part of any database. Defining a private relvar *V* shall have the effect of initializing *V* to some value—either a value specified explicitly as part of the operation that defines *V*, or the empty relation of type RELATION *H* otherwise (where RELATION *H* is the type of relvar *V*).

15. Every relvar shall have at least one **candidate key**. At least one such key shall be defined, explicitly or implicitly, at the time the relvar in question is defined, and it shall not be possible to destroy all of the candidate keys of a given relvar other than by destroying the relvar itself.

16. A **database** shall be a named container for relvars; the content of a given database at any given time shall be a set of database relvars. The necessary operators for defining and destroying databases shall have no effect, when invoked, on any current transactions (see RM Prescription 17 and OO Prescriptions 4 and 5), nor on the **D** environment in which any such transaction is operating.

17. Each **transaction** shall interact with exactly one database. However, distinct transactions shall be allowed to interact with distinct databases, and distinct databases shall not necessarily be disjoint. Also, **D** shall provide facilities for a transaction to define new relvars, or destroy existing ones, within its associated database (see RM Prescription 13). Every execution of every **statement** (other than a "begin transaction" statement—see OO Prescription 4) shall be performed within the context of some transaction. Every statement execution shall be **semantically atomic** (i.e., it shall be as if either the statement executes in its

entirety or it fails to execute at all), except possibly if either of the following is the case:

a. The statement in question is not syntactically atomic (i.e., it contains another statement nested inside itself).

b. The statement in question represents the invocation of a user defined update operator.

18. **D** shall support the usual operators of the **relational algebra** (or some logical equivalent thereof). All such operators shall be expressible without excessive circumlocution. **D** shall support **type inference** for relation types, whereby the type of the result of evaluating an arbitrary relational expression shall be well defined and known to both the system and the user. *Note:* It follows from this prescription that **D** shall also support type inference for tuple types, whereby the type of the result of evaluating an arbitrary tuple expression shall be well defined and known to both the system and the user.

19. **Variable references** and **constant references** shall be valid expressions. The expression V, where V is a variable reference, shall be regarded as an invocation of a read-only operator that returns the current value of variable V. The expression C, where C is a constant reference, shall be regarded as an invocation of a read-only operator that returns the value of constant C.

20. **D** shall provide facilities for users to define and destroy their own **tuple operators** (*user defined* tuple operators) and **relational operators** (*user defined* relational operators), and paragraphs a.-c. from RM Prescription 3 shall apply, mutatis mutandis. **Recursion** shall be permitted in operator definitions.

21. **D** shall support the **assignment** operator ":=" for every type T. The assignment shall be referred to as a scalar, tuple, or relation (or relational) assignment according as T is a scalar, tuple, or relation type. Let V and v be a variable and a value, respectively, of the same type. After assignment of v to V (the "target variable"), the equality comparison $V = v$ shall evaluate to TRUE (see RM Prescription 8).

    D shall also support a **multiple** form of assignment, in which several individual assignments shall be performed as a single semantically atomic operation. Let *MA* be the multiple assignment

```
A1 , A2 , ... , An ;
```

(where *A1*, *A2*, ..., *An* are individual assignments, each assigning to exactly one target variable, and the semicolon marks the overall end of the operation). Then the semantics of *MA* shall be defined by the following pseudocode (Steps a.-d.):

a. For $i := 1$ to n, expand any syntactic shorthands involved in *Ai*. After all such expansions, let *MA* take the form

```
V1 := X1 , V2 := X2 , ... , Vz := Xz ;
```

for some $z \geq n$, where *Vi* is the name of some variable not defined in terms of any others and *Xi* is an expression of declared type the same as that of *Vi*.

b. Let p and q ($1 \leq p < q \leq z$) be such that *Vp* and *Vq* are identical and there is no r ($r < p$ or $p < r < q$) such that *Vp* and *Vr* are identical. Replace *Vq* := *Xq* in *MA* by an assignment of the form

```
Vq := WITH ( Vq := Xp ) : Xq
```

and remove *Vp* := *Xp* from *MA*. Repeat this process until no such pair p and q remains. Let *MA* now consist of the sequence

```
U1 := Y1 , U2 := Y2 , ... , Um := Ym ;
```

where each *Ui* is some *Vj* ($1 \leq i \leq j \leq m \leq z$).

c. For $i := 1$ to m, evaluate *Yi*. Let the result be *yi*.

d. For $i := 1$ to m, assign *yi* to *Ui*.

Note: Step b. of the foregoing pseudocode makes use of the WITH construct of **Tutorial D**. For further explanation, see [*the answer to Exercise 2 in Chapter 1 of the present book*].

22. **D** shall support certain **comparison operators**, as follows:

a. The operators for comparing scalars shall include "=", "≠", and (for ordered types) "<", ">", etc.

b. The operators for comparing tuples shall include "=" and "≠" and shall not include "<", ">", etc.

c. The operators for comparing relations shall include "=", "≠", "⊆" ("is a subset of"), and "⊇" ("is a superset of") and shall not include "<", ">", etc.

d. The operator "∈" for testing membership of a tuple in a relation shall be supported.

In every case mentioned except "∈" the comparands shall be of the same type; in the case of "∈" they shall have the same heading. *Note:* Support for "=" for every type is in fact required by RM Prescription 8.

23. **D** shall provide facilities for defining and destroying **integrity constraints** (**constraints** for short). Let *C* be a constraint. Then *C* can be thought of as a boolean expression (though it might not be explicitly formulated as such); it shall be **satisfied** if and only if that boolean expression evaluates to TRUE, and **violated** if and only if it is not satisfied. No user shall ever see a state of affairs in which *C* is violated. There shall be two kinds of constraints:

a. A **type** constraint shall specify the set of values that constitute a given type.

b. A **database** constraint shall specify that, at all times, values of a given set of database relvars taken in combination shall be such that a given boolean expression (which shall mention no variables other than the database relvars in question) evaluates to TRUE. Insofar as feasible, **D** shall support **constraint inference** for database constraints, whereby the constraints that apply to the result of evaluating an arbitrary relational expression shall be well defined and known to both the system and the user.

Note: Let database relvars *R1* and *R2* be distinct and let database constraint *DBC* mention them both; then assignment of some relation *r1* to *R1* will in general require assignment of some relation *r2* to *R2* in order that *DBC* not be violated. The individual assignments *R1 := r1* and *R2 := r2* shall be executed as part of the same multiple assignment operation (see RM Prescription 21).

Moreover, if (a) the user requests the assignment $R1 := r1$ without requesting, as part of the same multiple assignment, some assignment to $R2$, but (b) the system is able to determine $r2$ (from *DBC* or otherwise) for itself, then (c) the assignment $R2 := r2$ shall be performed automatically (though not necessarily without the user's knowledge) unless (d) such automatic assignments have been declaratively prohibited.

24. Let *DB* be a database; let *DBC1*, *DBC2*, ..., *DBCn* be all of the database constraints defined for *DB* (see RM Prescription 23); and let *DBC* be any boolean expression that is logically equivalent to

```
( DBC1 ) AND ( DBC2 ) AND ... AND ( DBCn ) AND TRUE
```

Then *DBC* shall be the **total database constraint** for *DB*.

25. Every database shall include a set of database relvars that constitute the **catalog** for that database. **D** shall provide facilities for assigning to relvars in the catalog. *Note:* Since assignments in general are allowed to be multiple assignments in particular (see RM Prescription 21), it follows that **D** shall permit any number of operations of a definitional nature—defining and destroying types, operators, variables, constraints, and so on—all to be performed as a single semantically atomic operation.

26. **D** shall be constructed according to well established principles of **good language design**.

RM PROSCRIPTIONS

1. **D** shall include no concept of a "relation" whose attributes are distinguishable by ordinal position. Instead, for every relation r expressible in **D**, the attributes of r shall be distinguishable by *name*.

2. **D** shall include no concept of a "relation" whose tuples are distinguishable by ordinal position. Instead, for every relation r expressible in **D**, the tuples of r shall be distinguishable by *value*.

3. **D** shall include no concept of a "relation" containing two distinct tuples $t1$ and $t2$ such that the comparison "$t1 = t2$" evaluates to TRUE. It follows that (as

already stated in RM Proscription 2), for every relation *r* expressible in **D**, the tuples of *r* shall be distinguishable by value.

4. **D** shall include no concept of a "relation" in which some "tuple" includes some "attribute" that does not have a value.

5. **D** shall not forget that relations with no attributes are respectable and interesting, nor that candidate keys with no components are likewise respectable and interesting.

6. **D** shall include no constructs that relate to, or are logically affected by, the "physical" or "storage" or "internal" levels of the system.

7. **D** shall support no tuple level operations on relvars or relations.

8. **D** shall not include any specific support for "composite" or "compound" attributes, since such functionality can more cleanly be achieved, if desired, through the type support already prescribed.

9. **D** shall include no "domain check override" operators, since such operators are both ad hoc and unnecessary.

10. **D** shall not be called SQL.

OO PRESCRIPTIONS

1. **D** shall permit **compile time type checking**.

2. If **D** supports **type inheritance**, then such support shall conform to the inheritance model defined in Part IV of the *Manifesto* book (as revised in Chapter 19 of the book *Database Explorations*, by Hugh Darwen and myself (Trafford, 2010) [*and as further revised in my book Type Inheritance and Relational Theory (O'Reilly, 2016)*]).

3. **D** shall be **computationally complete**. **D** may support, but shall not require, invocation from "host programs" written in languages other than **D**. **D** may also

support, but shall not require, the use of other languages for implementation of user defined operators.

4. **D** shall provide **explicit transaction** support, according to which:

a.   Transaction initiation shall be performed only by means of an explicit **"begin transaction"** statement.

b.   Transaction termination shall be performed only by means of a **"commit"** or **"rollback"** statement; commit must always be explicit, but rollback can be implicit (if and only if the transaction fails through no fault of its own).

If transaction *TX* terminates with commit ("normal termination"), changes made by *TX* to the applicable database shall be committed. If transaction *TX* terminates with rollback ("abnormal termination"), changes made by *TX* to the applicable database shall be rolled back.

Optionally, **D** shall also provide **implicit** transaction support, according to which any request to execute some statement *S* (other than a "begin transaction," "commit," or "rollback" statement) while no transaction is in progress shall be treated as if that statement *S* is immediately preceded by a "begin transaction" statement and immediately followed by either a "commit" statement (if statement *S* executes successfully) or a "rollback" statement (otherwise).

5. **D** shall support **nested transactions**—i.e., it shall permit a parent transaction *TX* to initiate a child transaction *TX'* before *TX* itself has terminated, in which case:

a.   *TX* and *TX'* shall interact with the same database (as is in fact required by RM Prescription 17).

b.   Whether *TX* shall be required to suspend execution while *TX'* executes shall be implementation defined. However, *TX* shall not be allowed to terminate before *TX'* terminates; in other words, *TX'* shall be wholly contained within *TX*.

c.   Rollback of *TX* shall include the rolling back of *TX'* even if *TX'* has terminated with commit. In other words, "commit" is always interpreted within the parent context (if such exists) and is subject to override by the parent transaction (again, if such exists).

6. Let *AggOp* be an **aggregate** operator (other than one that simply returns the cardinality of its operand relation), and let the relation over which the aggregation is to be done in some given invocation of *AggOp* be *r*. Without loss of generality, let the items to be aggregated in that invocation of *AggOp* be just the appearances of values within some attribute *A* of *r*. If all of the following are true:

   a. *AggOp* is essentially just shorthand for some iterated dyadic operator *Op* (e.g., the dyadic operator is "+" in the case of SUM)

   b. An identity value *i* exists for *Op* (e.g., the identity value is zero in the case of "+")

   c. The semantics of *AggOp* are not such as to require the result of an invocation to be a value appearing in *A*

then the invocation is equivalent to *i Op x1 Op x2 ... Op xn*, where *n* ($n \geq 0$) is the cardinality of *r* and *x1*, *x2*, ..., *xn* are the *n* appearances of values for *A* in *r*, arbitrarily ordered.

OO PROSCRIPTIONS

1. Relvars are not domains.

2. No database relvar shall include an attribute of type *pointer.*

RM VERY STRONG SUGGESTIONS

1. **D** should provide a mechanism according to which values of some specified candidate key (or specified components thereof) for some specified relvar are **supplied by the system**. It should also provide a mechanism according to which an arbitrary relation can be extended to include an attribute whose values (a) are

unique within that relation (or within certain partitions of that relation), and (b) are once again **supplied by the system**.

2. Let *RX* be a relational expression. By definition, *RX* can be thought of as designating a relvar, *R* say—either a user defined relvar (if *RX* is just a relvar name) or a system defined relvar (otherwise). It is desirable, though perhaps not always feasible, for the system to be able to **infer the candidate keys** of *R*, such that:

a. If *RX* constitutes the defining expression for some virtual relvar *R'*, then those inferred candidate keys can be checked for consistency with the candidate keys explicitly defined for *R'* (if any) and—assuming no conflict—become candidate keys for *R'*.

b. Those inferred candidate keys can be included in the information about *R* that is made available (in response to a "metaquery") to a user of **D**.

D should provide such functionality, but without any guarantee (a) that such inferred candidate keys are not proper supersets of actual candidate keys ("proper superkeys") or (b) that such an inferred candidate key is discovered for every actual candidate key.

3. **D** should support **transition constraints**—i.e., constraints on the transitions that a given database can make from one value to another.

4. **D** should provide some shorthand for expressing **quota queries**. It should not be necessary to convert the relation concerned into (e.g.) an array in order to formulate such a query.

5. **D** should provide some shorthand for expressing the **generalized transitive closure** operation, including the ability to specify generalized *concatenate* and *aggregate* operations.

6. **D** should provide some means for users to define their own generic **operators**, including in particular generic **relational** operators.

7. **SQL** should be implementable in **D**—not because such implementation is desirable in itself, but so that a painless migration route might be available for

current SQL users. To this same end, existing SQL databases should be convertible to a form that **D** programs can operate on without error.

OO VERY STRONG SUGGESTIONS

1. **Type inheritance** should be supported (in which case, see OO Prescription 2).

2. Let operator *Op* have a parameter of declared type *T*. Then the definition of *Op* should be **logically distinct** from the definition of *T*, not "bundled in" with this latter definition. *Note:* The operators required by RM Prescriptions 4, 5, 8, and 21 might be exceptions in this regard.

3. **D** should support the concept of **single level storage**.

Appendix B

Glossary of Terms

This appendix contains definitions, mostly in abbreviated and somewhat rough and ready form, for many of the technical terms used in the body of the text. The definitions are based on ones in my book *The New Relational Database Dictionary* (O'Reilly, 2016).

ad hoc polymorphism Overloading.

argument The operand that replaces a given parameter of a given operator on a given invocation of the operator in question.

assignment An operator (":=") that assigns a value (the source, denoted by an expression) to a variable (the target, denoted by a variable reference); also, the operation performed when that operator is invoked. The source and target must be of the same type, and the operation overall must abide by *The Assignment Principle*. Every update operator invocation is logically equivalent to some assignment operation, albeit possibly a multiple one.

Assignment Principle Immediately following assignment of value v to variable V, the comparison $v = V$ evaluates to TRUE.

attribute An ordered pair of the form $<A,T>$, where A is the name of the attribute in question and T is the name of the corresponding type (though T is often ignored in informal contexts).

attribute (SQL) A component of a structured type.

bag A collection of elements in which any given element can appear more than once.

base relation The value of a given base relvar at a given time.

base relvar A relvar not defined in terms of others.

body A set of tuples all of the same type.

candidate key Key. The qualifier "candidate" is a hangover from older writings and can usually be omitted without loss.

cardinality The number of elements in a bag or set.

cartesian product Let relations r_1 and r_2 have no attribute names in common. Then the expression

    r_1 TIMES r_2

denotes the cartesian product of r_1 and r_2, and it returns the relation with heading the set theory union of the headings of r_1 and r_2 and body the set of all tuples t such that t is the set theory union of a tuple from r_1 and a tuple from r_2.

coercion Implicit type conversion.

constraint Either a database constraint or a type constraint; usually taken to refer to a database constraint, unless the context demands otherwise.

data independence The ability to change either the physical or the logical design of a database without having to make corresponding changes in the way the database is perceived by users. The terms *physical data independence* and *logical data independence* refer to the two cases.

data model A theory of data; an abstract, self-contained, logical definition of the data structures, data operators, and so forth, that together make up the abstract machine with which users interact.

database Strictly, a database value; more commonly used, in this book in particular, to refer to what would more accurately be called a database variable.

database constraint An integrity constraint that's not a type constraint.

declared type Same as type, except possibly if inheritance is in effect.

degree The number of attributes in a given heading.

dereferencing *See* referencing.

difference Let relations r_1 and r_2 be of the same type T. Then the expression

```
r₁ MINUS r₂
```

denotes the difference between r_1 and r_2 (in that order), and it returns the relation of type T with body the set of all tuples t such that t appears in r_1 and not in r_2.

DISTINCT type (SQL) *See* user defined type (SQL).

domain Type. The term *type* is preferred, partly because it has a longer pedigree (in computing contexts, at least), and partly because *domain* has a somewhat different meaning in mathematics.

encapsulated Scalar. (The term has an extended meaning in OO contexts, but that meaning is deprecated because it mixes model and implementation.)

equality A truth valued operator ("="); two values are equal if and only if they're the very same value.

expression A read-only operator invocation; thus, a construct that denotes a value (in effect, a rule for computing, or determining, the value in question).

extension Let relation r not have an attribute called A. Then the expression

```
EXTEND r : { A := exp }
```

denotes an extension of r, and it returns the relation with heading the heading of r extended with attribute A and body the set of all tuples t such that t is a tuple of r extended with a value for A that's computed by evaluating the expression *exp* on that tuple of r.

field (SQL) A component of a row type.

first normal form Relation *r* is in first normal form (1NF)—equivalently, *r* is normalized—if and only every tuple in *r* contains a single value in every attribute position. All relations are in 1NF. *Note:* Higher normal forms (2NF, etc.) do exist, but they apply to relvars, not relations.

function (mathematics) Given sets *X* and *Y*, not necessarily distinct, a rule pairing each element *x* of *X* with exactly one element *y* of *Y*; equivalently, the set of ordered pairs <*x,y*> that constitutes that pairing.

function (programming languages) A read-only operator. Note, however, that the programming language construct denoted by this term is—or at least should be—precisely a function in the mathematical sense; thus, there's really just one concept here, not two.

generated type A type obtained by invoking a type generator.

generic constraint A constraint that's automatically enforced in connection with every type that's produced by invocation of some given type generator.

generic operator An operator that's available in connection with every type that's produced by invocation of some given type generator.

generic polymorphism The kind of polymorphism exhibited by a generic operator.

heading A set of attributes such that distinct attributes in the set have distinct names.

immutable object (OO) A value. *See also* mutable object.

implementation A physical realization on a physical computer system of the abstract machine that constitutes some given data model.

implementation defined (SQL) Term used to refer to a feature whose specifics can vary from one implementation to another but do at least have to be defined for any individual implementation.

implementation dependent (SQL) Term used to refer to a feature whose specifics can vary from one implementation to another and don't even have to be defined for any individual implementation.

Information Principle The database as seen by the user contains relvars, and nothing but relvars.

intersection Let relations r_1 and r_2 be of the same type T. Then the expression

```
r₁ INTERSECT r₂
```

denotes the intersection of r_1 and r_2, and it returns the relation of type T with body the set of all tuples t such that t appears in each of r_1 and r_2.

join Let relations r_1 and r_2 be joinable. Then the expression

```
r₁ JOIN r₂
```

denotes the join—sometimes referred to more specifically as the *natural* join—of r_1 and r_2, and it returns the relation with heading the set theory union of the headings of r_1 and r_2 and body the set of all tuples t such that t is the set theory union of a tuple from r_1 and a tuple from r_2.

joinable Relations r_1 and r_2 are joinable if and only if attributes with the same name are of the same type—equivalently, if and only if the set theory union of their headings is a legal heading.

literal A self-defining symbol; a symbol that denotes a value that's known and determined at compile time.

logical difference A difference that's logical, not (e.g.) merely psychological, in nature.

message (OO) Operator invocation.

method (OO) Either an operator as such (a model concept) or an implementation of some operator (an implementation concept).

most specific type Same as type, except possibly if inheritance is in effect.

multiple assignment An operation that allows several individual assignments all to be performed in parallel (in effect, simultaneously).

multiset Bag.

mutable object (OO) A variable. *See also* immutable object.

mutator (OO) An update operator.

natural join *See* join.

nonscalar Having user visible component parts.

normalized First normal form. Sometimes also used to refer to some higher normal form, but such usage is deprecated.

object (OO) A value or a variable.

object ID (OO) Either the address of the pertinent object, if the object is a variable, or the object itself, if the object is a value.

observer (OO) A read-only operator.

operation Either the execution of some operator or an operator as such, depending on context.

overloading Using the same name for two or more different operators.

parameter A formal operand in terms of which some operator is defined, to be replaced by an argument when the operator in question is invoked.

physical representation Internal representation of data in physical storage.

pointer An implementation construct (basically an address).

possible representation Let T be a scalar type, and let v be an appearance in some context of some value of type T; then v has exactly one physical representation and at least one possible representation. If T is user defined, then at least one possible representation ("possrep" for short) for values of type T must be explicitly declared; if T is system defined, one or more possreps for values of type T might be explicitly declared, but don't have to be. Each possrep consists of zero or more components, where each such component consists in turn of a name and a corresponding declared type.

possibly nondeterministic (SQL) Term used to refer to the fact that the results of evaluating certain SQL expressions are unpredictable.

POSSREP The **Tutorial D** construct that defines a possible representation.

projection Let relation r have attributes $A_1, A_2, ..., A_n$ (and possibly others), of types $T_1, T_2, ..., T_n$, respectively. Then the expression

```
r { A₁ , A₂ , ..., Aₙ }
```

denotes the projection of r on those attributes, and it returns the relation with heading $\{<A_1,T_1>, <A_2,T_2>, ..., <A_n,T_n>\}$ and body consisting of all tuples t such that there exists a tuple in r that has the same value for attributes $A_1, A_2, ..., A_n$ as t does.

pseudovariable reference The use of an operational expression to denote the target for some update operation (usually explicit assignment).

read-only operator A function; an operator that, when invoked, updates nothing (except possibly variables local to the implementation of the operator in question) but returns a value, of a type declared when the operator in question is defined.

REF type (SQL) If T is a structured type, then defining T causes automatic definition of an associated REF type, denoted REF (T), whose values are "references" to rows in some "typed table" that's defined to be "of" type T. Thus, REF is really a type generator, and values of a REF type are SQL's analog of object IDs. In other words, they're pointers.

referencing An operator that, given a variable *V*, returns a pointer to—in other words, the address of—*V*. *Note:* Languages that support pointers usually support an operator called *dereferencing* as well, which, given a pointer *p*, returns the variable *V* that *p* points to. In SQL, however, (a) the dereferencing operator returns a value, not a variable—namely, the value of whatever it is that its pointer argument points to—and (b) the corresponding referencing operator doesn't exist.

RELATION In **Tutorial D**, the type generator for relation types. Also used in **Tutorial D** to denote a relation selector.

relation A relation value. *Note:* The term is also commonly used to refer to a relation variable, of course, but that usage is strongly deprecated as the source of much confusion.

relation selector Let *T* be a relation type; then the corresponding selector is an operator that allows a relation of type *T* to be selected, or specified, by supplying a set of tuples of the appropriate type.

relation type Let *H* be a heading; then all relations and all relvars with heading *H* are of a certain relation type (denoted RELATION *H* in **Tutorial D**), and no other relation and no other relvar is of that type.

relation value Let *H* be a heading, let *B* be a body consisting of tuples with heading *H*, and let *r* be the pair <*H,B*>. Then *r* is a relation value with heading *H* and body *B*, and with the same degree and attributes as *H* and with the same cardinality as *B*.

relation valued attribute An attribute whose type is some relation type.

relation variable A variable whose type is some relation type. Let relation variable *R* be of declared type *T*; then *R* has the same heading (and therefore the same attributes and degree) as type *T* does. Let the value of *R* at some given time be *r*; then *R* has the same body and cardinality at that time as *r* does.

relational assignment An operation that assigns a relation value to a relation variable. The relational INSERT, DELETE, and UPDATE operators are special cases.

relational database A database that abides by *The Information Principle*.

relvar Relation variable.

repeating group Let some table have a column C of type T. Then C is a repeating group column if and only if the values appearing in C aren't values of type T but are, rather, collections (i.e., sets or bags or sequences or arrays or ...) of values of type T. Relations in the relational model aren't allowed to have repeating group attributes (which is why this definition is phrased in terms of tables and columns instead of relations and attributes); in fact, a "relation" with a repeating group "attribute" is a contradiction in terms. *Note:* Technically, the foregoing definition might be considered as defining a repeating field rather than a repeating group. A repeating group would then be a repeating field in which the pertinent "field" is actually a combination of two or more columns, considered as a unit.

restriction Let r be a relation and let bx be a restriction condition. Then the expression

```
r WHERE bx
```

denotes the restriction of r according to bx, and it returns the relation with heading the same as that of r and with body consisting of just those tuples of r for which bx evaluates to TRUE.

restriction condition Let r be a relation; then a restriction condition on r is a boolean expression in which all attribute references are references to attributes of r and there are no relvar references.

scalar (*Of a type, attribute, value, or variable*) Having no user visible component parts. The term is also used as a noun, in which case it refers to a scalar value specifically. (*Of an operator*) Returning a scalar result.

selector An operator for selecting, or specifying, an arbitrary value of a given type. Literals are a special case.

signature Let *Op* be an operator; then *Op* has a signature, denoting that operator as perceived by the user and consisting of (a) the operator name *Op*, (b) the declared types of the parameters to *Op*, and either (c) the declared type of the result, if any, of executing *Op* or (d) an indication of which parameters to *Op*, if any, that are subject to update. *Note:* To what extent signatures in SQL conform to the foregoing definition isn't entirely clear.

strong typing A programming language is strongly typed if and only if every expression of the language is of a known type and type errors are always detected (preferably at compile time).

structured type (SQL) *See* user defined type (SQL).

system defined type A built-in type.

THE_ operator Let *T* be a scalar type. Then definition of a possrep *PR* for *T* causes automatic definition of a set of operators of the form THE_*A*, THE_*B*, …, THE_*C* (**Tutorial D** syntax), where *A*, *B*, ..., *C* are the names of the components of *PR*. Let *v* be a value of type *T*, and let *PR(v)* denote the possible representation corresponding to *PR* for that value *v*. Then invoking THE_*X* on *v* (*X* = *A*, *B*, …, *C*) returns the value of the *X* component of *PR(v)*.

THE_ pseudovariable A THE_ operator invocation used to specify the target of an assignment.

TUPLE In **Tutorial D**, the type generator for tuple types. Also used in **Tutorial D** to denote a tuple selector.

tuple A tuple value.

tuple assignment An operation that assigns a tuple value to a tuple variable.

tuple selector Let *T* be a tuple type; then the corresponding selector is an operator that allows a tuple of type *T* to be selected, or specified, by supplying values for the pertinent attributes.

tuple type Let H be a heading; then all tuples and all tuplevars with heading H are of a certain tuple type (denoted TUPLE H in **Tutorial D**), and no other tuple and no other tuplevar is of that type.

tuple value Let H be a heading, and let t be a set of triples of the form $<A,T,v>$, called components, obtained from H by extending each attribute $<A,T>$ in H to contain some value v of type T, called the attribute value in t for attribute A. Then t is a tuple value with heading H and the same degree and same attributes as H.

tuple variable A variable whose type is some tuple type. Let tuple variable V be of type T; then V has the same heading (and therefore the same attributes and same degree) as type T does.

tuplevar Tuple variable.

TYPE In **Tutorial D**, the type generator for scalar types.

type A named, and in practice finite, set of values.

type constraint A definition of the values that make up a given type. The type constraint for type T is checked, in effect, whenever some selector is invoked for that type T; in other words, a type constraint error ("type error" for short) occurs if and only if some selector is invoked with arguments that cause it to violate the applicable type constraint.

type generator An operator that's invoked at compile time instead of run time and returns a type instead of a value.

type inheritance An organizing principle according to which one type can be defined as a subtype of one or more other types, called supertypes (of the type in question). If T' is a subtype of supertype T, then all values of type T' are also values of type T, and read-only operators and type constraints that apply to values of type T therefore also apply to (i.e., "are inherited by") values of type T'. However, values of type T' will have read-only operators and type constraints of their own that don't apply to values that are only of type T and not of type T'.

union Let relations r_1 and r_2 be of the same type T. Then the expression

```
r₁ UNION r₂
```

denotes the union of r_1 and r_2, and it returns the relation of type T with body the set of all tuples t such that t appears in at least one of r_1 and r_2.

update operator An operator that, when invoked, returns no value but updates a variable (usually an argument) that's not local to the implementation of the operator in question.

user defined type A type defined by some agency other than the system.

user defined type (SQL) SQL divides user defined types into two kinds, DISTINCT types and structured types. In essence:

- A DISTINCT type D (a) is defined in terms of just one underlying type T (where T is system defined, scalar, explicitly visible to the user, and is in fact the physical—not just some possible—representation for values of type D); (b) has no type constraint apart from the obvious one that values of type D must be representable as values of type T; (c) inherits comparison and assignment operators, but no other operators, from type T; (d) effectively does have selector and THE_ operators, though the associated terminology and syntax differ from the way such things are defined in connection with such operators in this book; and (e) can't have proper subtypes.

- A structured type S (a) is defined in terms of a construct somewhat akin to a possrep, except that the "possrep" in question is really the physical (not just some possible) representation for values of type S; (b) has no type constraint apart from the obvious one that values of type S must be representable in terms of that specified physical representation; (c) has no known comparison operators (not even "=") other than ones explicitly defined by means of a special and separate CREATE ORDERING operator; (d) effectively does have assignment, selector, and THE_ operators, though the associated terminology and syntax differ from the way such things are defined in connection with such operators in this book; and (e) can have proper subtypes.

value An "individual constant" (for example, the individual constant three, denoted by the integer literal 3).

variable A holder for a representation of a value. Unlike values, variables (a) have location in time and space and (b) can be updated (that is, the current value of the variable in question can be replaced by another value).

WITH A syntactic device, supported by **Tutorial D** in particular, for introducing names for the results of subexpressions. The introduced names are then available for subsequent use (but only within the overall expression or statement of which the WITH specification forms a part) to denote those results.

Note: SQL also supports a WITH construct, with semantics similar but not identical to those of the **Tutorial D** construct—and, it has to be said, with much less practical utility, owing to the fact that SQL's support for any given relational operator is, in general, quite hard to disentangle from its support for other such operators. (Simplifying slightly, the problem is that, in SQL, the subexpressions whose results can be named via WITH can't be anything less than an entire SELECT expression.)

Index

For alphabetization purposes, (a) differences in fonts and case are ignored; (b) quotation marks are ignored; (c) other punctuation symbols—hyphens, underscores, parentheses, etc.—are treated as blank spaces; (d) numerals precede letters; (e) blank spaces precede everything else. The appendixes are mostly not indexed.

example value, *see* initial value
expression, 65,236
    vs. statement, 92
EXTEND, 259

factorial, 83
FETCH, 65
field (SQL), 82,194
    ordered left to right, 82,195
    unnamed, 195
FINAL vs. NOT FINAL, 179-180,201-202
First Axiom of Equality, 93
first normal form (1NF), 33,37,46,66-67
foreign key, 52,212,228-229
function (math), 14
    directional, 14
    vs. binary relation, 15
function (SQL), 185

generated type, 44,52,132-136
generic polymorphism, 136,156
generic type, 59
Gray, James, 13
GROUP, 58-59

heading
    defined, 16
    of tuple, 44
Hurwitz, W. A., xi

image (function), 14
implementation defined, 72
implementation dependent, 72
inclusion polymorphism, 156
indeterminacy, 78-81,90-92
Information Principle, 45,218

inheritance
    model, 11,156
    not discussed, xii,37-38,57,177
    OO, 181
    SQL, 180-181
initial value, 142-144
INSERT, 19
intersection, 261
instance, 226-227
INSTANTIABLE, 226
integrity constraint, *see* constraint
Ireland, 198
irrational number, 24

Jacobson, Ivar, 21
join, 161,261
joinable, 161,261

key, 7,18

Lindsay, Bruce G., 13
literal, 50,149,236
logical difference, 3

Maier, David, 13,100
Melton, Jim, 177,178,187,200,202,215,216,217,225,226
Melzak, Z. A., xi
method, 185,187
    invocation, 191
    lockstep definition, 189
    selfish, 190
MINUS, *see* difference
most specific type, 150
    can't be changed (SQL), 225
multiple assignment, 128-131,157-158
    repeated target, 130-131

www.ingramcontent.com/pod-product-compliance
Lightning Source LLC
Chambersburg PA
CBHW080630060326
40690CB00021B/4874